Journalism in an Era of Big Data

T0330891

Big data is marked by staggering growth in the collection and analysis of digital trace information regarding human and natural activity, bound up in and enabled by the rise of persistent connectivity, networked communication, smart machines, and the internet of things. In addition to their impact on technology and society, these developments have particular significance for the media industry and for journalism as a practice and a profession. These data-centric phenomena are, by some accounts, poised to greatly influence, if not transform, some of the most fundamental aspects of news and its production and distribution by humans and machines.

What such changes actually mean for news, democracy, and public life, however, is far from certain. As such, there is a need for scholarly scrutiny and critique of this trend, and this volume thus explores a range of phenomena—from the use of algorithms in the newsroom, to the emergence of automated news stories—at the intersection between journalism and the social, computer, and information sciences. What are the implications of such developments for journalism's professional norms, routines, and ethics? For its organizations, institutions, and economics? For its authority and expertise? And for the epistemology that underwrites journalism's role as knowledge-producer and sense-maker in society? Altogether, this book offers a first step in understanding what big data means for journalism. This book was originally published as a special issue of Digital Journalism.

Seth C. Lewis is the inaugural Shirley Papé Chair in Electronic and Emerging Media in the School of Journalism and Communication at the University of Oregon, Eugene, OR, USA. He is also a visiting fellow with the Information Society Project at Yale Law School, New Haven, CT, USA. His widely published research explores the digital transformation of journalism, with a focus on the human–technology interactions and media innovation processes associated with data, code, analytics, social media, and related phenomena. He is co-editor of *Boundaries of Journalism: Professionalism, Practices, and Participation* (Routledge, 2015), and is on the editorial boards of *New Media & Society*, *Social Media + Society*, *Digital Journalism*, and *Journalism & Mass Communication Quarterly*, among other journals. He is a two-time winner (2013 and 2016) of the Outstanding Article of the Year in Journalism Studies Award, from the Journalism Studies Division of the International Communication Association.

Journalism Studies: Theory and Practice
Series editor: Bob Franklin, *Cardiff School of Journalism, Media and Cultural Studies, Cardiff University, UK*

The journal *Journalism Studies* was established at the turn of the new millennium by Bob Franklin. It was launched in the context of a burgeoning interest in the scholarly study of journalism and an expansive global community of journalism scholars and researchers. The ambition was to provide a forum for the critical discussion and study of journalism as a subject of intellectual inquiry but also an arena of professional practice. Previously, the study of journalism in the UK and much of Europe was a fairly marginal branch of the larger disciplines of media, communication and cultural studies; only a handful of Universities offered degree programmes in the subject. *Journalism Studies* has flourished and succeeded in providing the intended public space for discussion of research on key issues within the field, to the point where in 2007 a sister journal, *Journalism Practice,* was launched to enable an enhanced focus on practice-based issues, as well as foregrounding studies of journalism education, training and professional concerns. Both journals are among the leading ranked journals within the field and publish six issues annually, in electronic and print formats. More recently, 2013 witnessed the launch of a further companion journal *Digital Journalism* to provide a site for scholarly discussion, analysis and responses to the wide ranging implications of digital technologies for the practice and study of journalism. From the outset, the publication of themed issues has been a commitment for all journals. Their purpose is first, to focus on highly significant or neglected areas of the field; second, to facilitate discussion and analysis of important and topical policy issues; and third, to offer readers an especially high quality and closely focused set of essays, analyses and discussions.

The *Journalism Studies: Theory and Practice* book series draws on a wide range of these themed issues from all journals and thereby extends the critical and public forum provided by them. The Editor of the journals works closely with guest editors to ensure that the books achieve relevance for readers and the highest standards of research. rigour and academic excllence. The series makes a significant contribution to the field of journalism studies by inviting distinguished scholars, academics and journalism practitioners to discuss and debate the central concerns within the field. It also reaches a wider readership of scholars, students and practitioners across the social sciences, humanities and communication arts, encouraging them to engage critically with, but also to interrogate, the specialist scholarly studies of journalism which this series provides.

Journalism in an Era of Big Data

Cases, concepts, and critiques

Edited by
Seth C. Lewis

Routledge
Taylor & Francis Group

LONDON AND NEW YORK

First published 2017 by Routledge

2 Park Square, Milton Park, Abingdon, Oxfordshire OX14 4RN
711 Third Avenue, New York, NY 10017

Routledge is an imprint of the Taylor & Francis Group, an informa business

First issued in paperback 2018

British Library Cataloguing in Publication Data
A catalogue record for this book is available from the British Library

ISBN 13: 978-1-138-69203-9 (hbk)
ISBN 13: 978-0-367-02841-1 (pbk)

Typeset in Myriad Pro
by RefineCatch Limited, Bungay, Suffolk

Publisher's Note
The publisher accepts responsibility for any inconsistencies that may have arisen during the conversion of this book from journal articles to book chapters, namely the possible inclusion of journal terminology.

Disclaimer
Every effort has been made to contact copyright holders for their permission to reprint material in this book. The publishers would be grateful to hear from any copyright holder who is not here acknowledged and will undertake to rectify any errors or omissions in future editions of this book.

Contents

Citation information

The chapters in this book were originally published in *Digital Journalism*, volume 3, issue 3 (June 2015). When citing this material, please use the original page numbering for each article, as follows:

Introduction

Journalism in an Era of Big Data: Cases, concepts, and critiques
Seth C. Lewis
Digital Journalism, volume 3, issue 3 (June 2015) pp. 321–330

Chapter 1

Clarifying Journalism's Quantitative Turn: A typology for evaluating data journalism, computational journalism, and computer-assisted reporting
Mark Coddington
Digital Journalism, volume 3, issue 3 (June 2015) pp. 331–348

Chapter 2

Between the Unique and the Pattern: Historical tensions in our understanding of quantitative journalism
C. W. Anderson
Digital Journalism, volume 3, issue 3 (June 2015) pp. 349–363

Chapter 3

Data-driven Revelation? Epistemological tensions in investigative journalism in the age of "big data"
Sylvain Parasie
Digital Journalism, volume 3, issue 3 (June 2015) pp. 364–380

Chapter 4

From Mr. and Mrs. Outlier to Central Tendencies: Computational journalism and crime reporting at the Los Angeles Times
Mary Lynn Young and Alfred Hermida
Digital Journalism, volume 3, issue 3 (June 2015) pp. 381–397

Chapter 5

Algorithmic Accountability: Journalistic investigation of computational power Structures
Nicholas Diakopoulos
Digital Journalism, volume 3, issue 3 (June 2015) pp. 398–415

Chapter 6

The Robotic Reporter: Automated journalism and the redefinition of labor, compositional forms, and journalistic authority
Matt Carlson
Digital Journalism, volume 3, issue 3 (June 2015) pp. 416–431

Chapter 7

Waiting for Data Journalism: A qualitative assessment of the anecdotal take-up of data journalism in French-speaking Belgium
Juliette De Maeyer, Manon Libert, David Domingo, François Heinderyckx and Florence Le Cam
Digital Journalism, volume 3, issue 3 (June 2015) pp. 432–446

Chapter 8

Big Data and Journalism: Epistemology, expertise, economics, and ethics
Seth C. Lewis and Oscar Westlund
Digital Journalism, volume 3, issue 3 (June 2015) pp. 447–466

For any permission-related enquiries please visit:
http://www.tandfonline.com/page/help/permissions

Notes on Contributors

C.W. Anderson is Associate Professor in the Department of Media Culture, College of Staten Island, New York City, New York, USA. He holds a Ph.D. from Columbia University and is a visiting fellow at Yale Law School's Information Society Project. His current research examines the changing relationship between digital journalism and American politics.

Matt Carlson is Associate Professor in the Department of Communication, Saint Louis University, USA, where he teaches and researches in the area of media and journalism studies. He is author of the forthcoming book, *Journalistic authority: A relational approach*.

Mark Coddington is Assistant Professor in the Department of Journalism and Mass Communications, Washington and Lee University, Lexington, Virginia, USA. His research explores how the professional production of news is being changed through its encounter with participatory technologies. He is also a former journalist.

Juliette De Maeyer is Assistant Professor in the Department of Communication, Université de Montréal, Canada. Her current research explores journalism and the media, with a particular focus on the journalistic production process.

Nicholas Diakopoulos is an Assistant Professor at the University of Maryland, College Park Philip Merrill College of Journalism, with courtesy appointments in the College of Information Studies and Department of Computer Science. He is Director of the Computational Journalism Lab at UMD, a member of the Human-Computer Interaction Lab (HCIL) at UMD, a Tow Fellow at Columbia University School of Journalism, and Associate Professor II at the University of Bergen Department of Information Science and Media Studies. His research is in computational and data journalism with emphases on algorithmic accountability and social computing in the news. He received his Ph.D. in Computer Science from the School of Interactive Computing at Georgia Tech, where he co-founded the program in Computational Journalism in 2006.

David Domingo is Chair of Journalism at the Department of Information and Communication Sciences at Université Libre de Bruxelles, Belgium. His research focuses on innovation processes in online communication, with a special interest in the (re)definition of practices and identities involved in news production, circulation and use.

Alfred Hermida is Associate Professor and Director of the School of Journalism, University of British Columbia, Canada, and co-founder of The Conversation Canada.

A former BBC broadcast and online journalist, his research examines the impact of digital technologies on journalistic norms and practices, with a focus on data and computational journalism, and on social media. He is author of the award-winning book, *Tell Everyone: Why We Share and Why It Matters* (DoubleDay, 2014), co-editor of *The Sage Handbook of Digital Journalism* (Sage, 2016) and co-author of *Participatory Journalism: Guarding Open Gates at Online Newspapers* (Wiley Blackwell, 2011). (Wiley Blackwell, 2011).

François Heinderyckx is Professor and Dean of the Faculty of Letters, Translation and Communication, Université libre de Bruxelles, Belgium, and Chang Jiang Professor at the Communication University of China. He is co-editor of the recently published, *Gatekeeping in Transition* (Routledge, 2015).

Florence Le Cam is Chair of Journalism in the Department of Information and Communication Sciences, Université libre de Bruxelles, Belgium. Her research interests are the professional identities of journalists and the history of journalism as a profession.

Seth C. Lewis is the inaugural Shirley Papé Chair in Electronic and Emerging Media in the School of Journalism and Communication at the University of Oregon, Eugene, OR, USA. He is also a visiting fellow with the Information Society Project at Yale Law School, New Haven, CT, USA. His widely published research explores the digital transformation of journalism, with a focus on the human–technology interactions and media innovation processes associated with data, code, analytics, social media, and related phenomena. He is co-editor of *Boundaries of Journalism: Professionalism, Practices, and Participation* (Routledge, 2015).

Manon Libert is a graduate student in the Department of Information and Communication Sciences, Université libre de Bruxelles, Belgium.

Sylvain Parasie is Assistant Professor of Sociology at the University of Paris-Est Marne-la-Vallée, France. His current research focuses on the socio-political aspects of technological innovation in news organizations. He is author of the book, *Et maintenant, une page de pub: une histoire morale de la publicité à la télévision française, 1968–2008*.

Oscar Westlund is Associate Professor in the Department of Journalism, Media and Communication at the University of Gothenburg, Sweden. Westlund has researched the production, distribution and consumption of news through various methods for a decade, focusing especially on the shifts towards digital technologies such as mobile media. Westlund has authored more than 100 publications, including articles in approximately 20 journals, official inquiries for the Swedish government and the EU Commission, and many book chapters. In 2016, one of his co-authored articles with Seth C. Lewis was awarded the Wolfgang Donsbach Outstanding Article of Year Award by the International Communication Association.

Mary Lynn Young is Associate Professor at the School of Journalism, University of British Columbia, Canada. Her research interests include gender and the media, newsroom sociology, media credibility and representations of crime. She has also worked as an editor, business columnist and senior crime reporter at major daily newspapers in Canada and the United States. Her publications can be found in journals such as *Digital Journalism* and the *Canadian Journal of Communication*.

JOURNALISM IN AN ERA OF BIG DATA
Cases, concepts, and critiques

Seth C. Lewis

This special issue examines the changing nature of journalism amid data abundance, computational exploration, and algorithmic emphasis—developments with wide meaning in technology and society at large, and with growing significance for the media industry and for journalism as practice and profession. These data-centric phenomena, by some accounts, are poised to greatly influence, if not transform over time, some of the most fundamental aspects of news and its production and distribution by humans and machines. While such expectations may be overblown, the trend lines are nevertheless clear: large-scale datasets and their collection, analysis, and interpretation are becoming increasingly salient for making sense of and deriving value from digital information, writ large. What such changes actually mean for news, democracy, and public life, however, is far from certain. As such, this calls for scholarly scrutiny, as well as a dose of critique to temper much celebration about the promise of reinventing news through the potential of "big data." This special issue thus explores a range of phenomena at the junction between journalism and the social, computer, and information sciences. These phenomena are organized around the contexts of digital information technologies being used in contemporary newswork—such as algorithms and analytics, applications and automation—that rely on harnessing data and managing it effectively. What are the implications of such developments for journalism's professional norms, routines, and ethics? For its organizations, institutions, and economics? For its authority and expertise? And for the epistemology that undergirds journalism's role as knowledge-producer and sense-maker in society?

Before getting to those questions, however, let us begin more prosaically: *What is the big deal about big data?* That may be a curious way to open a special issue on the subject, but the question is an important starting point for at least three reasons. First, it is *the* question being asked, whether directly or indirectly, in many policy, scholarly, and professional circles, on many a panel at academic and trade conferences, and across the pages of journals and forums in seemingly every discipline. This is especially true in the social sciences and humanities generally and in communication, media, and journalism specifically. While exploring the methods of computational social science (Lazer et al. 2009; see also Busch 2014; Lewis, Zamith, and Hermida 2013; Mahrt and Scharkow 2013; Oboler, Welsh, and Cruz 2012), scholars are also wrestling with the conceptual implications of digital datasets and dynamics that, in sheer size and scope, may challenge how we think about the nature of mediated communication (Boellstorff 2013; Bruns 2013; Couldry and Turow 2014; Driscoll and Walker 2014; Karpf 2012). Second, this opening query calls up the skepticism that is quite needed, for there is good reason to question not only whether big data is a "thing," but also in whose interests, toward what purposes, and with what consequences the very term is being promulgated as a "solution" to unlocking various social problems (Crawford, Miltner, and Gray 2014; cf. Morozov 2013). Finally, to open with such an audacious question is to acknowledge at the outset that the processes and philosophies associated with big data, in the broadest sense, are very much in flux: an indeterminate set of leading-edge activities and approaches that may prove to be innovative, inconsequential, or something else entirely. What, then, *is* the big deal?

It is for this reason that I emphasize the deliberate naming of this special issue: "Journalism *in an era of* big data." While historical hindsight can make any naming of an "era" a fool's game, there also seems to be broad agreement that, in the developed world of digital information technologies, we are situated in a moment of data deluge. This moment, however loosely bounded, is noted for at least two major developments that have accelerated in recent years. The first is the overwhelming volume and variety of digital information produced by and about human (and natural) activity, made possible by the growing ubiquity of mobile devices, tracking tools, always-on sensors, and cheap computing storage, among other things. As one report described it: "In a digitized world, consumers going about their day—communicating, browsing, buying, sharing, searching—create their own enormous trails of data" (Manyika et al. 2011, 1). "This data layer," noted another observer, "is a shadow. It's part of how we live. It is always there but seldom observed" (quoted in Bell 2012, 48). The second major development involves rapid advances in and diffusion of computing processing, machine learning, algorithms, and data science (Manovich 2012; Mayer-Schönberger and Cukier 2013; O'Neil and Schutt 2013; Provost and Fawcett 2013). Put together, these developments have enabled corporations, governments, and researchers to more readily navigate and analyze this shadow layer of public life, for better or worse, and much to the chagrin of critics concerned about consumer privacy and data ethics (boyd and Crawford 2012; Oboler, Welsh, and Cruz 2012). Thus, whether dubbed "big" or otherwise, this moment is one in which *data*—its collection, analysis, and representation, as well as associated data-driven techniques of computation and quantification—bears particular resonance for understanding the intersection of media, technology, and society (González-Bailón 2013).

Computation and Quantification in Journalism

What is the big deal, then, for journalism? By now, there is no shortage of accounts about the implications of technology change for the most fundamental aspects of gathering, filtering, and disseminating news; similarly, much has been written about such changes and their implications for journalistic institutions, business models, distribution channels, and audiences (for an overview of recent scholarly work in this broad terrain, see Franklin 2014; see also Anderson, Bell, and Shirky 2012; Lewis 2012; Ryfe 2012; Usher 2014). Yet, in comparison to the large body of literature, for instance, on the role of Twitter in journalism (Hermida 2013), the particular role of *data* in journalism—as well as interrelated notions of algorithms, computer code, and programming in the context of news—is only beginning to receive major attention in the scholarly and professional discourse. Among scholars, there is a rapidly growing body of work focused on unpacking the nature of computation and quantification in news. The scholarly approaches include case studies of journalists within and across news organizations (e.g., Appelgren and Nygren 2014; Fink and Anderson 2014; Karlsen and Stavelin 2014; Parasie and Dagiral 2013), theoretical undertakings that often articulate concepts of computer science and programming in the framework of journalism (e.g., Anderson 2013; Hamilton and Turner 2009; Flew et al. 2012; Gynnild 2014; Lewis and Usher 2013), and analyses that take a more historical perspective in comparing present developments with computer-assisted reporting (e.g., Parasie and Dagiral 2013; Powers 2012). More oriented to journalism professionals, there are a growing number of handbooks on data journalism (Gray, Bounegru, and Chambers 2012), industry-facing reports on the likes of data (Howard 2014), algorithms (Diakopoulos 2014), and sensors (Pitt 2014), and conferences on "quantifying journalism" via data, metrics, and computation.

Data journalism, as Fink and Anderson (2014, 1) note bluntly, is seemingly "everywhere," based on the industry buzz and accelerating scholarly interest. "[W]hether and how data journalism actually exists as a thing in the world, on the other hand, is a different and less understood question." This special issue is a systematic effort to address that issue. It aims to outline the state of research in this emerging domain, bringing together some of the most current and critical scholarship on what is becoming of journalism—from its reporting practices to its organizational arrangements to its discursive interpretation as a professional community—in a moment of experimentation with digital data, computational techniques, and algorithmic forms of representing and interpreting the world.

"Journalism in an era of big data" is thus a way of seeing journalism as interpolated through the conceptual and methodological approaches of *computation* and *quantification*. It is about both the ideation and implementation of computational and mathematical mindsets and skill sets in newswork—as well as the necessary deconstruction and critique of such approaches. Taking such a wide-angle view of this phenomenon, including both practice and philosophy within this conversation, means attending to the social/cultural dynamics of computation and quantification—such as the grassroots groups that are seeking to bring pro-social "hacking" into journalism (Lewis and Usher 2013, 2014)—as well as the material/technological characteristics of these developments. It means recognizing that algorithms and related computational tools and techniques "are neither entirely material, nor are they entirely human—they are hybrid, composed of both human intentionality and material obduracy" (Anderson 2013, 1016). As such, we need a set of perspectives that highlight the distinct and interrelated roles of social actors and technological actants at this emerging intersection of journalism (Lewis and Westlund 2014a).

To trace the broad outline of journalism in an era of big data, we need (1) empirical cases that describe and explain such developments, whether at the micro (local) or macro (institutional) levels of analysis; (2) conceptual frameworks for organizing, interpreting, and ultimately theorizing about such developments; and (3) critical perspectives that call into question taken-for-granted norms and assumptions. This special issue takes up this three-part emphasis on *cases*, *concepts*, and *critiques*. Such categories are not mutually exclusive nor exhaustively reflective of what is covered in this issue; indeed, various elements of case study, conceptual development, and critical inquiry are evident in all of the articles here. In that way, these studies provide a blended set of theory, practice, and criticism upon which scholars may develop future research in this important and growing area of journalism, media, and communication.

Cases, Concepts, and Critiques

For a set of phenomena as uncertain as journalism in an era of big data, conceptual clarity is the first order of business. What used to be a coherent notion of computer-assisted reporting (CAR) in the 1990s "has splintered into a set of ambiguously related practices" that are variously described in terms such as computational journalism, data journalism, programmer-journalism, and so on (Coddington 2014). Reviewing the state of the field thus far, Mark Coddington finds "a cacophony of overlapping and indistinct definitions that forms a shaky foundation for deeper research into these practices." As data-driven forms of journalism become more central to the profession, "it is imperative that scholars do not treat them as simple synonyms but think carefully about the significant differences between the forms they take and their implications for changing journalistic practice as a whole." Against that backdrop, Coddington opens this special issue by clarifying this "quantitative turn" in journalism, offering a typology of three dominant approaches: computer-assisted reporting, data journalism, and computational journalism. While there are overlaps in practice among these forms of quantitative journalism, there are also key distinctions:

> CAR is rooted in social science methods and the deliberate style and public-affairs orientation of investigative journalism, data journalism is characterized by its participatory openness and cross-field hybridity, and computational journalism is focused on the application of the processes of abstraction and automation to information.

Having classified them as such, Coddington differentiates them further according to their orientation on four dimensions: (1) professional expertise or networked participation, (2) transparency or opacity, (3) big data or targeted sampling, and (4) a vision of an active or passive public. His typology points to "a significant gap between the professional and epistemological orientations of CAR, on the one hand, and both data journalism and computational journalism, on the other." Open-source culture, he suggests, is a continuum through which to see distinctions among these forms: CAR reflecting a professional, less "open" approach to journalism, on one end, with data journalism being situated as a professional–open hybrid in the middle, and computational journalism hewing most closely to the networked, participatory values of open source (cf. Lewis and Usher 2013).

Building on Coddington's conceptualization of quantitative journalism, C. W. Anderson (2014) offers a historically based critique that reveals, at least in the US context, how "the underlying ideas of data journalism are not new, but rather can be traced back in history and align with larger questions about the role of quantification in journalistic practice." He takes what he calls an "objects of journalism-oriented" approach to studying data and news, one that pays attention (in this case historically) to how data is embodied in material "objects" such as databases, survey reports, and paper documents as well as how journalists situate their fact-building enterprise in relation to those objects of evidence. This object orientation is connected with actor-network theory (ANT) and its way of seeing news and knowledge work as an "assemblage" of material, cultural, and practice-based elements. It allows Anderson to take "a longer historical trajectory that grapples with the very meaning of 'the quantitative' for the production of knowledge," with a particular emphasis on "the epistemological dimensions of these quantitative practices" (emphasis original). By examining several historical tensions underlying journalists' use of data—such as the document-oriented shift from thinking about news products as "records" to thinking about them as "reports" that occurred in the early nineteenth century—Anderson offers an important critique. He challenges prevailing wisdom about the orderly progression of data and visualization, showing instead that "the story of quantitative journalism in the United States is less one of sanguine continuity than it is one of rupture, a tale of transformed techniques and objects of evidence existing under old familiar names." The ultimate payoff in this approach, he argues, is both a backward-looking reappraisal of history and a forward-looking lens for examining the quantitative journalism of the future: not merely in how it embraces big data, but "rather the ways in which it reminds us of *other* forms of information that are not data, *other* types of evidence that are not quantitative, and *other* conceptions of what counts as legitimate public knowledge" (original emphasis).

With its emphasis on epistemology and materiality, Anderson's historical account sets up the contemporary case study by Sylvain Parasie (2014). He examines the San Francisco-based Center for Investigative Reporting (CIR) to explore the question: To what extent does big-data processing influence how journalists produce knowledge in investigative reporting? Parasie extends (and critiques) previous research on journalistic epistemologies in two ways, firstly by more fully taking into account "how journalists rely on the material environment of their organization to decide whether their knowledge claims are justified or not." These material factors include databases and algorithms, which "are not black boxes providing unquestionable results, and [thus] we need to examine the material basis on which they collectively hold a specific output as being justified." Secondly, Parasie sheds light on "the often tortuous history of how justified beliefs are collectively produced in relation to artifacts," following the lead of Latour and Woolgar (1979) in their study of how science is produced in the laboratory. In studying a 19-month investigation by CIR, Parasie shows how a heterogeneous team of investigative reporters, computer-assisted reporters, and programmer-journalists works through epistemological tensions to develop a shared epistemic culture, one connected with the material artifacts of data-oriented technologies. In all, Parasie makes key distinctions between "hypothesis-driven" and "data-driven" paths to journalistic revelations, in line with Coddington's conceptual mapping; he also highlights the interplay of materiality, culture, and practice, much as Anderson prescribes.

These articles are followed by three that take up algorithms and automation, pointing to matters of "autonomous decision-making" (Diakopoulos 2014) and the journalistic consequences of such developments for organizational and professional norms and routines. In the first article, Mary Lynn Young and Alfred Hermida (2014) examine the emergence of computationally based crime news at *The Los Angeles Times*. Following Boczkowski's (2004) theorizing about technological adaptation in news media organizations, they find that "computational thinking and techniques emerged in a (dis)continuous evolution of organizational norms, practices, content, identities, and technologies that interdependently led to new products." Among these products was a series of automatically generated crime stories, or "robo-posts," to a blog tracking local homicides. This concept of "algorithm as journalist," they argue, raises questions about "how decisions of inclusion and exclusion are made, what styles of reasoning are employed, whose values are embedded into the technology, and how they affect public understanding of complex issues."

This interest in interrogating the algorithm is further developed in Nicholas Diakopoulos' (2014) provocative notion of "algorithmic accountability reporting," which he defines as "a mechanism for elucidating and articulating the power structures, biases, and influences that computational artifacts exercise in society." In effect, he argues for flipping the computational journalism paradigm on its head, at least in this instance: instead of building another computational tool to enable news storytelling, technologists and journalists instead can use reverse engineering to investigate the algorithms that govern our digital world and unpack the crux of their power: autonomous decision-making. Understanding algorithmic power, in this sense, means analyzing "the atomic decisions that algorithms make, including *prioritization, classification, association,* and *filtering*" (original emphasis). Furthermore, Diakopoulos uses five case studies to consider the opportunities and challenges associated with doing algorithm-focused accountability journalism. He thus contributes to the literature both a theoretical lens through which to scrutinize the relative transparency of public-facing algorithms as well as an empirical starting point for understanding the potential for and limitations of such an approach, including questions of human resources, law, and ethics.

Lastly among these three, Matt Carlson (2014) explains what begins to happen as "the role of big data in journalism shifts from reporting tool to the generation of news content" in the form of what he calls "automated journalism." The term refers to "algorithmic processes that convert data into narrative news texts with limited to no human intervention beyond the initial programming." Among the data-oriented practices emerging in journalism, he says, "none appear to be as potentially disruptive as automated journalism," insofar as it calls up concerns about the future of journalistic labor, news compositional forms, and the very foundation of journalistic authority. By analyzing Narrative Science and journalists' reactions to its automated news services, Carlson shows how this "technological drama" (cf. Pfaffenberger 1992) reveals fundamental tensions not only about the work practices of human journalists but also what a future of automated journalism may portend for "larger understandings of what journalism is and how it ought to operate." Among other issues going forward, he says, "questions need to be asked regarding whether an increase in algorithmic judgment will lead to a decline in the authority of human judgment."

Before rushing headlong into robot journalism, however, quantitative journalism in its most basic form is still searching for institutional footing in many parts of the world. In exploring the difficulties for data journalism in French-speaking Belgium, Juliette de Maeyer et al. (2014) offer a much-needed reminder that the take-up of such journalism is neither consistent nor complete. Moreover, they argue that journalism (and hence data journalism) must be understood "as a socio-discursive practice: it is not only the production of (data-driven) journalistic artefacts that shapes the notion of (data) journalism, but also the discursive efforts of all the actors involved, in and out of the newsrooms." By mapping the discourse within this small media system, they uncover "a cartography of who and what counts as data journalism," within which they find divisions around the duality of "data" and "journalism" and between "ordinary" versus "thorough" forms of data journalism. These discourses disclose the various obstacles, many of them structural and organizational, that hinder the development of data journalism in that region. Among their respondents who have engaged in the actual practice of data journalism, there seems to be an overall feeling of resignation. There might have been a brief euphoric phase after the first encounter with the concept of data journalism, but journalists who return from trainings full of ideas and ambitious projects are quickly caught again in the constraints of routinized news production.

Like Anderson and Parasie in this issue, the authors draw upon Bruno Latour (2005), in this case to suggest that data journalism is clearly a "matter of concern" in French-speaking Belgium even while there is a relative absence of data journalism artifacts, or "matters of fact" that can be displayed as evidence. Overall, de Maeyer and colleagues demonstrate how data journalism may "exist as a discourse (re)appropriated by a range of actors, originating from different—and sometimes overlapping—social worlds," allowing us to understand the uneven and sometimes incoherent path through which experimentation may lead to implementation (or not).

Finally, and befitting the opening discussion about the big deal of big data, the concluding article takes up this question: If big data is a wide-scale social, cultural, and technological phenomenon, what are its particular implications for journalism? Seth Lewis and Oscar Westlund (2014b) suggest four conceptual lenses—epistemology, expertise, economics, and ethics—through which to understand the present and potential applications of big data for journalism's professional logic and its industrial production. These conceptual approaches, distinct yet interrelated, show "how journalists and news media organizations are seeking to make sense of, act upon, and derive value from big data." Ultimately, the developments of big data, Lewis and Westlund posit, may have transformative meaning for "journalism's ways of *knowing* (epistemology) and *doing* (expertise), as well as its negotiation of *value* (economics) and *values* (ethics)." As quantitative journalism becomes more central to journalism's professional core, and as computational and algorithmic techniques likewise become intertwined with the business models on which journalism is supported, critical questions will continually emerge about the socio-material relationship of big data, journalism, and media work broadly. To what extent are journalism's cultural authority and technological practices changing in the context of (though not necessarily because of) big data? And how might such changes be connected with news audiences, story forms, organizational arrangements, distribution channels, and news values and ethics, among many other things? The articles in this issue—their cases, concepts, and critiques—offer a starting point for exploring such questions in the future.

REFERENCES

Anderson, C. W. 2013. "Towards a Sociology of Computational and Algorithmic Journalism." *New Media & Society* 15 (7): 1005–1021. doi:10.1177/1461444812465137.

Anderson, C. W. 2014. "Between the Unique and the Pattern: Historical Tensions in Our Understanding of Quantitative Journalism." *Digital Journalism*. [This issue] doi:10.1080/21670811.2014.976407.

Anderson, C. W., Emily Bell, and Clay Shirky. 2012. *Post-industrial Journalism: Adapting to the Present*. New York: Tow Center for Digital Journalism, Columbia University.

Appelgren, Ester, and Gunnar Nygren. 2014. "Data Journalism in Sweden: Introducing New Methods and Genres of Journalism into 'Old' Organizations." *Digital Journalism* 2 (3): 394–405. doi:10.1080/21670811.2014.884344.

Bell, Emily. 2012. "Journalism by Numbers." *Columbia Journalism Review* 51 (3): 48–49.

Boczkowski, Pablo J. 2004. *Digitizing the News: Innovation in Online Newspapers*. Cambridge, MA: MIT Press.

Boellstorff, Tom. 2013. "Making Big Data, in Theory." *First Monday* 18 (10). doi:10.5210/fm.v18i10.4869. http://firstmonday.org/ojs/index.php/fm/article/view/4869/3750.

boyd, danah, and Kate Crawford. 2012. "Critical Questions for Big Data: Provocations for a Cultural, Technological, and Scholarly Phenomenon." *Information, Communication & Society* 15 (5): 662–679. doi:10.1080/1369118X.2012.678878.

Bruns, Axel. 2013. "Faster than the Speed of Print: Reconciling 'Big Data' Social Media Analysis and Academic Scholarship." *First Monday* 18 (10). doi:10.5210/fm.v18i10.4879. http://firstmonday.org/ojs/index.php/fm/article/view/4879.

Busch, Lawrence. 2014. "A Dozen Ways to Get Lost in Translation: Inherent Challenges in Large Scale Data Sets." *International Journal of Communication* 8. http://ijoc.org/index.php/ijoc/article/view/2160.

Carlson, Matt. 2014. "The Robotic Reporter: Automated Journalism and the Redefinition of Labor, Compositional Forms, and Journalistic Authority." *Digital Journalism*. [This issue] doi:10.1080/21670811.2014.976412.

Coddington, Mark. 2014. "Clarifying Journalism's Quantitative Turn: A Typology for Evaluating Data Journalism, Computational Journalism, and Computer-Assisted Reporting." *Digital Journalism*. [This Issue] doi:10.1080/21670811.2014.976400.

Couldry, Nick, and Joseph Turow. 2014. "Advertising, Big Data and the Clearance of the Public Realm: Marketers' New Approaches to the Content Subsidy." *International Journal of Communication* 8. http://ijoc.org/index.php/ijoc/article/view/2166.

Crawford, Kate, Kate Miltner, and Mary L. Gray. 2014. "Critiquing Big Data: Politics, Ethics, Epistemology." *International Journal of Communication* 8. http://ijoc.org/index.php/ijoc/article/view/2167/1164.

Diakopoulos, Nicholas. 2014. *Algorithmic Accountability Reporting: On the Investigation of Black Boxes*. New York: Tow Center for Digital Journalism, Columbia University. doi:10.1080/21670811.2014.976411.

Diakopoulos, Nicholas. 2014. "Algorithmic Accountability: Journalistic Investigation of Computational Power Structures." *Digital Journalism*. [This Issue]. doi:10.1080/21670811.2014.976411.

Driscoll, Kevin, and Shawn Walker. 2014. "Working within a Black Box: Transparency in the Collection and Production of Big Twitter Data." *International Journal of Communication* 8. http://ijoc.org/index.php/ijoc/article/view/2171

Fink, Katherine, and C. W. Anderson. 2014. "Data Journalism in the United States: Beyond the 'Usual Suspects'." *Journalism Studies*. doi:10.1080/1461670X.2014.939852.

Flew, Terry, Christina Spurgeon, Anna Daniel, and Adam Swift. 2012. "The Promise of Computational Journalism." *Journalism Practice* 6 (2): 157–171. doi:10.1080/17512786.2011.61665.

Franklin, Bob. 2014. "The Future of Journalism: In an Age of Digital Media and Economic Uncertainty." *Digital Journalism* 2 (3): 254–272.

González-Bailón, Sandra. 2013. "Social Science in the Era of Big Data." *Policy & Internet* 5 (2): 147–160. doi:10.1002/1944-2866.POI328.

Gray, Jonathan, Liliana Bounegru, and Lucy Chambers. 2012. *The Data Journalism Handbook*. Sebastopol, CA: O'Reilly Media.

Gynnild, Astrid. 2014. "Journalism Innovation Leads to Innovation Journalism: The Impact of Computational Exploration on Changing Mindsets." *Journalism* 15 (6): 713–730. doi:10.1177/1464884913486393.

Hamilton, James T., and Fred, Turner. 2009. "Accountability through Algorithm: Developing the Field of Computational Journalism." Report from the Center for Advanced Study in the Behavioral Sciences, Summer Workshop 27-41, Duke University, Durham, NC.

Hermida, Alfred. 2013. "#Journalism: Reconfiguring Journalism Research about Twitter, One Tweet at a Time." *Digital Journalism* 1 (3): 295–313. doi:10.1080/21670811.2013.808456.

Howard, Alexander Benjamin. 2014. *The Art and Science of Data-Driven Journalism*. New York: Tow Center for Digital Journalism, Columbia University.

Karlsen, Joakim, and Eirik Stavelin. 2014. "Computational Journalism in Norwegian Newsrooms." *Journalism Practice* 8 (1): 34–48. doi:10.1080/17512786.2013.813190.

Karpf, David. 2012. "Social Science Research Methods in Internet Time." *Information, Communication & Society* 15 (5): 639–661. doi:10.1080/1369118X.2012.665468.

Latour, Bruno. 2005. *Reassembling the Social: An Introduction to Actor-Network-theory*. New York: Oxford University Press.

Latour, Bruno, and Steve Woolgar. 1979. *Laboratory Life. the Construction of Scientific Facts*. Princeton, NJ: Princeton University Press.

Lazer, David, Alex (Sandy) Pentland, Lada Adamic, and Sinan Aral et al. 2009. "Life in the Network: The Coming Age of Computational Social Science." *Science* 323 (5915): 721–723.

Lewis, Seth C. 2012. "The Tension between Professional Control and Open Participation: Journalism and Its Boundaries." *Information, Communication & Society* 15 (6): 836–866. doi:10.1080/1369118X.2012.674150.

Lewis, Seth C., Rodrigo Zamith, and Alfred Hermida. 2013. "Content Analysis in an Era of Big Data: A Hybrid Approach to Computational and Manual Methods." *Journal of Broadcasting & Electronic Media* 57 (1): 34–52. doi:10.1080/08838151.2012.761702.

Lewis, Seth C., and Nikki Usher. 2013. "Open Source and Journalism: Toward New Frameworks for Imagining News Innovation." *Media, Culture & Society* 35 (5): 602–619. doi:10.1177/0163443713485494.

Lewis, Seth C., and Nikki Usher. 2014. "Code, Collaboration, and the Future of Journalism: A Case Study of the Hacks/Hackers Global Network." *Digital Journalism* 2 (3): 383–393. doi:10.1080/21670811.2014.895504.

Lewis, Seth C., and Oscar Westlund. 2014a. "Actors, Actants, Audiences, and Activities in Cross-Media News Work: A Matrix and a Research Agenda." *Digital Journalism*. doi:10.1080/21670811.2014.927986.

Lewis, Seth C., and Oscar Westlund. 2014b. "Big Data and Journalism: Epistemology, Expertise, Economics, and Ethics." *Digital Journalism*. [This issue] doi:10.1080/21670811.2014.976418.

Mahrt, Merja, and Michael Scharkow. 2013. "The Value of Big Data in Digital Media Research." *Journal of Broadcasting & Electronic Media* 57 (1): 20–33. doi:10.1080/08838151.2012.761700.

de Maeyer, Juliette, Manon Libert, David Domingo, François Heinderyckx, and Florence Le Cam. 2014. "Waiting for Data Journalism: A Qualitative Assessment of the Anecdotal Take-up of Data Journalism in French-speaking Belgium." *Digital Journalism*. [This issue] doi:10.1080/21670811.2014.976415.

Manovich, Lev. 2012. "Trending: The Promises and the Challenges of Big Social Data." In *Debates in the Digital Humanities*, edited by M. K. Gold, 460–475. Minneapolis, MN: The University of Minnesota Press.

Manyika, James, Michael Chui, Brad Brown, Jacques Bughin, Richard Dobbs, Charles Roxburgh, and Angela H. Byers. 2011. *Big Data: The Next Frontier for Innovation, Competition, and Productivity*. McKinsey Global Institute. http://www.mckinsey.com/insights/mgi/research/technology_and_innovation/big_data_the_next_frontier_for_innovation.

Mayer-Schönberger, Viktor, and Kenneth Cukier. 2013. *Big Data: A Revolution That Will Transform How We Live, Work, and Think*. Boston, MA: Houghton Mifflin Harcourt.

Morozov, Evgeny. 2013. *To Save Everything, Click Here: The Folly of Technological Solutionism*. New York: PublicAffairs.

Oboler, Andre, Kristopher Welsh, and Lito Cruz. 2012. "The Danger of Big Data: Social Media as Computational Social Science." *First Monday* 17 (7–2). http://firstmonday.org/htbin/cgiwrap/bin/ojs/index.php/fm/article/view/3993/3269.

O'Neil, Cathy, and Rachel Schutt. 2013. *Doing Data Science: Straight Talk from the Frontline*. Sebastpol, CA: O'Reilly Media.

Parasie, Sylvain. 2014. "Data-driven Revelation: Epistemological Tensions in Investigative Journalism in the Age of 'Big Data'." *Digital Journalism*. [This issue] doi:10.1080/21670811.2014.976408.

Parasie, Sylvain, and Eric Dagiral. 2013. "Data-driven Journalism and the Public Good: 'Computer-Assisted-Reporters' and 'Programmer-journalists' in Chicago." *New Media & Society* 15 (6): 853–871. doi:10.1177/1461444812463345.

Pfaffenberger, Bryan. 1992. "Technological Dramas." *Science, Technology & Human Values* 17 (3): 282–312. doi:10.1177/016224399201700302.

Pitt, Fergus. 2014. *Sensors and Journalism*. New York: Tow Center for Digital Journalism, Columbia University.

Powers, Matthew. 2012. "'In Forms That Are Familiar and Yet-to-Be Invented': American Journalism and the Discourse of Technologically Specific Work." *Journal of Communication Inquiry* 36 (1): 24–43. doi:10.1177/0196859911426009.

Provost, Foster, and Tom Fawcett. 2013. "Data Science and Its Relationship to Big Data and Data-Driven Decision Making." *Big Data* 1 (1): 51–59. doi:10.1089/big.2013.1508.

Ryfe, David M. 2012. *Can Journalism Survive? An Inside Look at American Newsrooms*. Cambridge; Malden, MA: Polity Press. Web.

Usher, Nikki. 2014. *Making News at The New York Times*. Ann Arbor: University of Michigan Press.

Young, Mary Lynn, and Alfred Hermida. 2014. "From Mr. and Mrs. Outlier to Central Tendencies: Computational Journalism and Crime Reporting at the Los Angeles Times." *Digital Journalism*. [This Issue] doi:10.1080/21670811.2014.976409.

CLARIFYING JOURNALISM'S QUANTITATIVE TURN

A typology for evaluating data journalism, computational journalism, and computer-assisted reporting

Mark Coddington

As quantitative forms have become more prevalent in professional journalism, it has become increasingly important to distinguish between them and examine their roles in contemporary journalistic practice. This study defines and compares three quantitative forms of journalism—computer-assisted reporting, data journalism, and computational journalism—examining the points of overlap and divergence among their journalistic values and practices. After setting the three forms against the cultural backdrop of the convergence between the open-source movement and professional journalistic norms, the study introduces a four-part typology to evaluate their epistemological and professional dimensions. In it, the three forms are classified according to their orientation toward professional expertise or networked participation, transparency or opacity, big data or targeted sampling, and a vision of an active or passive public. These three quantitative journalistic forms are ultimately characterized as related but distinct approaches to integrating the values of open-source culture and social science with those of professional journalism, each with its own flaws but also its own distinct contribution to democratically robust journalistic practice.

Introduction

Professional journalism has historically been built around two elements—textual and visual. Numbers have long had a role in journalism as well, but American journalists have consistently downplayed their importance in making up their professional skillset, leading to a notorious difficulty in presenting numerical data accurately and responsibly (Maier 2002). A notable exception has been the professional subfield of computer-assisted reporting (CAR), which has focused on journalistically analyzing quantitative data for at least 40 years. Over the past several years, this data-driven strain of journalism has become more prominent within the profession as it has converged with the increasingly ubiquitous digitization of information both personal and public. As more information has become ones and zeroes at its most elemental level, more journalism has involved gathering, analyzing, and computing that information as quantitative data as well. Journalism appears to be taking, as Petre (2013) puts it, "a quantitative turn."

This wave of quantitatively oriented journalism has deep democratic roots; various forms of it are tied to open government advocacy (Parasie and Dagiral 2013) and the public-service tradition of investigative journalism (Cox 2000). It has great potential to broaden journalism's ability to make democratic institutions more responsive and legible to the public, but even within this sub-area of journalism, views of the public and the journalistic process are broadly disparate. Where the CAR of the 1990s was generally a single, unified concept for both professionals and scholars, the area has splintered into a set of ambiguously related practices variously termed by researchers computational journalism (Flew et al. 2012; Karlsen and Stavelin 2014), programmer-journalism (Parasie and Dagiral 2013), open-source journalism (Lewis and Usher 2013), or data journalism (Appelgren and Nygren 2014; Fink and Schudson 2014; Gynnild 2014), among others.

The journalists engaged in these practices seem particularly unconcerned with classifying their work *vis-à-vis* professional journalism, a sentiment most famously expressed in a short blog post by developer Adrian Holovaty (2009) that answered the question "Is data journalism?" with "Who cares?" This has resulted in several of the aforementioned terms being thrown together within professional discourse as synonyms. For researchers, however, these definitional questions are fundamental to analyzing these practices as sites of professional and cultural meaning, without which it is difficult for a coherent body of scholarship to be built. Indeed, the nascent scholarship in the area is often characterized by initial attempts to define these forms of journalism, each of which has largely been well-conceived and conceptually useful. But taken collectively, they have produced a cacophony of overlapping and indistinct definitions that forms a shaky foundation for deeper research into these practices. As these data-driven forms of journalism move closer to the center of professional journalistic practice, it is imperative that scholars do not treat them as simple synonyms but think carefully about the significant differences between the forms they take and their implications for changing journalistic practice as a whole.

Building on the work of Parasie and Dagiral (2013), Gynnild (2014), and Stavelin (2014) to delineate differences between these practices, this study is an attempt to develop a typology for analyzing forms within this quantitative area of journalism. It examines three professional practices—CAR, data journalism, and computational journalism—along four professional and epistemological dimensions. The analysis will begin with a brief discussion of the cultural background against which these practices are operating, then proceed with an introduction to the three practices, and finally an evaluation of each practice against each of the four dimensions.

Open-source Culture

These new forms of journalistic practice are emerging within an increasing interaction between programmers and journalists, as more programmers have begun to move into professional newsrooms and professional journalists have become increasingly drawn to programming's technical capabilities and cultural norms, which have been heavily influenced by the open-source movement.

The term "open source" as a technological principle was born in the late 1990s as a more palatable and widely accessible offshoot of the free software movement. Both movements focused on the ability to freely access, modify, and redistribute software as a manifestation of the universal right to access to information and knowledge (Coleman 2013; Kelty 2008). While open-source is intrinsically oriented not toward journalism but toward software, Lewis and Usher (2013) explained its application to journalism through four principles: transparency, iteration, tinkering, and participation. Each of those principles arises from the process of collaboratively building and sharing software, the practice at the core of the open-source software movement. And as Lewis and Usher explained, each is gradually becoming more prevalent within professional journalistic culture as a small subset of more computing-oriented journalists are drawn to the open-source ideals of creativity, experimentation, and liberation of information. In this way, the principles of open source have been an important common ground for bringing together "hacks" (journalists) and "hackers" (technologists).

Data-driven Journalism Practices

The three journalistic practices examined here are not mutually exclusive. Since they have very similar professional and epistemological roots, they will inevitably overlap, in some cases significantly. Actual cases of these practices will often display characteristics of more than one of these categories, as well as the marks of open-source principles. Key institutions have been involved in the perpetuation of more than one of these practices; for example, the National Institute for Computer-Assisted Reporting (NICAR) was the central organization in computer-assisted reporting during the 1990s and is now a central organization in connecting and training those who practice data journalism (Fink and Anderson 2014). In addition, many of the journalists who engage in these practices themselves tend to emphasize their continuity; data journalists generally characterize themselves as following in the same tradition as CAR. But there are significant differences between these forms of practice, and the following is an attempt to pull them apart and clarify them conceptually. This paper relies heavily on research into these practices within the United States and Scandinavia, since those have been the most thoroughly studied geographical settings for this work. It thus broadly describes the forms as they are generally practiced in those environments, though national and local variations certainly exist, both within these areas and outside them.

Computer-assisted Reporting

Though the use of computers in journalism dates back to the 1950s (Cox 2000), the *de facto* godfather of CAR is Philip Meyer, who outlined a new form called precision journalism in a book of the same name (Meyer 1973). Precision journalism was modeled after social science, using empirical methods (particularly surveys and content analysis) and statistical analysis to achieve more definitive answers to journalistic questions. It was not until the late 1980s and early 1990s that precision journalism, since recast as

CAR, began to make significant inroads into newsrooms, led by several high-profile, Pulitzer Prize-winning stories that became an important vehicle for professional valida- tion (Houston 1996).

CAR became closely tied to investigative reporting, often being seen as an auxil- iary tool to aid in long-term, public-affairs journalism projects (Cox 2000; Gynnild 2014; Parasie and Dagiral 2013). Though CAR journalists often fought against the perception that their practices were only for time-consuming investigative story packages—an asso- ciation that may ultimately have limited CAR's adoption within professional journalism (Gynnild 2014), they also encouraged it at times, characterizing it as, in the words of one CAR pioneer, "the new investigative journalism" (Jaspin 1993). The term CAR has fallen out of favor since the early 2000s as its technology has broadly diffused throughout newsrooms; Meyer himself called in 1999 for the moniker to be retired, describing it as an "embarrassing reminder that we are entering the 21st century as the only profession in which computer users feel the need to call attention to ourselves" (Meyer 1999, 4). Meyer's call ultimately went unheeded, as CAR continues to be practiced in journalism, though it appears to be invoked more often as a historical mode of quantitative journal- ism than a contemporary practice. A comparison between CAR and data journalism or computational journalism, as this paper undertakes, is thus a characterization more of change in practice over time than a comparison of contemporaneous practices.

While CAR had its roots in social science-based statistical methods, it came to embody two sets of practices: the data gathering and statistical analysis descended from Meyer's precision journalism, and more general computer-based information- gathering skills such as online and archival research and even email interviews (Miller 1998; Yarnall et al. 2008). The more general information-gathering skills have become so elemental a part of journalistic work that they can no longer be considered, in Powers' (2011) terms, "technologically specific work," though the statistical- and data- oriented forms of CAR remain such because of their relative lack of diffusion. This is the form of CAR that this paper refers to with the term, and the one that serves as the foundation for the modern approaches of data journalism and computational journal- ism (Gynnild 2014).

Data Journalism

Sometimes referred to as data-driven journalism, data journalism seems to have taken up the mantle of CAR in contemporary professional journalism. Though it is less preferred by scholars, data journalism appears to be the term of choice in the news industry for journalism based on data analysis and the presentation of such analysis (though note the ambivalence toward the term found by Appelgren and Nygren 2014). Professional definitions have tended to be broad, characterizing data journalism as essentially any activity that deals with data in conjunction with journalistic reporting and editing or toward journalistic ends, as in Stray's (2011) definition of data journalism as "obtaining, reporting on, curating and publishing data in the public interest." Several others have defined data journalism in terms of its convergence between several dispa- rate fields and practices, characterizing it as a hybrid form that encompasses statistical analysis, computer science, visualization and web design, and reporting (Bell 2012; Bradshaw 2010; Thibodeaux 2011). Data journalism has also been closely associated with the use and proliferation of open data and open-source tools to analyze and display that data (Gynnild 2014), though open data is not necessarily or exclusively a part of its domain of practice (Parasie and Dagiral 2013).

Data journalism has been ascendant since the late 2000s, before which time most data analysis within newsrooms had either been in the form of CAR or in news organizations that dealt largely in specialist financial information (Bell 2012). Though it is not a central element of professional journalistic work, it has made significant inroads into the news industry, with heavy demand throughout the profession despite a relatively small number of dedicated data journalists and relative rarity outside of the most resource-rich news organizations (Fink and Anderson 2014; Howard 2014). Young and Hermida (2014) argue that a new professional class of data journalists is beginning to form, though they have often appropriated computational methods to fit dominant professional practices. One particularly celebrated example of data journalism was *The Guardian*'s 2009–10 project reporting on the expense claims of Members of the United Kingdom's Parliament, in which the newspaper published 460,000 pages of expense reports online and asked their readers to sort through them and flag questionable claims. The project resulted in investigative reports and data visualizations led many Members of Parliament to re-examine and re-pay some of their claims. This project exemplifies the data journalism model in its focus on opening data to the public and its use of public input to drive data analysis, visualization, and reporting (Gray, Bounegru, and Chambers 2012).

While data journalism is often used within the context of investigative projects such as *The Guardian*'s, it is much more loosely coupled with investigative journalism than was CAR. Some scholars and professionals have emphasized the continuity between CAR and data journalism (e.g., Gordon 2013; Gray, Bounegru, and Chambers 2012), but data journalism's decoupling with investigative journalism and integration into broader journalistic practices marks a significant break between CAR and data journalism (Gray, Bounegru, and Chambers 2012; Marshall 2011; Minkoff 2010). Other distinctions include data journalism's emphasis on visualization as a core practice through a close connection between visualization design and journalistic values (Gordon 2013; Weber and Rall 2013), and an epistemological break in which data journalism views readers as co-constructors of truths and moral claims (Parasie and Dagiral 2013).

Computational Journalism

Computational journalism has at times been used by scholars to include CAR and data journalism, conflating the previous two forms; indeed, the most common definition of computational journalism seems to encompass both CAR and data journalism: "the combination of algorithms, data, and knowledge from the social sciences to supplement the accountability function of journalism" (Hamilton and Turner 2009, 2). But by defining them so broadly, this definition does not allow much room to draw significant distinctions between each of the three practices. Instead, following Diakopoulos (2011), I define computational journalism here as a strand of technologically oriented journalism centered on the application of computing and computational thinking to the practices of information gathering, sense-making, and information presentation, rather than the journalistic use of data or social science methods more generally.

Stavelin (2014) helpfully emphasizes the application of computational tools and methods in the service of journalistic aims in his definition of computational journalism, though he notes that it goes beyond a particular set of tools to a set of processes built on a particular mode of thought known as computational thinking. This form of thinking—developed as a concept by Wing (2006, 2008) but with roots in mid-twentieth-century computer science (National Research Council of the National Academies 2010)—is built around abstraction and automation. Abstraction, the ability to break down information or problems beyond their immediate material context, is the central element of computational thinking. It is a cognitive process, rather than a practice necessarily done by computer; computing, then, is simply the automation of abstracted information and processes (Wing 2008). These automation processes often take the form of algorithms, which are occasionally considered a third element of computational thinking (Flew et al. 2012). Algorithms are the abstraction of a step-by-step procedure taking an input and producing an output to accomplish a defined outcome (Diakopoulos 2014a; Wing 2008). Algorithms can prioritize, classify, and filter information, and can be involved in journalism at several stages, including distribution—as in search results and audience metrics—determining topics to cover, or even writing stories themselves (Anderson 2013a; Carlson 2014).

Even with this narrowed definition of computational journalism, there are a variety of types of projects that might fit under its umbrella. Diakopoulos (2014a) describes the use of algorithmic processes in reporting on other algorithms, such as ProPublica's recreation of the algorithm used to send personalized campaign emails in the 2012 US presidential campaign or *The Wall Street Journal*'s use of simulated user profiles to determine the algorithms governing price discrimination in online commerce. More directly, computational processes can produce the news content itself, as in Narrative Science's use of structured data to produce automated financial and sports articles (Bell 2012). A more widely applicable example of computational journalism may be DocumentCloud, founded by ProPublica and *New York Times* journalists in 2008, which hosts user-submitted and user-annotated documents and provides computational tools to process them, such as optical character recognition (Cohen et al. 2011). Though they involve different stages of the journalistic process and different levels of human involvement, each of these examples involve the core elements of computational journalism—practices or services built around computational tools in the service of journalistic ends.

Like data journalism, computational journalism has been characterized as a descendant of CAR. Gynnild (2014) identifies Philip Meyer as an ahead-of-his-time pioneer of computational thinking's application to journalism, and others have said that journalists have been practicing computational journalism (or computational thinking) for decades without labeling it as such (e.g., Linch 2010). Indeed, CAR is built in part around the use of simple computational processes—most commonly database analysis—to sort information. However, as Diakopoulos (2011) notes, computational journalism goes beyond CAR in its focus on the processing capabilities of computing, particularly aggregating, automating, and abstracting information. Likewise, there is also significant commonality between data journalism and computational journalism in the use of computational tools and collaborative processes to analyze and present data. But, as Stray (2011) points out, not all data journalism is computational; computational journalism works primarily through abstraction of information to produce computable models, while data journalism works primarily through analysis of data sets to produce data-oriented stories (Stavelin 2014). The three practices, then, are distinct quantitatively oriented journalistic forms: CAR is rooted in social science methods and the deliberate style and public-affairs orientation of investigative journalism, data journalism is characterized by its participatory openness and cross-field hybridity, and computational journalism is focused on the application of the processes of abstraction and automation to information.

Typology

Having outlined each of the concepts, we now turn toward the effort to classify and differentiate them. The typology (visualized in Figure 1) that follows examines four dimensions: two of them are professional—professional expertise versus networked information and transparency versus opacity. One, big data versus targeted sampling, is epistemological, and the final one has a professional/moral dimension—the vision of an active versus passive public. The dimensions of this typology are ideal types (Weber 1947), generalized forms not meant to capture the details of a particular case, but instead intended to serve as ideal forms against which individual cases and genres might be compared. As such, the classification of each form of journalism into this typology necessarily involves broad generalizations. Because of the overlap in practice among CAR, data journalism, and computational journalism, the typology is not meant to be a definitive placement of these genres regarding each type, but rather an initial guide used to evaluate any computational or data-oriented project, tool, or organization.

This typology was developed through a close reading of about 90 texts on CAR, data journalism, and computational journalism, within both academic and professional discourse. The professional discourse on the subject consisted largely of articles in journalism reviews such as the *Columbia Journalism Review* and *Nieman Journalism Lab*, textbooks, and other blog posts and articles by data and computational journalism professionals, gathered through several years of personal collection, augmented by archive searches of journalism publications and snowball-style data gathering through hyperlinks and citations. After analysis of a subset of these texts, an initial typology was developed; the analytical corpus was expanded and the typology revised and refined after academic feedback.

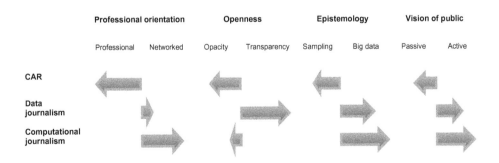

FIGURE 1
A visualized typology of data-driven journalism forms

Professional Expertise Versus Networked Information

The first dimension of the typology is an orientation toward openness and broad participation on one end and professional expertise and limited participation on the other. Expressed organizationally, it is the difference between a production process limited to professionals within institutional organizations and one open to a networked, loosely joined group consisting of both professionals and non-professionals. More acutely, it addresses the practices' relationship to the norms and practices of traditional professional journalism, particularly the degree to which they are subordinated to the specialized knowledge and institutionalized routines of traditional reporting. This tension between broad participation and professional control has been a defining one in twenty-first-century journalism (Lewis 2012), though it is magnified at the intersection between computing and journalism, as distributed participation is a fundamental element of open-source practice (Lewis and Usher 2013).

Throughout its history, CAR has been continually subordinated to professional norms and framed as a way to enhance professional expertise. Books and articles defending CAR and explaining its practices are filled with admonitions that CAR does not replace or threaten traditional reporting, depicting it as simply a new tool in the service of existing practices, rather than a new way of seeing news or information. "Nothing can replace good, old-fashioned reporting, but CAR is an additional tool," said one investigative reporter in a typical statement (Garrison 1996, 116). Data is similarly seen within CAR as entirely secondary to human-oriented aspects of a story—that is, the ones that must be gathered through traditional, "shoe-leather" practices of interviewing and direct observation (e.g., Houston 1996; Jaspin 1993; Miller 1998). This subjugation to the methods of professional methods is also evident in CAR's close ties to investigative journalism, which sits at the core of journalists' professional identity (Ettema and Glasser 1998). In CAR, claims from data are precipitated by leads based on reporting and are subjected to journalistic practices such as cross-checking and interviewing that are drawn from and subordinated to investigative journalism (Parasie 2014). The effect is that, as Philip Meyer put it, CAR is "the same old journalism but with better tools" (Miller 1988, 36).

This placement of CAR strictly in the service of professional norms and practices puts it squarely within the professionalist, "high modern" paradigm prevalent in journalism during the era in which it developed (Flew et al. 2012). In this model, data held no value of their own except to produce stories, and "the computer-assisted reporter was still primarily a journalist rather than a technologist; the underlying goal was to produce a better story" (Lewis and Usher 2013, 605; Parasie and Dagiral 2013). This foregrounding of story has continually pulled CAR back into the realm of the investigative reporting-oriented professional practices, like interviewing and examination of documents, around which journalists are most keen to build their professional expertise and identity (Coddington 2014). As Meyer (2002) argues, CAR has also existed in tension with the professional journalistic norms into which it is embedded. In particular, CAR's emphasis on the analysis of data collected according to social scientific principles is a real challenge to traditional journalism, which tends to defer to the expertise of official sources and the authority of anecdotal example and personal experience. Still, by and large, CAR is a form of data processing that is subordinated almost completely under the principles of professional journalism.

Data journalism retains CAR's emphasis on subordinating data to the professional journalistic value of narrative and the "story." Just as in CAR, data journalism discourse foregrounds telling the story over using data, though it is looser in its connection to traditional journalistic practices in producing those narratives (Fink and Anderson 2014; Stavelin 2014). As Howard (2014, 5) asserts in his definition of the practice: "data journalism is telling stories with numbers, or finding stories in them." In data journalism, however, the expertise needed to determine the story has spread beyond the strictly professional realm of CAR. This storytelling work no longer requires interviews and other professional journalistic practices, but only examination of the data. This opens up the expertise of using data to tell stories to anyone capable of accurately drawing meaning from that data, professional journalist or not. Data journalist and researcher Liliana Bounegru explains this shift aptly:

> By enabling anyone to drill down into data sources and find information that is rele-
> vant to them, as well as to verify assertions and challenge commonly received assump-
> tions, data journalism effectively represents the mass democratisation of resources,
> tools, techniques and methodologies that were previously used by specialists—whether
> investigative reporters, social scientists, statisticians, analysts or other experts. (Gray,
> Bounegru, and Chambers 2012, "Data Journalism in Perspective")

In practical terms, this openness toward non-professional involvement leads many data journalism projects to involve opening data sets to the audience and developing tools for them to explore or personalize them (Parasie and Dagiral 2013), as well as crowdsourcing the data and analysis stemming from it—inverting the normal computa-tional mode of using software to compute human data by instead providing data to humans to process (Appelgren and Nygren 2014; Stavelin 2014, 44). Data journalism retains an emphasis on editorial selection and professional news judgment in analyzing and presenting data (Stray 2010), but it does so while also building around a recognition that expertise in analyzing and drawing meaning from that data often exists outside of the profession, among the audience. Though data journalists see their work as fundamentally sense-making as other professional journalists do, they have opened up that sense-making process to be a collective one, bringing the citizen alongside the professional (Parasie and Dagiral 2013).

A distributed information production process is even more central to computa-tional journalism than to data journalism. Much like open-source journalism, computa-tional journalism and computational thinking are at their core collaborative processes. Computational thinking is fundamentally a group phenomenon rather than an individ-ual one (National Research Council of the National Academies 2010), and computational journalism is oriented around the belief that human expertise is located in crowds, rather than small, closely guarded enclaves. Computational journalism is an effort to harness that expertise, taking advantage of emerging sets of tools that allow for broad, many-to-many collaboration (Cohen et al. 2011; Flew et al. 2012). Computational jour-nalism can shed the emphasis on narrative and storytelling that tends to draw CAR and data journalism back toward professional journalistic practices and news judgment, as it tends to be more focused on producing a tangible product or platform than a narrative (Diakopoulos 2013; Stavelin 2014), though Diakopoulos (2011, 2014b) also details forms of computational journalism that are oriented toward finding and telling stories.

There are limits to the distributed structure and practices of computational journalism. It is much more reliant on technical expertise—most notably, advanced programming skills—that while not limited to a particular profession (and certainly not journalism) can nonetheless be quite difficult to acquire. Additionally, Karlsen and Stavelin (2014) found that even those highly specialized technical skills can still be subordinated to journalistic ones when computational journalism is practiced within a traditional newsroom. Still, of the three forms examined here, computational journalism is least wedded to professional journalistic norms and practices and most essentially distributed and networked in its practice.

Transparency Versus Opacity

Transparency has been an ascendant journalistic value over the past decade, one characterized as a crucial element to establishing credibility with an increasingly mistrustful public (Karlsson 2010; Plaisance 2007). Though professional journalists have long advocated for open information for themselves, they have been much less willing to open up the process by which they produce news to the public. Lewis and Usher (2013) describe transparency as a key element of the open-source movement, though journalists have been slow to pick the value up because of their concerns about its threat to their professional autonomy. Karlsson (2010) classifies two distinct strains of journalistic transparency: disclosure transparency, or openness about how news is produced, and participatory transparency, or the ability of those outside the profession to participate in the journalistic process. I will focus here on disclosure transparency, which Karlsson notes was technically achievable in the pre-digital media system, but was largely barred by a closed professional culture.

CAR is grounded in the same modernist professional journalistic culture that has typically resisted efforts to make its professional practices transparent to the public. Though it has exhibited a stronger inclination toward disclosure transparency than that culture through the transparency of social science methods (Meyer 2002), some traces of that opacity are evident. In CAR, as Taylor (2009) notes, the data are meant to be invisible within a story—something to be included, but downplayed so as not to detract from the story's core human elements. The advice given in Miller's (1998) CAR textbook comports with this description: choose carefully what numbers to include, and only lead with those numbers when they are particularly compelling. Otherwise, the data should recede into the background. As for the process by which those numbers are gathered, Miller advocates transparency, but equally emphasizes how it should be limited: "Explain, when necessary and relevant, how you gathered your information. But don't go overboard" (Miller 1998, 225). In the CAR paradigm, neither methods nor the data itself are the story, so both should be set in the background to the extent that they infringe on journalists' professional abilities to filter data and find meaning in it for the audience.

By contrast, transparency of both process and product are a core element of data journalism. Some of that transparency has come to data journalism by way of the open-source philosophy, as Gynnild (2014) characterized the use of open-source tools and open data as a defining element of data journalism. Unlike in CAR, publishing the data alongside articles based on it is so fundamental to the practice of data journalism that it is described as something that "goes without saying" (Gray, Bounegru, and Chambers 2012, "Engaging People Around Your Data"). *The Guardian*'s Simon Rogers (Stray 2010) described this data publication as the primary difference between how his paper approaches data now and how it did so a decade prior, during the heyday of CAR. In Rogers' account, the shift has been a response to demand driven by the access to unfiltered information elsewhere on the internet. Online audiences, Rogers said, "want the interpretation and the analysis from people, but they also want the veracity of seeing the real thing, without having it aggregated or put together. They just want to see the raw data" (Stray 2010). In data journalism, displaying this kind of transparency does not undermine the story the journalist is trying to convey; it simply adds to it.

The role of transparency is much less settled within computational journalism, thanks to particular obstacles endemic to computational work. Algorithmic transparency, Diakopoulos (2014b) argues, is much more difficult than data transparency, as it involves additional labor costs for both creating and making sense of an algorithm for public consumption. Likewise, Stavelin (2014) contends that software is opaque by nature, and thus any transparency in computational journalism is chiefly borrowed from professional journalistic values, rather than coming from within its own native framework. Computational journalism does, however, have its own normative well from which to draw an orientation toward transparency—namely the influence of the open-source software movement (Lewis and Usher 2013; Parasie and Dagiral 2013), whose commitment to transparency far outstrips that of professional journalism. To the degree, then, that computational journalists adhere to the ideals of that movement, they may be able to overcome the barriers to disclosure that exist within the work they do. Diakopoulos (2014b) offers a promising model to incorporate transparency into the journalistic use of algorithms, though he acknowledges the tensions inherent in such an adaptation of journalistic norms.

Targeted Sampling Versus Big Data

The third dimension of the typology is epistemological, having to do with how data is gathered and analyzed in order to generate conclusions and knowledge. On one pole is data gathered through targeted means such as sampling, with conclusions reached through inference and causality placed at a premium. This is generally the epistemological approach of classic social science. On the other pole is a focus on large data sets or collections of information that are obtained through attempts at capturing the totality of a phenomenon, with an emphasis on exploratory analysis and simple correlation rather than causation. This roughly corresponds to the epistemology of the "big data" movement, which Mayer-Schönberger and Cukier (2013) have helpfully set in stark contrast to that of traditional social science. From a big-data perspective, simple correlation and exploratory rather than hypothesis-driven analysis are often sufficient because the size of the database overcomes any analytical shortcomings with it (Bollier 2010; Mayer-Schönberger and Cukier 2013).

CAR is located toward the targeted sampling pole of this dimension. Meyer's (2002) precision journalism philosophy out of which CAR grew is not just deeply rooted in the practice of social science; it *is* social science, simply translated for journalists. CAR remained rooted in that social science mindset with an emphasis on hypothesis testing and survey research, especially early on. As CAR grew, however, more of its projects demonstrated an openness to more complete data and less statistically rigorous analysis. As we will see, data journalism and computational journalism are in part responses to a dramatic rise in information scale, and CAR was also a response to certain forms of information abundance (Parasie and Dagiral 2013). But it typically dealt with a somewhat smaller scale of data, and it often—but not always—used sampling and statistical analysis as a method to produce intelligibility for large data sets.

Data journalists often emphasize the exponential increase in the amount of data being collected and the size of individual data sets as a key element of what is new about their practice (Gray, Bounegru, and Chambers 2012; Howard 2014; Rogers 2011). When the primary task shifts from finding and collecting data to processing it, the analysis of that data accordingly shifts from being driven by hypotheses that spurred the gathering of that data to a more inductive and exploratory approach. Tellingly, while Appelgren and Nygren (2014) described the data journalists they studied as being tied to Meyer's methods, none of those journalists mentioned social scientific methods, instead emphasizing the size of the data sets they dealt with. Rogers (2011) also ties this change to the increasing speed of data journalism, noting that the old form of the practice often involved weeks of in-depth data analysis, while the new form prioritizes producing analyses as quickly as possible. Both the scale of the data and the pace of the work, then, push data journalism toward a more exploratory, big-data form of analysis.

Computational journalism is similarly oriented to a big-data epistemology, largely because it is responding, just as data journalism is, to a shift toward increasing information abundance (Flew et al. 2012). The speed issue faced by data journalism is much less present here, but the foregrounding of computational methods encourages a particular inclination toward use of unaltered large data sets. Such computational methods allow extremely large data sets to be handled in full, thus eliminating the need for sampling. Parasie and Dagiral (2013) explain that the programmer-journalists in their study "do not consider statistics as a major tool because, in their opinion, data do not hide anything if they are granular and complete" (863). They eschew sampling because they do not believe such procedures can produce new knowledge from data. Instead, that intelligibility comes from the ability to access complete data through skilled use of computational tools.

Vision of the Public: Active Versus Passive

The conception of the public has been a central element of modern professional journalism; its invocation has been a foundation for journalistic claims of authority. Journalism has historically seen the public as a unitary, rational, and fixed body, but the online environment has deeply complicated this vision, at once revealing the public as fragmented and creating the potential for a more interactive and participatory public (Anderson 2013b). This vision of a fragmented and participatory public creates tension with journalists' professional norms of autonomy and authority, leading journalists to continue to resist seeing the public as a productive and interactive part of the journalistic process (Lewis 2012). Each of these three forms acts on a vision of a more active public than does traditional professional journalism, though the degree of that public's activity and generative value varies widely.

The public is crucial to the work of CAR, but in a much less active way than in data journalism. As a form closely tied to investigative journalism, CAR relies on the public to supply the moral outrage that it works to produce. As Ettema and Glasser (1998) argue, the normative aim of investigative journalism is to highlight violations of the moral order, as determined by the public for which those journalists write, and their response to the story. In this way, "*every* investigation must be understood as a call to the conscience of a community" (Ettema and Glasser 1998, 187)—a test of the public's consensus on community values. The public's role is to respond to the perceived moral outrage in a way that upholds their community values and condemns violators. This role for the public typically does not involve analyzing or contributing to the data themselves; CAR aims to use the truths in public data to set the public agenda, rather than giving the public an active role in determining its own meaning from data (Parasie and Dagiral 2013).

Like CAR, data journalism is also built around informing the public about critical issues, but the public is involved to a greater degree and to different ends. The goal of data journalism is to allow the public to analyze and draw understanding from data themselves, with the data journalist's role being to access and present the data on the public's behalf. This has a substantial influence on the process of data journalism itself, which is oriented around creating utility for the user. In developing data journalism products—often data visualization or Web applications—their usefulness to the audience is a prime consideration (Gray, Bounegru, and Chambers 2012; Stray 2010). Consider the contrast with CAR, whose primary measure of "impact" is in influence not on the public itself, but on institutions or officials through public outrage. In data journalism, the public plays a much more direct role, as the goal is more simply to provide a useful way for the public to enhance its own understanding of, and draw its own meaning from, public issues. On the other hand, as Fink and Anderson (2014) note, while many data journalists profess a devotion to serving an active public, their conception of that public is still primarily rationalized and anonymized through online metrics, rather than as a personal or reciprocal participant in the journalistic process.

Computational journalism also views its public as a collection of rational, participatory users who are capable of producing understanding from data themselves. The members of the public, in this view, expect to interact with the information they encounter, and the goal of computational journalism is to provide them with the tools they need to perform their own filtering and abstraction with it (Flew et al. 2012; Hamilton and Turner 2009). As Gynnild (2014) notes, the computational view of the audience as autonomous and creative enough to perform their own searches of data—allowed by computational tools—is part of what enables the publication of data in itself to be considered journalistic. This overall view of an interactive, autonomous public that expects to be engaged with data is very similar to that of data journalism; if anything, computational journalism's envisioned public is even more empowered in its ability to do its own computational thinking on the data it can access.

Conclusion

This typology is only an initial attempt to classify more systematically these data-driven journalistic practices. These dimensions are hardly the only ones differentiating them, and this area of journalism remains unsettled, so new dimensions and forms of practice may emerge over the next several years. Still, this typology indicates a significant gap between the professional and epistemological orientations of CAR, on the one hand, and both data journalism and computational journalism, on the other (see Figure 1). This divide has its origins in the cultural background from which each has approached journalism: CAR arose out of an effort to marry social science with modern professional journalism, and especially investigative journalism. Data journalism and computational journalism, on the other hand, have arisen from the intersection of professional journalism with open-source culture. Each represents a different amalgam between those two social realms, but the fact that those combinations are being made from very similar raw cultural materials gives them much more in common with each other than with CAR.

As it stands, data journalism is the closest we have to the melding of professional journalism and both open-source and computational principles, as advocated by Lewis and Usher (2013) and others. Data journalists' statements that narrative, storytelling, and traditional reporting are still important parts of good data journalism (e.g., Gray, Bounegru, and Chambers 2012) are attempts to closely link themselves to the dominant professional view of journalism. By reiterating the importance of traditional journalistic work, they help to ensure that their own work is taken seriously by professional journalism—that they are seen as continuing its practices, rather than harming them (Powers 2011).

Like data journalism, computational journalism is a blend between professional journalism and open-source culture, though through its tighter connection to programming it moves closer to the influence of open-source culture than does data journalism. Computational journalism thus inherits a strong emphasis on open and networked workflows but also remains more materially and technically oriented than data journalism. The bridge to professional journalism and to CAR is a bit further here than with data journalism: the concept of computational thinking, of abstracting data when approaching complex tasks or objects of news down to granular, discrete elements, does not appear to have a precedent or analog in pre-computer-age journalism. Gynnild (2014) does, however, identify Meyer as an ahead-of-his-time pioneer of computational thinking's application to journalism. Though computational journalism differs significantly from CAR in many of its emphases and animating principles, its emphasis on abstracting journalistic inquiries to large-scale and quantifiable forms, and using computational methods to filter and analyze large bodies of information, can be traced to CAR's influence.

Despite its generalized nature and the fluidity of the practices it covers, this typology offers a useful orienting framework for future research into these emergent forms. It highlights several under-researched dimensions that may be especially fruitful for gaining a fuller understanding of data-driven journalistic practices and their relationship to both professional journalism and the public. First, scholars would do well to focus more closely on the epistemological elements of each of the forms—the ways in which their constructions of facts and knowledge compare and contrast to each other and to other professional journalistic practices. This is one of data-driven journalism's starkest points of divergence from the modern professional journalistic mindset, and further work that fleshes out the epistemological roots of these practices, such as Parasie (2014) in this issue, would be most helpful in outlining its contours.

Second, research should delve deeper into the shifting position of data-driven journalism in relationship to the larger field of professional journalism. On this point, I echo Anderson's (2013a) call to approach these forms of journalism from an institutional or field perspective, examining the social and cultural power struggles within this emerging field and in relation to adjacent fields such as traditional journalism or computer science. As this field grows and coheres, its autonomy from and flows of influence and capital between adjacent fields may be crucial in shaping broader journalistic practice.

Finally, beyond general statements about commitment to openness and participation, the relationship between these journalistic forms and the public has received little scrutiny. Research should more fully examine these journalists' vision of the public and their relationship to it, including their audiences' reception of their work. We have little knowledge of whether data journalists' openness to the public is being substantively reciprocated, or the epistemological and attitudinal frameworks in which audiences are consuming and evaluating the journalism they produce. Research from such an audience-centric perspective could extend our currently one-dimensional understanding of data-driven journalism and the public. To the extent that a quantitative turn is indeed occurring within journalism, it becomes particularly important to examine the ways such a turn changes its alignment with both the profession's traditional values and practices as well as the public.

ACKNOWLEDGEMENTS

The author thanks Steve Reese and Seth Lewis, as well as the anonymous reviewers for *Digital Journalism*, for their feedback on earlier drafts of this paper.

REFERENCES

Anderson, C. W. 2013a. "Towards a Sociology of Computational and Algorithmic Journalism." *New Media and Society* 15: 1005–1021.

Anderson, C. W. 2013b. *Rebuilding the News: Metropolitan Journalism in the Digital Age*. Philadelphia, PA: Temple University Press.

Appelgren, Ester, and Gunnar Nygren. 2014. "Data Journalism in Sweden: Introducing New Methods and Genres of Journalism into 'Old' Organizations." *Digital Journalism* 2: 394–405. doi:10.1080/21670811.2014.884344.

Bell, Emily. 2012. "Journalism by Numbers." *Columbia Journalism Review*. September 5. http://www.cjr.org/cover_story/journalism_by_numbers.php?page=all.

Bollier, David. 2010. *The Promise and Peril of Big Data*. Washington, DC: The Aspen Institute.

Bradshaw, Paul. 2010. "How to Be a Data Journalist." *The Guardian*, October 1. http://www.theguardian.com/news/datablog/2010/oct/01/data-journalism-how-to-guide.

Carlson, Matt. 2014. "The Robotic Reporter: Automated Journalism and the Redefinition of Labor, Compositional Forms, and Journalistic Authority." *Digital Journalism*. doi:10.1080/21670811.2014.976412.

Coddington, Mark. 2014. "Defending Judgment and Context in 'Original Reporting': Journalists' Construction of Newswork in a Networked Age." *Journalism* 15: 678–695.

Cohen, Sarah, Chengkai Li, Jun Yang, and Cong Yu. 2011. "Computational Journalism: A Call to Arms to Database Researchers." Paper presented at the 5th Biennial Conference on Innovative Data Systems Research (CIDR '11), Asilomar, CA, January 9–12. http://ranger.uta.edu/~cli/pubs/2011/cjdb-cidr11-clyy-nov10.pdf.

Coleman, E. Gabriella. 2013. *Coding Freedom: The Ethics and Aesthetics of Hacking*. Princeton, NJ: Princeton University Press.

Cox, Melisma. 2000. "The Development of Computer-assisted Reporting." Paper presented at AEJMC 2000, Phoenix, AZ, August 9–12. http://com.miami.edu/car/cox00.pdf.

Diakopoulos, Nicholas. 2011. "A Functional Roadmap for Innovation in Computational Journalism." April 22. http://www.nickdiakopoulos.com/2011/04/22/a-functional-roadmap-for-innovation-in-computational-journalism/.

Diakopoulos, Nicholas. 2013. "Finding Tools Vs. Making Tools: Discovering Common Ground between Computer Science and Journalism." *Nieman Journalism Lab*, February 14. http://www.niemanlab.org/2013/02/finding-tools-vs-making-tools-discovering-common-ground-between-computer-science-and-journalism/.

Diakopoulos, Nicholas. 2014a. "Algorithmic Accountability: Journalistic Investigation of Computational Power Structures." *Digital Journalism*. doi:10.1080/21670811.2014.976411.

Diakopoulos, Nicholas. 2014b. *Algorithmic Accountability Reporting: On the Investigation of Black Boxes*. New York: Tow Center for Digital Journalism.

Ettema, James S., and Theodore L. Glasser. 1998. *Custodians of Conscience: Investigative Journalism and Public Virtue*. New York: Columbia University Press.

Fink, Katherine, and C. W. Anderson. 2014. "Data Journalism in the United States: Beyond the 'Usual Suspects'." *Journalism Studies*. doi:10.1080/1461670X.2014.939852.

Fink, Katherine, and Michael Schudson. 2014. "The Rise of Contextual Journalism, 1950s–2000s." *Journalism* 15: 3–20.

Flew, Terry, Christina Spurgeon, Anna Daniel, and Adam Swift. 2012. "The Promise of Computational Journalism." *Journalism Practice* 6: 157–171.

Garrison, Bruce. 1996. "Tools Daily Newspapers Use in Computer-Assisted Reporting." *Newspaper Research Journal* 17 (1): 113–126.

Gordon, Rich. 2013. "Want to Build a Data Journalism Team? You'll Need These Three People." *Northwestern University Knight Lab*, June 28. http://knightlab.northwestern.edu/2013/06/28/want-to-build-a-data-journalism-team-youll-need-these-three-people/.

Gray, Jonathan, Liliana Bounegru, and Lucy Chambers, eds. 2012. *The Data Journalism Handbook*. http://datajournalismhandbook.org/1.0/en/index.html.

Gynnild, Astrid. 2014. "Journalism Innovation Leads to Innovation Journalism: The Impact of Computational Exploration on Changing Mindsets." *Journalism* 15: 713–730. doi:10.1177/1464884913486393.

Hamilton, James T., and Fred Turner. 2009. "Accountability through Algorithm: Developing the Field of Computational Journalism." Report given at the Behavioral Sciences Summer Workshop, Stanford, CA, July 27–31. http://www.stanford.edu/~fturner/Hamilton%20Turner%20Acc%20by%20Alg%20Final.pdf.

Hermida, Alfred, and Mary-Lynn Young. 2014. "From Mr. and Mrs. Outlier to Central Tendencies: Computational Journalism and Crime Reporting at the *Los Angeles Times*." *Digital Journalism*. doi:10.1080/21670811.2014.976409.

Holovaty, Adrian. 2009. "The Definitive, Two-Part Answer to 'is Data Journalism?'" May 21. http://www.holovaty.com/writing/data-is-journalism/.

Houston, Brant. 1996. *Computer-assisted Reporting: A Practical Guide*. New York: St. Martin's.

Howard, Alexander Benjamin. 2014. *The Art and Science of Data-driven Journalism*. New York: Tow Center for Digital Journalism. http://towcenter.org/wp-content/uploads/2014/05/Tow-Center-Data-Driven-Journalism.pdf.

Jaspin, Elliot. 1993. "The New Investigative Journalism: Exploring Public Records by Computer." In *Demystifying Media Technology*, edited by John V. Pavlik and Everette E. Dennis, 142–149. Mountain View, CA: Mayfield.

Karlsen, Joakim, and Eirik Stavelin. 2014. "Computational Journalism in Norwegian Newsrooms." *Journalism Practice* 8: 34–48. doi:10.1080/17512786.2013.813190.

Karlsson, Michael. 2010. "Rituals of Transparency: Evaluating Online News Outlets' Uses of Transparency Rituals in the United States, United Kingdom and Sweden." *Journalism Studies* 11: 535–545.

Kelty, Christopher M. 2008. *Two Bits: The Cultural Significance of Free Software*. Durham, NC: Duke University Press.

Lewis, Seth C. 2012. "The Tension between Professional Control and Open Participation: Journalism and Its Boundaries." *Information, Communication and Society* 15: 836–866. doi:10.1080/1369118X.2012.674150.

Lewis, Seth C., and Nikki Usher. 2013. "Open Source and Journalism: Toward New Frameworks for Imagining News Innovation." *Media, Culture and Society* 35: 602–619. doi:10.1177/0163443713485494.

Linch, Greg. 2010. "Why Computational Thinking Should be the Core of the New Journalism Mindset." *Publish2*, April 30. http://blog.publish2.com/2010/04/30/computational-thinking-new-journalism-mindset/.

Maier, Scott R. 2002. "Numbers in the News: A Mathematics Audit of a Daily Newspaper." *Journalism Studies* 3: 507–519.

Marshall, Sarah. 2011. "10 Things Every Journalist Should Know about Data." *News: Rewired*, April 26. http://www.newsrewired.com/2011/04/26/10-things-every-journalist-should-know-about-data/.

Mayer-Schönberger, Viktor, and Kenneth Cukier. 2013. *Big Data: A Revolution That Will Transform How We Live, Work, and Think*. New York: Eamon Dolan/Houghton Mifflin Harcourt.

Meyer, Philip. 1973. *Precision Journalism*. Bloomington, IL: Indiana University Press.

Meyer, Philip. 1999. "The Future of CAR: Declare Victory and Get out!." In *When Nerds and Words Collide: Reflections on the Development of Computer Assisted Reporting*, edited by Nora Paul, 4–5. St. Petersburg, FL: Poynter Institute.

Meyer, Philip. 2002. *Precision Journalism*. 4th ed. Lanham, MD: Rowman and Littlefield.

Miller, Tim. 1988. "The Data-base Revolution." *Columbia Journalism Review* 27 (3): 35–38.

Miller, Lisa C. 1998. *Power Journalism: Computer-assisted Reporting*. Fort Worth, TX: Harcourt Brace and Co.

Minkoff, Michelle. 2010. "Bringing Data Journalism into Curricula." March 24. http://michellem inkoff.com/2010/03/24/bringing-data-journalism-into-curricula/.

National Research Council of the National Academies. 2010. *Report of a Workshop on the Scope and Nature of Computational Thinking*. Washington, DC: National Academies Press.

Parasie, Sylvain. 2014. "Data-driven Revelation? Epistemological Tensions in Investigative Journalism in the Age of 'Big Data'." *Digital Journalism*. doi:10.1080/21670811.2014.976408.

Parasie, Sylvain, and Eric Dagiral. 2013. "Data-driven Journalism and the Public Good: 'Computer-Assisted Reporters' and 'Programmer-Journalists' in Chicago." *New Media and Society* 15: 853–871.

Petre, Caitlin. 2013. "A Quantitative Turn in Journalism?" *Tow Center for Digital Journalism*, October 30. http://towcenter.org/blog/a-quantitative-turn-in-journalism/.

Plaisance, Patrick L. 2007. "Transparency: An Assessment of the Kantian Roots of a Key Element in Media Ethics Practice." *Journal of Mass Media Ethics* 22: 187–207.

Powers, Matthew. 2011. "'In Forms that are Familiar and Yet-to-Be Invented': American Journalism and the Discourse of Technologically Specific Work." *Journal of Communication Inquiry* 36: 24–43.

Rogers, Simon. 2011. "Data Journalism at the Guardian: What is It and How Do We Do It?" *The Guardian*, July 28. http://www.theguardian.com/news/datablog/2011/jul/28/data-journalism.

Stavelin, Eirik. 2014. *Computational Journalism: When Journalism Meets Programming*. PhD diss., Norway: University of Bergen.

Stray, Jonathan. 2010. "How the Guardian is Pioneering Data Journalism with Free Tools." *Nieman Journalism Lab*, August 5. http://www.niemanlab.org/2010/08/how-the-guardian-is-pioneering-data-journalism-with-free-tools/.

Stray, Jonathan. 2011. "A Computational Journalism Reading List." January 31. http://jonathanstray.com/a-computational-journalism-reading-list.

Taylor, Megan. 2009. "How Computer-Assisted Reporters Evolved into Programmer/Journalists." *PBS MediaShift*, August 7. http://www.pbs.org/mediashift/2009/08/how-computer-assisted-reporters-evolved-into-programmerjournalists219.

Thibodeaux, Troy. 2011. "5 Tips for Getting Started in Data Journalism." *Poynter*, October 6. http://www.poynter.org/how-tos/digital-strategies/147734/5-tips-for-getting-started-in-data-journalism/.

Weber, Max. 1947. *The Theory of Social and Economic Organization*. Translated and edited by Talcott Parsons. New York: Free Press.

Weber, Wibke, and Hannes Rall. 2013. "'We Are Journalists': Production Practices, Attitudes and a Case Study of the New York times Newsroom." In *Interaktive Infografiken*, edited by Wibke Weber, Miguel Burmester, and Ralph Tille, 161–172. Wiesbaden, Germany: Springer Vieweg.

Wing, Jeannette M. 2006. "Computational Thinking." *Communications of the ACM* 49 (3): 33–35.

Wing, Jeannette M. 2008. "Computational Thinking and Thinking about Computing." *Philosophical Transactions. Series A, Mathematical, Physical, and Engineering Sciences* 366: 3717–3725.

Yarnall, Louise, J. T. Johnson, Luke Rinne, and Michael Andrew Ranney. 2008. "How Post-Secondary Journalism Educators Teach Advanced CAR Data Analysis Skills in the Digital Age." *Journalism and Mass Communication Educator* 63: 146–164.

BETWEEN THE UNIQUE AND THE PATTERN
Historical tensions in our understanding of quantitative journalism

C. W. Anderson

This article proposes that the underlying ideas of data journalism are not new, but rather can be traced back in history and align with larger questions about the role of quantification in journalistic practice. This article sketches out a theoretical frame (assemblage theory) in which quantitative journalism is best understood by examining the objects of evidence that journalism mobilizes on its behalf. The article illustrates this perspective by outlining three historical tensions in notions of quantitative journalism: tensions between records and reports, individuality and social science, and isolated facts and broader patterns.

Introduction

The year was 1946, and newspaper journalism in the United States was in trouble. Such, at least, was the opinion of Kenneth Stewart, writing in the illustrated monthly magazine *The Survey Graphic*. Among the problems for news outlined by Stewart were monopoly ownership, the growth of newspaper chains, a reliance of too many news outlets on information from the Associated Press and other wire services, and collusion on the part of the American Newspaper Publishers Association to fix prices. Worst of all, Stewart lamented, was the fact that so many cities relied on only one source of information for their news:

> We have lost one thousand dailies and over three thousand weeklies in the past few decades. Only 117 cities continue to have competing newspaper ownership. In more than one hundred areas the only newspaper owns the only radio station. Five movie producers dominate the screen of the nation, through ownership of key theaters. On top of all this, some trade unions, by feather-bed rules, have placed undue and uneconomic burdens on free enterprise in the mass-media fields. (Stewart 1946, 453)

Accompanying this litany of statistics was a large informational graphic, titled "Newspapers" and produced by someone known only as "The Chartmakers" (Figure 1). The graphic was designed to visualize the arresting statistic that "only 1 city out of 12 has competing daily newspapers" (Stewart 1946, 453).

This chapter is adapted from the forthcoming *Journalistic Cultures of Truth: Data in the Digital Age* (Oxford University Press).

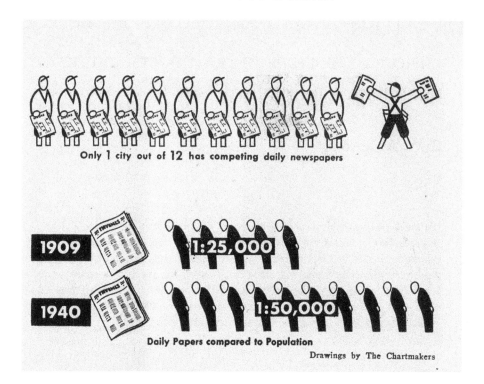

Only 1 city out of 12 has competing daily newspapers

1909

1:25,000

1940

1:50,000

Daily Papers compared to Population

Drawings by The Chartmakers

FIGURE 1

Uncredited Illustration from "Freedom to Read: Newspapers," published in Volume 39 of the Survey Graphic (1946)

This type of illustration was common in the publication appropriately titled *The Survey Graphic* and which, as part of its mission, attempted to make what its editors called "social work concerns" accessible to a broader public. *The Survey Graphic* had existed for more than 25 years, ever since it was decided to bolster the professional journal *The Survey* by publishing a more general-interest magazine designed less for social workers and more for everyday people who cared about social issues. Most importantly for the purposes of this essay, *The Survey Graphic* was designed to stand at the intersection of the world of research, the world of data, and the world of journalism; it attempted to "carry forward swift first hand investigations with a procedure comparable to that of scientific research ... interpret the findings of others ... employ photographs, maps, charts, the arts in gaining a hearing from two to twenty times that of formal books and reports (Finnegan 2003). The 1946 article on newspaper circulation, discussed above, is representative of this drive to meld statistics, contextual journalism, and striking illustrations in order to make a point. What I am calling "quantitative journalism," following the example of Mark Coddington (2014), seems at first glance many decades old.

In some ways, this brief trip back to the 1940s is a comforting one. The use of data to tell stories, it would appear, is not some recent imposition by statisticians and computer scientists on journalism's more humanistically inclined spirit. Data aggregation and information visualization have been part of journalism for a long time. Perhaps there is even something like a human need for data and for pictures built around data, a need that journalists, with the advent of new technologies, can finally satisfy. One way to understand quantitative journalism in 2014 is thus to find traces of its past in its present and of its present in its past; perhaps we can then even speculate intelligently about its future.

But in other ways the story of quantitative journalism in the United States is less one of sanguine continuity than it is one of rupture, a tale of transformed techniques and objects of evidence existing under old familiar names. I think, in other words, that the continuity perspective mentioned above is deeply and fundamentally flawed. The producers of *The Survey Graphic* understood the meaning and purpose of data very differently than most reporters and editors working today. The varieties and forms of data that journalists have available to them in the early twenty-first century are different, as are the techniques journalists use to gather, process, and display that data. Thinking about the history of quantitative journalism in this way—as transformation and rupture—is less likely to offer us comfort and more likely to unsettle us. But perhaps it will also help us reframe our current understanding of data and journalism as a *contingent understanding*, less inevitable and timeless than it is the product of deliberate choices intersecting with historical structures and filtered through an intellectually precarious profession. What I am proposing to sketch out in the pages that follow, in other words, is a genealogy of quantitative journalism. There is no entirely unproblematic understanding of quantitative journalism, I hope to argue below; its history is not determined by its purpose and use, but rather its purpose and use are enabled through its tangled history. As Nietzsche noted, in a passage from the *Genealogy of Morals* that held particular resonance for Foucault:

> the "development" of a thing, a practice, or an organ has nothing to do with its progress towards a single goal, even less is it the logical and shortest progress reached with the least expenditure of power and resources. Rather, it is the sequence of more or less profound, more or less mutually independent processes of overpowering that take place on that thing, together with the resistance that arises against that overpowering each time, the changes of form which have been attempted for the purpose of defense and reaction, as well as the results of successful counter-measures. Form is fluid; the "meaning," however, is even more so. (Nietzsche [1887] 2006, 51)

This article proposes that we ought to approach the question of data journalism by studying its history, and by conducting the kind of history that Foucault called "genealogy." That is, we ought to study the process by which journalism engages in a form of public "world building": the way that a variety of processes, technologies, and evidentiary objects contribute to this crafting of publics and public issues; and the manner in which these materialities and discourses have been loaded with different meanings at different times. From this perspective, "big data" might be seen as another object of evidence that enters the journalistic bloodstream at a particular moment or moments. This genealogical perspective can, in turn, shed light on why the relationship of journalism to big data matters in a more normative sense. I want to note, at the outset, that this overview is part of an in-progress monograph on the socio-cultural history of quantitative journalism. While the paper primarily draws on a wide variety of secondary literature, it is also informed by extensive archival research, including in the Franklin H. Giddings archive at Columbia University and the Paul Kellogg archive at the University of Minnesota. Although rarely directly cited in this overview article, the time I have already spent in the archives has played a key role in helping me to formulate the typologies and overall direction of this paper.

In the first section of this article, I want to make the case for conducting a genealogy of quantitative journalism in a particular fashion, what I call an "objects of journalism-oriented" approach to studying data and news (Anderson and DeMaeyer, forthcoming). To understand the operation of data within the news production process, we need to understand both how that data was embodied in particular social and material "objects" like databases, bound survey reports, and even paper documents, as well as the way that journalists understand their own professional relationship to those objects of evidence. In the second section, I want to move from the question of what an object-oriented approach might offer to the study of journalism to the reverse question: how analyzing the occupation of journalism might shed light on aspects of both our current "big data" moment as well as on general processes of fact-building within a variety of knowledge-oriented disciplines. The final section of the paper will be devoted to sketching four "critical moments" in journalism history, moments whose nuances might contribute to the genealogical understanding of quantitative journalism I propose above.

Material, Cultural, and Practice Perspectives on Journalistic Assemblage

When burrowing into quantitative journalism's past, it is helpful to think broadly about journalism as a process of *assemblage*. Thinking about journalism as assemblage directs our scholarly attention to the interlocking *material*, *cultural*, and *practice-based* underpinnings of data journalism—perspectives that simultaneously broaden the notion of data beyond simply bites, bits, and digital traces to include a variety of evidentiary objects such as documents, maps, surveys, informational graphics, opinion polls, variable-based social science formulas, and computational techniques. Data journalism, from this perspective, has a history—but it is more a history of jagged edges and discontinuities of practice rather than a continuing unfolding of ever more sophisticated quantitative work. Thinking of journalism as assemblage allows us to see journalism as just one among many knowledge-building process in which heterogeneous "fact-fragments" are assembled into a variety of journalistic products. News stories are assemblages of social and material artifacts (documents, interviews, data, links, etc.), as are the very organizations that do this assembling (constructed as they are out of human workers, specific technologies, office buildings, work routines, content management systems, and so forth). This perspective on newswork, which itself draws upon Latour (2005) and others working in the tradition of actor-network theory (Anderson 2013; Weiss and Domingo 2010; Hemmingway and van Loon 2011) should be seen as less of an explanatory theory about the world and more of a particular orientation toward news production that allows us to ask interesting questions in new ways. These questions include: How does knowledge get produced? Do the changing material conditions of evidence change the mechanisms through which facts are generated and verified? And do the changing material substrates of knowledge generate different professional understandings of which facts matter, and why?

This assemblage perspective on journalistic work thus demonstrates that there are several lenses through which we might choose to historicize journalistic practice, including the practices we now subsume under the label of "data journalism." We can examine the materiality of the objects that journalists use as evidence, the meaning attributed to these material artifacts by journalists and others, and the actual work process through which these various fact fragments are assembled, and the way that materiality and culture intersect with those practices. In other words, a materialist-assemblage perspective on digital journalism would ask, first, what evidentiary facts do journalists assemble, and what facts do they ignore (what is the materiality of data journalism, and how has that material substrate changed)? Second, *how are* these fact-fragments assembled (what are the practices and routines of data journalism, and how have they evolved)? And finally, how do journalists *understand* what they are doing when they assemble certain facts in certain ways (is there a culture of data journalism, and what is the history of that culture)?

The focus on which evidentiary facts get assembled by journalists is, inevitably, partially a material focus, and I see this analysis of quantitative journalism as contributing toward the recent "material turn" in communication studies. As Diana Coole and Samantha Frost summarize in *New Materialisms: Ontology, Agency, and Politics*:

> everywhere we look, it seems to us, we are witnessing scattered but insistent demands for more materialist modes of analysis and for new ways of thinking about matter and processes of materialization. We are also aware of the emergence of novel if still diffuse ways of conceptualizing and investigating material reality. This is especially evident in disciplines across the social sciences. (Coole and Frost 2010, 2–3)

Has there been a similar material turn in the study of journalism? This is a particularly fraught question for communication scholars insofar as many discussions of technology and communicative processes are met with standard warnings against "technological determinism," usually accompanied by the invocation of the specter of Marshall McLuhan and a warning that while ordinary folk and political leaders speak of technology as driving history, more informed and nuanced social scientists understand that most technologies are really just a social construction. As John Durham Peters has convincingly argued, however, "'technological determinism' or more recently 'technodeterminism' is a notion in desperate need of a critical intellectual history and reappraisal. It is a doctrine more often attributed than advocated" (Peters 2011). This paper tries to follow Peters' advice and consider one particular case of the material underpinnings of communication—the role of data in the construction of journalistic knowledge—without paying ritual homage to the notion that "the social" stands as the ultimate arbiter of all materialist processes and affordances. Indeed, the field of communications and journalism studies has its own set of canonical theorists who have provided it with a rich set of writings on the relationship between media and materiality (Packer and Wiley 2012)—among them the much-maligned but much-cited Marshall McLuhan (1962), as well as Eric Havelock (1963), James Carey (1992), Harold Innis (1951), and Walter Ong (1958). Of these, it is perhaps Innis (the Canadian political economist) and Havelock (the theorist of Greek orality) who have received the least sustained attention from the broader set of new materialist theorists working in the social sciences; both of them, however, devoted particular attention to the complex intersection between orality and inscription, as well as to the tripartite relationship between materiality, spatial coordination, and temporal power. Materiality, space, and time are all deeply implicated in both the journalistic *understanding of* and *occupational relationship to* data, and thus the insights of Innis and Havelock may be particularly helpful when thinking through the full history and genealogy of quantitative journalism.

A focus on materiality alone, of course, is not enough to do justice to the full complexity of quantitative journalism's genealogical trajectory. Material artifacts must be assembled into facts by news workers, and in this sense, materials are filtered through, though they are not reducible to, journalistic practices and routines. How do facts get *built* in journalism, both historically and in this new world of data? Are the procedures through which journalists build facts different now than they were in earlier historical eras? For contemporary practices, we can turn to ethnographic research; for past eras we must turn to the analysis of news content, the memoirs of different communication workers and social activists, and interviews with theorists and practitioners of quantitative journalism. Practices add nuance and texture to what might first appear to be a blunt, deterministic focus on materiality by showing how journalists, sociologists, and activists made use of particular technological affordances (Graves 2007) to shape discrete news products.

Finally, the third lens on the practice and history of quantitative journalism turns our attention to issues of how journalists *understand* the meaning of the material they assemble, the reasons why they draw on some kinds of facts and not others, and the way the material underpinnings of those facts affect this conception of "what counts" as important of valid evidence. Journalists could, after all, construct all of their news stories by conducting a daily séance and transcribing the voices and paranormal knockings into a coherent view of the latest news. They obviously do not, and there are important reasons why this is so. Less facetiously, American journalists have moved from valuing documents as a record of the goings on of a distant government to embracing, in the mid-nineteenth century, the then-alien concept of the interview (Schudson 1995) and relegating material documents (and with them, perhaps, the notion of "data") to a minor role in news reporting. Combining these three lenses, the materiality of particular facts intersects with the routines that make use of them and cultural understandings of what facts matter, when they matter, and why they matter. By starting from an "objects of journalism" approach to the study of data, and by unspooling that approach historically, across time, we can gain deep insights into our present communicative and journalistic moment.

Periodizing Quantitative Journalism

In his article in this special issue, Coddington (2014) argues that we ought to periodize quantitative news production—dividing it into the ideal types of computer-assisted reporting, data journalism, and computational journalism—and further argues that each of these types is distinguished by a particular species of practice, an epistemological orientation, and a particular vision of the audience. The remainder of this paper can be seen as both an expansion and narrowing of Coddington's focus—an expansion because I seek to place quantitative journalism within a longer historical trajectory that grapples with the very meaning of "the quantitative" for the production of knowledge, and a narrowing insofar as I focus primarily on the *epistemological* dimensions of these quantitative practices. In particular, this analysis tries to bring the material, cultural, and practice-oriented perspectives on journalistic assemblage to bear on developing a history of quantitative journalism.

This section sketches three historical tensions underlying journalists' use of data, filtered through a lens that sees this cultural understanding of data as related to different journalistic attitudes toward a wide variety of material journalistic objects. First, I discuss the contrast between the idea of a journalistic "record" and journalistic "report" in the early nineteenth century. Second, I explore the tension between journalism as individualized narrative and more of a social science, a tension that found real, material embodiment in the use of documents in journalism over the course of the twentieth century. Third, and finally, I discuss how focusing on the material objects of journalistic evidence helps glimpse an emerging tension between data collection as a process by which hidden facts are brought to light versus data collection as a process in which previously known information is organized into comprehensible patterns.

Records and Reports

What were the objects undergirding most journalism in the United States in the decades before the rise of the penny press in the 1830s? Primarily, ensembles of journalistic evidence before the mid-nineteenth century were centered on documents. Although it has rarely been framed in quite this fashion, it is possible to argue that the major evidentiary shift in journalistic processes and procedures in the middle of the nineteenth century consisted in transition of the form from a written to an oral form of knowledge production. Although the journalistic use of documents before the 1830s may seem remote from our understanding of the journalistic use of data in the twenty-first century, a materialist perspective on journalistic work can help us understand that the affinities between documentary evidence and data-oriented evidence go beyond the perceived transience and permanence of the different evidentiary forms.

Discussion of this transformation in the journalism studies literature tends to focus on *what was new* about the penny press in the 1830s: the interview. The news interview, according to a definition in the *International Encyclopedia of Communication*, is defined by its focus "on matters related to recent news events, its highly formal character, and its [management] primarily through questions and answers" (Clayman 2008, 2510). In Schudson's (1995, 24) language, "interviewing, all but unknown in 1865, had become a common activity for reporters in the 1870s and 1880s, was widely practiced by 1900, and was a mainstay of American journalism by World War I." Not only does the interview have a chronological history, however; it can also be examined cross-culturally. Høyer and Pöttker's (2005) overview of the "diffusion of the news paradigm" between 1850 and 2000 is perhaps the most ambitious and wide-ranging example of this type of analysis, but credit for launching this strain of comparative research belongs to Chalaby (1996), with his work on the "Anglo-American" origins of journalism and his argument that "the interview is an Anglo-American invention." More than simply a historical and cultural artifact, the interview also has a material and technological basis. Lee (2008), along with other scholars working broadly in the tradition of science and technology studies, has documented the importance of technological artifacts and recording technologies in the emergence of the interview in sociological research.

But what did the interview replace as the center of the journalistic evidentiary ensemble? What was the nature of the document as evidence in the colonial and early Federalist newspaper era, and what changed after the rise of the penny press? Around the time of the emergence of the penny press, journalists began to articulate a new and shifting relationship toward material evidence, an attitude that helped to reorder the evidentiary value of the human beings, paper documents, and news reporters that together assembled in the journalistic story. Following some brief but intriguing remarks by Hazel Dicken-Garcia (1989) in her monograph *Journalistic Standards in Nine-teenth-century America*, I contend that it is helpful to think of this shift from "paper to people" as part of a broader shift in American journalism from thinking of news products as *records* to thinking of them as *reports*. The key shift here lies at the nexus between materiality, time, and the larger structures and cultures of newsgathering; it occurred between the invention of the penny press and the conclusion of the Civil War. In Dicken-Garcia's (1989, 54) words, "if information is thought of as a record, its value is principally the same whether it is a week or a year old, and this value may, in fact, increase with time. But if it is regarded as a report, recency is its most valuable quality." The insatiable demand for information about the bloody Civil War, she argues, shifted the public appetite for news irrecoverably in the direction of demanding news reports. This demand, in turn, activated a variety of latent potentials in the news production process. Techniques such as the eyewitness observation, the interview, and the cultivation of army officers as sources all emerged from the battlefield campgrounds of the war. Technologies also played a role, though primarily a reactive one, with already-existing techniques such as photography and the telegraph assuming a more prominent role in the assemblage practices of newspapers.

While Dicken-Garcia discusses the role played by technology in news production as a largely reactive affair, it seems clear that macro-changes in material infrastructures also played a role in the transformation of the journalistic record into the journalistic report. In that light, *Journalistic Standards in Nineteenth-century America* makes a subtle argument that the modern newspaper marked the culmination of a lengthy process of *documentary disenchantment*. "When printing techniques were expensive, laborious, and time-consuming, the tedious work of recording information confined printing to the absolutely essential; anything beyond was required to be of a nature that elevated and ennobled mankind ... a predominant view saw the press as the keeper of the record of human kind and civilization's store of knowledge" (Dicken-Garcia 1989, 117). The phrase "disenchantment of documents" points to a radical change, one in which print was used as much to convey the report (with its trivialities, its eyewitness accounts, and insider gossip) as for a record of the activities of government, foreign events, and profit-generating market news.

Framing this shift from record to report in terms of the role and status of the document, *vis-à-vis* the role and status of the news interview, allows us to leaven these vaguely Havelockian musings with a more granular focus on materiality and the actual data that underlies the work of reporting the news. What kinds of documents were actually used to generate news as a record? How did these documents diffuse across the United States in the eighteenth and nineteenth centuries? What was the goal of government record-keeping? How did what Garvey (2012) has called "scissors journalism" (the cutting and pasting of already-existing news reports and their interpolation into new publications) actually work? Given the fact that these cutting-and-pasting techniques lasted well into the nineteenth and even early twentieth century, were documents really centered on record-keeping in Dicken-Garcia's sense, or were they used in more trivial ways even from an early stage?

This tension—between paper and people, and between journalism as a record versus journalism as a report—can open our eyes to some of the questions that haunt the use of "big data" in news reporting well into our current era. One of the key questions in the use of data for journalistic purposes is whether it is extending the time horizon of reporting, shifting the focus from chronicling the daily or even hourly event in a de-contextualized fashion versus looking at longer trends over time, embedded in a variety of thickly nuanced places and times. Is there, in other words, a relationship between the materiality of the document and the idea of journalism as a record, versus the orality of the interview and the decontextualized notion of journalism as a report? In some ways, this is the implication of Dicken-Garcia's historical analogy, and it is an open and interesting question as to its resonance insofar as it relates to the current digitization of news.

Individuality and Social Science

These arguments relate to a second tension surrounding the use of data and documents in practices of news production: the question as to whether journalism ought to be seen as a narrative telling the story of individuals, or as a more structural mapping of trends à la formal social science. These fault lines crisscross journalistic history across the entire twentieth century. It is possible to tease from that history a few constitutive moments that shed light on the role played by documents and data in evolving journalistic practices.

The "precision journalism" movement of the 1960s is the natural end-point of this line of analysis, marking, as it did, the most explicit fusion of social science, data documentation, and journalistic practice. By founder Philip Meyer's own accounting, we also need to consider the origins of precision journalism against the backdrop of other journalistic reform movements that had begun percolating in the 1960s, particularly the "new journalism" of Tom Wolfe, Truman Capote, and others. Precision journalism, which spawned computer-assisted reporting (CAR) and a variety of related technological news practices, was less about computers than it was about applying social science methods, such as sample surveys, statistical methods, and hypothesis testing, to journalism. It was also, at least initially, seen as existing in opposition to narrative reporting of the "new journalistic" variety: "The narrative journalists ... are subjective to a degree that disturbs conventional journalists and horrifies precision journalists. In essence, all the other new journalists push reporting toward art. Precision journalists push it toward science" (Meyer 2012). "For decades," Meyer recalls,

> as a precision journalist I considered narrative journalists my natural enemies. It didn't help that the early practitioners sometimes got caught making things up. For example, Gail Sheehy wrote an article for *New York* magazine in 1973 that described in great detail the sexual and financial escapades of a prostitute in New York who was called "Redpants." Then *The Wall Street Journal* revealed that there was no "Redpants." Sheehy had used a composite of several different prostitutes to provide the dramatic compression needed to give her story the pace and depth of fiction. (Meyer 2012)

The rise of precision journalism was hastened by technological developments (such as advanced computing capacity and the ability to more easily tabulate and analyze large data sets) but not by technology alone. Along with the general mood of reform signaled by the new journalism and the rise of professionalization in the 1960s, we should also consider the increase in publicly accessible government record-keeping as helping to create a new way of understanding the document as evidence, an understanding that was also tangled up in shifting technologies of information storage, duplication, and retrieval.

In some ways, however, precision journalism only marks the culmination of a number of other document/data-based trends that would appear, disappear, and reappear over the course of the modern era. Phillip Meyer can only call for journalism to become more like a social science if a historical argument has already concluded it is not such a science. Precision journalism can only emerge after the *stabilization* of the boundary between professional journalism and social science; indeed, in the early decades of the twentieth century, the line dividing reformist sociology, muckraking, and academic quantification was far from clear. The early 1900s, for instance, would see the rise of the so-called survey movement, itself tied to the emergence of the progressive movement and concomitant with the growth of new techniques for collecting and visualizing social data. While this article can only gesture at the history and importance of the social survey, it relates to our genealogical excavation insofar as the progressive-era reform movement marked one of the first attempts to pioneer new mechanisms of document and data collection to understand and visualize poverty, and also cultivated ties with the local press in order to press them for favorable articles about the movement and the reprinting of striking data visualizations.

In the 1930s, as the increasing institutionalization of academic sociology led to the marginalization of progressive-era elements of academic inquiry like the survey movement, these earlier reformist impulses and visualizations found a new outlet in long-form magazines like *The Survey Graphic*. While the steady occupational differentiation of social science from social work is the primary narrative thread around which most standard histories of sociology turn, a focus on the materiality of data can also lead to a consideration of the relationship between social science and journalism, in part by examining the shifting discourse about journalism in the mainstream sociological journals, as well as the complex relationship between these journals and muckraking magazines. In particular, scholars of data journalism need to consider the manner in which those journals discussed, or did not discuss, the materiality of journalistic practices, as well as the different ways that professional journalism began to draw boundaries around its occupational role *vis-à-vis* both social science and reformist politics (for further discussion, see Anderson, forthcoming). In essence, while we cannot deny the relevance of precision journalism and the importance of organizations such as the National Institute for Computer-Assisted Reporting (NICAR) to the current big data movement in journalism, these developments are themselves crisscrossed by a number of additional tendencies, false starts, and aborted attempts to think through the relationship between social science and news reporting.

Arguments about the use of data to make sense of the world, the relationship between data and the paper document, and the question of how the "story" of that data should be told, are arguments at least a century old. How and why did journalism come to embrace social scientific methods, even as a minority practice? How did journalists come to incorporate a variety of socio-material practices—the regression equation, the census, the database, the public opinion poll—into their news practices? These questions are more relevant today, in this era of quantitative journalism, than they ever have been, and understanding the history of the relationship between the profession of journalism and the profession of social science can help us gain insight into today's empirical practices.

Hidden Facts and Building Patterns

In his article, "Morelli, Freud, and Sherlock Holmes: Clues and the Scientific Method," the historian Carlo Ginzburg (1980) compares the evolution of two distinct empirical methodologies. The first centers around the discovery and analysis of the *clue*, a practice, he writes, of empirical diagnosis common to art historians like Giovanni Morelli, psychoanalysts like Sigmund Freud, and fictional detectives like Sherlock Holmes. "In all three [of these] cases," Ginzburg notes, "tiny details provide the key to a deeper reality, inaccessible by other methods" (11). The procedural focus of this method is on "the qualitative, the individual case or situation or document itself" (15). The second evidence-building method, one that Ginzburg attributes to a more abstract scientific culture, "use[s] mathematics and the experimental method ... to measure and repeat phenomena" (15). "In the first decades of the 17th century," Ginzburg writes, "the influence of this [second], Galilean model ... would lead towards the study of the typical rather than the exceptional, towards a general understanding of the workings of nature rather than particularistic, conjectural knowledge" (20). It would lead, in short, to the displacement of the clue and the individual detail in favor of mathematical models of regularized phenomena.

Ginzburg contends that a reversal of this generalizing tendency—a re-animated focus on characters and clues—began in the nineteenth century. This rebirth of the "clue-method" thus existed alongside, though it did not displace, simultaneous attempts to understand collectives as generic, law-governed aggregates. "The time at which these [clue-based] principles came after so long to fruition was perhaps not altogether random," Ginzburg notes. "It coincided with the emergence of an increasingly clear tendency for state power to impose a close-meshed net of control on society, and once again the method used ... involved attributing identity through characteristics which were trivial" (24). The rise of the clue, Ginzburg concludes, coincided with a rapidly emerging state interest in understanding people and objects as *individual and unique.*

While Ginzburg discusses the emergence of the idea of "the clue" in psychology, political economy, art criticism, and detective fiction, historian David Paul Nord (1990) analyzes the invention of "reportorial empiricism" in early journalism itself. Examining the overlap between seventeenth-century Puritan sermons, with their simultaneous focus on bizarre events and the placement of those events within a general scheme of divine history, and an early New England journalism that did much the same thing, Nord probes the roots of the "eclectic, reportorial method of inquiry" (28). He thus describes a method of knowledge construction that bears a remarkable similarity to those described, in a different context, by Ginzburg:

By reportorial empiricism, I mean that the teleological news literature of seventeenth-century New England was highly empirical, but the style was eclectic and reportorial, not systematic and scientific. The methodology was essentially what we today call "news reporting": the routine collation and citation of statement and sources. The sources ranged widely, from leading scientists to folklore to average people with stories to tell. The role of the writer was not to conduct systematic empirical research, but rather to report the empirical statements of others. Such a methodology was empiricism without science. It was, in a word, journalism. (Nord 1990, 38)

Nord's historical research—while fascinating in its own right—also points us toward the contemplation of some thoroughly modern questions: Why has journalism placed so much value in the unique, the bizarre, and the individual rather than in the regular, law-like, and ordinary? How did it come to pass that such an important instrument of knowledge came to be dominated by procedures that strike most social scientists, and many outside observers, as empirically inadequate, to say the least? What do changes in these procedures—a greater reliance on data and algorithms, for instance—portend for the future of news reporting?

A more current way to consider these questions would be to compare the role played by the Pentagon Papers with the huge cache of files published by WikiLeaks known as the Iraq War Logs. The Pentagon Papers, in Ginzburg's terms, were a "clue"—a previously hidden evidentiary fragment that provided insight into a larger social, economic reality. The Iraq War Logs, while arguably hidden sources of information, did not obtain their value from the scarcity or their uniqueness, but rather the way that they worked as a pattern-creating ensemble of evidence that "made sense" out of data that was already known. Just as Watergate and the resignation of Richard Nixon became a central cultural touchstone for an increasingly powerful class of professional Washington reporters, so too the Pentagon Papers would mark a key moment in which a particular vision data and the document would be ratified within journalism's collective memory. The remembered story of the Pentagon Papers would crystallize a particular journalistic understanding of information as both *scarce and hidden*, with the document serving as a particularly powerful materialization of this hidden, yet certified, knowledge. This understanding of documentary evidence becomes even clearer when we turn to *Custodians of Conscience*, an in-depth examination of the practices of investigative journalism and their connection to various styles of moral and social inquiry (Ettema and Glasser 1998). Ettema and Glasser discuss the previously noted ontological status of the document at some length in their work, particularly the manner in which the accumulated "weight" of documentary evidence represents a key inflection point for ascertaining controversial truth claims about secret behavior.

The idea of the document as a signal flare revealing the central aspects of a hidden truth stands in contrast to an alternate idea of the document as only one scrap of evidence that goes into making up a larger—and not necessarily hidden—world of information. Herein lies the third tension in our genealogy of data journalism. On the one hand, we can see data, and the documents that underlie that data, as a hidden fragment of information waiting to be uncovered. On the other hand, we might envision data as a thing that is both massive and already known, where the journalistic value added lies not in the unmasking of a hidden truth but in putting the overwhelming torrent of information into patterned context. Neither of these cultural belief systems is necessarily truer than the other, but both are subject to professional negotiation, and both represent different ways of configuring technologies, institutions, and organizational practices in the digital information era.

Conclusion

This article proposed that we historicize the relationship between journalism and big data in order to subject that relationship to the genealogical gaze. It has further argued that we need to think of data as a particularly material procedural substrate—that is, we need to consider the material objects (whether interviews, documents, human observations, or other objects) that underlie journalistic processes. The payoff of thinking about data in this way is that it allows us to productively probe the tensions that lie at the heart of the journalism–data nexus, tensions that include, but are not limited to, thinking of journalism as a record versus a report, a social science versus a narrative about individuals, and a hidden source of secret information versus an already known stream of un-patterned knowledge.

I promised early in this article that an additional payoff for thinking about new forms of journalism genealogically might be that it could help provide a normative handle on data journalism, or at least answer the "so what" question about why this kind of journalism matters. To some degree, of course, it is dangerous to draw the implications of data journalism out too strongly; it is far from the dominant form of journalistic work today, as several other articles in this special issue make clear. Nevertheless, while Michael Schudson's (2013) trenchant observation that "journalism is neither all about data nor all about stories" is certainly accurate, it is also impossible to ignore the fact that the center of gravity between journalism-as-data and journalism-as-story *does* shift, and means different things at different times. That there is a difference in emphasis between the New Journalism of Tom Wolfe and the Precision Journalism of Philip Meyer seems beyond dispute, as does the fact that "audience data" as filtered through Chartbeat and audience dialog filtered through the lens of public journalism are dramatically different ways of understanding "the public."

Will the tension between "story" and "data" still be meaningful in a dozen years? To posit an initial answer to that question, by way of a conclusion, some perspective drawn from the past decade of journalism history might be helpful. In 2003, the idea that the "people formerly known as the audience" could contribute something to journalistic production was a radical notion, whether that argument was advanced by journalism scholars, technologists, activist journalists, or members of the "blogosphere." Today, in a world dominated by social media and the perpetual, occasionally newsworthy status update, it seems hard to imagine a journalistic world where the audience did not have something to contribute to the production of news. What is radical about journalism now, in a world of digital media, may be its very *conservatism*: the fact that it exists at all as a relatively professionalized cadre of public information producers whose agenda is not entirely determined by the wishes of the audience. What was once a conservative liability has now become a useful pushback against other trends in the digital world.

Ten years from now, we may look back on the big data debate as a similarly quaint exercise. It is highly likely that the world we live in will be filled with data of various kinds, with an increased focus on measurement, outcomes assessment, and increasingly narrow news production tailored to the consumption of niche audiences. In that world, what matters about journalism may not be the degree to which it embraces big data, but rather the ways in which it reminds us of *other* forms of information that are not data, *other* types of evidence that are not quantitative, and *other* conceptions of what counts as legitimate public knowledge. These other forms of knowing are possible because they once existed, and thus, they can exist again.

REFERENCES

Anderson, C. W. *Journalistic Cultures of Truth: Data in the Digital Age*, Oxford University Press, [In press].

Anderson, C. W. 2013. *Rebuilding the News: Metropolitan Journalism in the Digital Age*. Philadelphia, PA: Temple University Press.

Anderson, C. W., and Juliette DeMaeyer. Forthcoming. "Introduction: Objects of Journalism." *Journalism: Theory, Practice, Criticism*.

Carey, J. W. 1992. *Communication as Culture: Essays on Media and Society*. New York: Routledge.

Chalaby, Jean. 1996. "Journalism as an Anglo-American Invention: A Comparison of the Development of French and Anglo-American Journalism, 1830s–1920s." *European Journal of Communication* 11: 303–326.

Clayman, Steven E. 2008. "Interview as Journalistic Form." In *International Encyclopedia of Communication*, edited by Wolfgang Donsbach, 2509–2513. Oxford: Blackwell.

Coddington, Mark. 2014. Clarifying Journalism's Quantitative Turn: A Typology for Evaluating Data Journalism, Computational Journalism, and Computer-assisted Reporting. *Digital Journalism*. doi: 10.1080/21670811.2014.976400.

Coole, Danah, and Samantha Frost, eds. 2010. *New Materialisms: Ontology, Agency, and Politics*. Raleigh, NC: Duke University Press.

Dicken-Garcia, Hazel. 1989. *Journalistic Standards in Nineteenth-Century America*. Madison, WI: University of Wisconsin Press.

Ettema, James S., and Theodore L. Glasser. 1998. *Custodians of Conscience: Investigative Journalism and Public Virtue*. New York: Columbia University Press.

Finnegan, Cara. 2003. "Social Welfare and Visual Politics: The Story of Survey Graphic." Accessed June 13, 2014. http://newdeal.feri.org/sg/essay.htm

Garvey, Ellen. 2012. *Writing with Scissors: American Scrapbooks from the Civil War to the Harlem Renaissance*. New York: Oxford University Press.

Ginzburg, C. 1980. *The Cheese and the Worms: The Cosmos of a Sixteenth-century Miller*. Baltimore, MD: Johns Hopkins University Press.

Graves, Lucas. 2007. "The Affordances of Blogging: A Case Study in Culture and Technological Effects." *Journal of Communication Inquiry* 31 (4): 331–346.

Havelock, Eric. 1963. *Preface to Plato*. Cambridge, MA: Harvard University Press.

Hemmingway, Emma, and Joost van Loon. 2011. "'We'll Always Stay with a Live, until We Have Something Better to Go to…': The Chronograms of 24-Hour Television News." *Time and Society* 20 (2): 149–170.

Høyer, Svennik, and Horst Pöttker, eds. 2005. *Diffusion of the News Paradigm 1850–2000*. Göteborg: Nordicom.

Innis, Harold. 1951. *The Bias of Communication*. Toronto: University of Toronto Press.

Latour, Bruno. 2005. *Reassembling the Social: An Introduction to Actor-Network-Theory*. New York: Oxford University Press.

Lee, Raymond M. 2008. "David Riesman and the Sociology of the Interview." *The Sociological Quarterly* 49 (2): 285–307.

Marshall, Mc Luhan. 1962. *The Gutenberg Galaxy: The Making of Typographic Man*. Toronto: University of Toronto Press.

Nietzsche, Frederich. 2006 [1887]. *On the Genealogy of Morality and Other Writings (Cambridge Texts in the History of Political Thought)*. Cambridge: Cambridge University Press.

Nord, David P. 1990. "Teleology and the News: The Religious Roots of American Journalism." *The Journal of American History* 77 (1): 9–38.

Ong, Walter. 1958. *Ramus, Method, and the Decay of Dialogue: From the Art of Discourse to the Art of Reason*. Chicago, IL: University of Chicago Press.

Packer, Jeremy, and Sean Wiley. 2012. "Strategies for Materializing Communication." *Communication and Critical/Cultural Studies* 9 (1): 107–113.

Peters, John Durham 2011. "Two Cheers for Technological Determinism." *Annenberg Research Seminar*, September 19.

Schudson, Michael. 1995. *The Power of News*. Cambridge, MA: Harvard University Press.

Schudson, Michael. 2013. "A Spotlight, Not a Truth Machine." Neiman Journalism Lab. Accessed August 17, 2014. http://www.niemanlab.org/2013/12/a-spotlight-not-a-truth-machine

Stewart, Kristen. 1946. "The Freedom to Read: Newspapers." *The Survey Graphic* 39: 452–456. December.

Weiss, Amy Schmitz, and David Domingo. 2010. "Innovation Processes in Online Newsrooms as Actor-Networks and Communities of Practice." *New Media and Society* 12 (7): 1156–1171.

DATA-DRIVEN REVELATION?
Epistemological tensions in investigative journalism in the age of "big data"

Sylvain Parasie

As an increasing number of reporters see databases and algorithms as appropriate means of doing investigation, journalism has been challenged in recent years by the following question: to what extent would the processing of huge datasets allow journalists to produce new types of revelations that rely less on normative assumptions? Drawing on the analysis of a particular investigation by the San Francisco-based Center for Investigative Reporting, this article points out the existence of epistemological tensions in the making of journalistic revelations that involve the processing of vast amounts of data. First, I show that the design of data-processing artifacts can match the traditional epistemology of journalistic investigation, but only with great efforts and resources from the organization. Second, I point out that the use of these artifacts by journalists follows two opposite paths to produce the revelation: a "hypothesis-driven" path and a "data-driven" path. Such findings contribute to a better understanding of how news organizations produce justified beliefs, as data-processing artifacts become major components of the newsroom's environment.

Introduction

In the last decade, computer databases and algorithms have made their way into news organizations (Gray, Bounegru, and Chambers 2012; Lewis 2011), where they are used in particular as tools supporting journalistic investigation. With the rise of so-called "data journalism" in the United States as well as in Europe, a growing number of journalists and programmers see data-processing tools as appropriate means to uncover officials' wrongdoings, social inequities, or environmental issues (Cohen, Hamilton, and Turner 2011; Parasie and Dagiral 2013). Established news organizations (such as *The New York Times* or *The Guardian*) as well as nonprofit organizations (such as ProPublica) and less formal groups of investigative journalists have produced revelations based on data-processing techniques.

Such initiatives cannot be isolated from a wider phenomenon often labeled "big data." This popular expression refers to the processing of massive quantities of information—government records, genetic sequences, traces left by internet users, etc.—in various domains such as scientific research, public policies, or business. One of the promises of "big data" is that the statistical processing of huge datasets could facilitate revelations about nature or society without relying on any theoretical or normative assumptions (Anderson 2008). As the authors of a recent book suggest, "big data may offer a fresh look and new insights precisely because it is unencumbered by the conventional thinking and inherent biases implicit in the theories of a specific field" (Mayer-Schönberger and Cukier 2013, 71).

Journalists may be receptive to this renewed promise of objectivity. Since the late nineteenth century, the distinction between facts and values has indeed been a strong occupational norm for North American journalists, who have largely emphasized the ideal of a reporter gathering "facts" in a detached, unbiased, and impersonal manner (Schudson 1978, 2001). Also, if we consider investigative journalists especially, a realist conception of the truth is often said to be prevalent among them: in their opinion, there is only one true and complete statement of what happened; and what happened is independent of their investigation. But scholars have shown that, in practice, investigative journalists base their investigation on a strong interdependence between facts and values. The facts they collect in the investigative process are inherently value-loaded and, conversely, the values they rely on hold some facts (Ettema and Glasser 1998). This is why we have to ask: to what extent does the processing of vast amounts of data affect how journalists produce knowledge in the process of an investigation? Does it modify the way they distinguish between facts and values in the making of a revelation?

Studying the "epistemologies" of knowledge producers is a classical approach in the sociology of knowledge, and more broadly in the area of science and technology studies (Knorr-Cetina 1999). It implies analyzing how actors make knowledge claims that they collectively find acceptable, and not evaluating whether those claims are valid or not. In the area of journalism studies, James Ettema and Theodore Glasser (1998, 2005) have adopted this perspective fruitfully to study investigative journalists, and other scholars extended this questioning to other types of journalism (Godler and Reich 2013). Since the goal is not to evaluate whether journalists' knowledge claims are valid or not, but merely to examine what journalists consider to be acceptable claims, this has been a significant departure from many sociological works that have been skeptical about journalistic claims to objectivity (Tuchman 1972; Hallin 2005).

My approach differs in two respects from the usual research on journalistic epistemologies. First, I take into account, in greater depth than do previous works, how journalists rely on the material environment of their organization to decide whether their knowledge claims are justified or not. For journalists, databases and algorithms are not black boxes providing unquestionable results, and we need to examine the material basis on which they collectively hold a specific output as being justified. Second, following Bruno Latour and Steve Woolgar's account of how science is made in the laboratory (Latour and Woolgar 1979), I disregard innovators' public accounts of how technology affects the epistemology of reporting, and focus rather on the often tortuous history of how justified beliefs are collectively produced in relation to artifacts.

Drawing on the analysis of a particular investigation performed by a San Francisco-based news organization, this article shows the existence of epistemological tensions in the making of journalistic revelations that involve the processing of vast amounts of data. Given the empirical limitation of this case, my intention is not to identify emergent trends regarding the use of data-processing artifacts in newsrooms in the

United States and elsewhere. My aim is rather to point out the existence of epistemo-logical tensions affecting investigative projects that involve that kind of artifact. These tensions are of two types. First, I show that the design of data-processing artifacts can fit the traditional epistemology of journalistic investigation, but only as the result of a long and costly process. Second, I point out that the use of these artifacts by journalists follows two opposite paths to produce the revelation.

Methods

In April 2011, the Center for Investigative Reporting (CIR), based in the San Francisco Bay area, revealed that the State of California had failed to enforce earthquake safety standards in public schools. I studied that particular investigation for two main reasons. First, because a team composed of journalists with heterogeneous backgrounds performed it: experienced investigative reporters with few skills in data processing, journalists with a background in "computer-assisted reporting," and pro-grammer-journalists connected with the "data science" community that is very active in the area. Since the team had no shared culture concerning the design and use of data-processing artifacts, this project provided a good opportunity to examine the epistemo-logical tensions in the collective making of a revelation in relation to such artifacts. The second reason is that this 19-month investigation consisted of a combination of quanti-tative and qualitative research methods. Journalists not only designed databases, per-formed statistical analyses, and built an interactive map, they also collected interviews and documentation. This afforded us the opportunity to identify precisely how data processing gave rise to epistemological tensions, in relation to the use of more traditional methods.

The fieldwork was carried out in collaboration with Eric Dagiral in the San Francisco Bay area between mid-August and mid-September 2012. We conducted five in-depth interviews with journalists involved in the project. Our questions aimed at reconstructing the history of this investigation and of how the team collectively dealt with databases and algorithms over time. Analyzing the rise of certainties and doubts within the team and how they evolved over the 19-month period was a major concern in this study. I also analyzed several versions of the databases designed by the team, examining how they were structured over time and processed to design outputs (maps, tables, lists) used in the investigation.

The Problematic Epistemologies of a "Data-driven" Investigation

With the growth and spread of data-processing artifacts, several institutions have come to question the grounds of their knowledge production. Scientific institutions, notably, have been challenged by the idea that the statistical processing of huge data-sets might allow them to produce new types of revelations about nature or society that rely less on theoretical or normative assumptions. Scholars in the study of science and technology have shown the existence of epistemological tensions within some scientific areas, between "hypothesis-driven" and "data-driven" perspectives (Strasser 2012). In the biomedical sciences, for instance, Keating and Cambrosio (2012) have shown that the field of cancer research features conflict between bio-informaticians, who support a data-driven view, and biostatisticians, who support a hypothesis-driven view.

Although data-processing artifacts are obviously not as commonplace in journalism as they are in science, databases and algorithms have been used in journalistic investigation since the late 1960s within the North American tradition of "computer-assisted reporting" (Cox 2000), and have been increasingly regular tools for news organizations since the 1990s (Garrison 1998). Nevertheless, as the "data-driven approach" conflicts with the established epistemologies of investigative reporting and computer-assisted reporting, it may be problematic for investigative reporters to adopt it.

The Epistemology of Investigative Journalism

Ettema and Glasser (1998, 2005) offer us a compelling portrait of the epistemology of US investigative journalism in the late 1990s. They showed that this epistemology has three main elements. Firstly, investigative reporters rely on an "externalist" approach to the truth, assuming that "there is only one true and complete description of the way the world is" (Ettema and Glasser 1998, 134). They strongly believe they can and must find out what really happened. Secondly, investigative journalists collect several accounts of what happened from different sources—through interviews and documentation—and then produce a new account that they believe is more authoritative. What is really important to them is the correspondence not between reality and their account, but rather between the various accounts they have collected. According to Ettema and Glasser, investigative reporters build their new authoritative account on the assumption that the reality must be coherent, determinate, and non-contradictory (137). Thirdly, the facts and the story emerge simultaneously in the investigation. While on the one hand, the reporter collects documents and interviews on the basis of an initial story that identifies the issues, on the other hand, the collected facts limit his or her choice of a story.

Such an epistemology is far removed from a model where the facts are first collected with few assumptions, and are then analyzed and composed into a story. Identifying leads in the data, formulating hypotheses, and collecting facts on the basis of an already-structured story: all of this might cause some epistemological problems for journalists as they consider the adoption of a "data-driven approach" in investigative reporting.

The Epistemology of Computer-assisted Reporting

Dealing with data-processing artifacts in order to investigate is far from being a recent phenomenon in the United States. Since the late 1960s, the "computer-assisted reporting" tradition has not only fostered the adoption of these artifacts in North American newsrooms, but also developed a coherent framework of epistemological standards to make databases more regular aspects of investigation (Parasie and Dagiral 2013). Such standards have been explored and disseminated by the National Institute for Computer-Assisted Reporting (NICAR) and the various handbooks published on the topic (Garrison 1998; Houston, Bruzzese, and Weinberg 2002).

One major standard is that data has no journalistic value in and of itself: database-oriented operations are viewed as valuable only when they are subordinated to a story idea (Garrison 1998, 281). Accordingly, the reporter has to process the data on the basis of assumptions regarding the issue concerned, the actors involved, and their responsibilities. Another standard is that journalistic norms remain entirely valid in such operations: checking data for accuracy, cross-comparing the accounts from various sources, etc. Moreover, this framework does not attribute any significant value to the processing of huge and complete datasets; only the handling of samples is important (Parasie and Dagiral 2013). It thus follows that the epistemological framework conveyed by the computer-assisted reporting tradition conflicts with the "data-driven" approach to journalistic revelations.

But there may be a huge gap between how journalists view epistemology in their public accounts and the actual epistemological grounds of their investigation—as in science (Latour and Woolgar 1979). I therefore chose to document how journalists collectively produce a revelation based on the processing of vast amounts of data.

The Challenge of Adjusting the Artifacts to Established Epistemologies

On April 7, 2011, the San Francisco-based CIR revealed systemic breakdowns in the way the State of California enforced seismic safety standards in the construction of public school buildings. For 19 months a dedicated team within this nonprofit news organization relied on a combination of various methods to produce this revelation:

> Tonight, a 19-month investigation by the Center for Investigative Reporting finds the state is failing to enforce earthquake safety standards in Californian public schools. It uncovers faulty constructions as well as a troubling lack of oversight by those in charge of keeping our children safe. (Transcript from a KQED television special, April 15, 2011)

During the investigation, the team designed databases and algorithms that matched the established epistemologies of journalistic investigation. Accordingly, it rejected the idea that the artifacts could encapsulate a hidden truth. Thus, the adjustment that had been so problematical for a long time was finally made, but it was demanding in terms of the resources made available by the organization.

Revelation

A series of articles entitled "On Shaky Ground" were published on the CIR website in April 2011. They made the following assertions:

(1) State regulators have routinely failed to enforce California's landmark earthquake safety law for public schools, by allowing children and teachers to occupy buildings with potential safety hazards reported during construction.
(2) State regulators have approved for jobs most of the inspectors accused of falsification and absence.
(3) The state has made it virtually impossible for school districts to access a fund set aside for urgent seismic repairs.
(4) Lobbyists and private interests have largely captured the regulation of school seismic safety.

Those articles put the blame primarily on the Division of the State Architects (DSA), the agency in charge of enforcing the regulation, and claimed that children in California public schools were put at risk in case of an earthquake. Moreover, an interactive map was released on the website, allowing any user to check whether a particular school was reviewed as safe or not, and its proximity to seismic zones (Figure 1).

As Corey Johnson—the journalist who led the investigation—told us, "The thought from experts and the larger public was that all schools were complying. So it took a lot of them by surprise when we reported that they did not." And this revelation was taken seriously, not only by parents concerned about the safety of their children, but also by governments and other media organizations. This led to a nationwide scandal as local and national media spread the news and commented on it.[1] The majority leader of the California State Legislature said, "It is unacceptable to allow children to use facilities that are unsafe," and the state legislature initiated a public inquiry and introduced a bill intended to enhance the seismic safety of public schools.[2] The investigative team consequently received several professional awards, including a finalist honor for the Pulitzer Prize in 2012 and top distinction from the Investigative Reporters and Editors association in the same year.

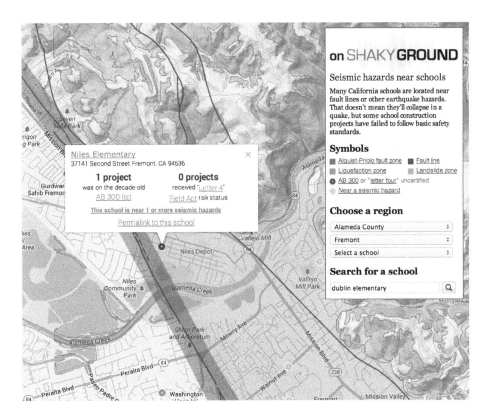

FIGURE 1
Interactive map of seismic hazards near Californian schools
Note: The picture shows the Niles Elementary School, in Fremont, California. This school is located near two seismic hazards and has one building project that is listed on a 2002 inventory of school buildings with potentially dangerous seismic hazards.

Origins of a "Big Story"

In September 2009, the reporter Corey Johnson was asked to write a story on the seismic safety of Californian schools for the 20th anniversary of the Loma Prieta earthquake.[3] At the time, the general opinion was that the Field Act was correctly enforced. Passed in 1933, this Act had created an agency, the DSA, whose mission is to approve school building projects and to regularly inspect the construction while underway.

As he started looking for information about the seismic safety of schools in California, Corey first interviewed a couple of experts. In order to obtain a list of unsafe schools, he submitted a data request to the DSA. The agency sent him back a spreadsheet indicating that more than 9000 schools in California did not comply with safety standards. At that point, Corey realized he was onto a "big story":

> Once I got that, that's when I knew that there was a big story here because the law was so strict that it said not one single school can violate this law—that 9000 in a list that appear to violate the law. So how does that happen? (Johnson, interview, August 31, 2012)

The spreadsheet enabled him to persuade his chief editors that he should have more time and resources to investigate deeper. This file appears to have been what he calls an "initial guide" in his investigation because it offered two important features. First, it gave quantified insight on the regulatory failure. Second, it offered information about the potentially unsafe schools, notably their names and addresses, which allowed him to believe that the investigation was "do-able." This initial view on the data in the investigative process has many similarities with the way in which investigative reporters assess the value of a tip (Ettema and Glasser 1998).

At this stage, the CIR chief editors strongly advised the team to design a comprehensive database of schools located in seismic hazard zones. The goal was then both to produce an artifact allowing reporters to evaluate and prove the massive regulatory breakdown, and to enable parents to check the safety of their children's school through an interactive map. This database was originally designed from three different datasets from government sources: one from the DSA regarding the safety status of every public school in California; another from the California Geological Survey—the agency in charge of the identification and the mapping of geological hazards in California—regarding the location of every seismic zone in the state; and another from the California Department of Education, which provided information about the location of every school building in the state. Throughout the investigation, this database was fed with several other datasets from the same and other institutions.

This database was designed essentially for gathering and collating, in the same artifact, various accounts held by different institutions. Since the accounts of the DSA were seriously questionable in a context of a massive regulatory crisis, the team saw the inclusion of other accounts from other agencies in the same database as a good means of producing a new authoritative account of the issue. Reporters could then collect information about the location of a particular school to point out that the fact of a school not having been inspected, or having been reviewed as unsafe because of its location near the fault—thus revealing a major failure of the regulatory agency. As noted above, this approach is largely in line with the established epistemology of investigative journalism.

"A Massive and Complicated Topic"

Once the journalists involved were convinced a "big story" was at stake, the investigation followed two different but connected paths: Corey Johnson collected interviews and documents to account for this massive regulatory crisis, while Agustin Armendariz, a "data analyst," was in charge of designing the database. However, as Agustin started merging the various datasets in October 2009, a host of difficulties arose, essentially due to the emergence of a gap between the epistemological framework that the journalists involved had relied on, and the features of the investigation.

The first difficulty stemmed from the extreme messiness of the data from state agencies. Schools were often labeled under different names in the DSA datasets and in those from the Department of Education. As there are tens of thousands of public schools in California, the merging of such messy datasets seemed almost impossible:

> It was a hard task. I mean, there was the messiness of the information. There was me trying to figure out how to convey to people what I think we can and can't do in a way that they would trust ... The big challenge of that process is that it was very much us getting to know each other and dealing with a massive, massive and complicated topic. (Armendariz, interview, September 12, 2012)

The inaccuracy of the data was another source of concern for Agustin and the journalists involved. Because state regulators seemed to have experienced major organizational issues, it appeared risky for the team to take it for granted that the regulators' records were accurate and factual. Moreover, as the datasets from the Department of Education were full of misspelled school names and poorly located school buildings, locating each school was very difficult. Because he used algorithms affecting the distance of each school from seismic zones, Agustin felt he could not guarantee the accuracy of the schools' location on the map:

> This is not survey data. I don't know how these things were projected, and I reprojected them when I stitched them together. I don't know how accurate that school point is. It's not the footprint of the school, and I don't even know where that building falls on campus. I can't make a 50-foot measurement like that. (Armendariz, interview, September 12, 2012)

The messiness and inaccuracy of the data also raised an ethical concern. As Agustin told us, it was very important for the CIR to avoid making wrong claims about the safety of a school. Falsely claiming that a school is unsafe for children might provoke unfounded reactions from people and ruin the reputation of the news organization:

> No information is ever clean. No data is ever perfect. I'm willing to accept that. But given that limitation, it's really important and really necessary and really hard to figure out what we can responsibly say with this information. (Armendariz, interview, September 12, 2012)

In the first six months of the investigation the most serious difficulties concerned the schools' location and the evaluation of their safety. For the journalists involved in the investigation, the geological data seemed the only element they could take for granted. Unlike government data, the geological information was produced by scientists. But in February 2010, Corey got a tip from a former geologist who used to work for the regulatory agency. According to this source, the geological map of seismic zones in California had changed substantially over the last decades, and not for scientific reasons. After checking state archives, Corey found out that the map had indeed been largely redrawn—under the pressure of private interests. Even geological data appeared to be political and, accordingly, largely questionable.

Designing a Database is a "Reporting Process"

A gap was opening up between the established epistemologies and the design of such a massive and comprehensive database. Moreover, it became obvious for the team that another big issue was the growing rift between the two fronts of the investigation. Whereas Corey was collecting enormous amounts of information that consisted mostly of qualitative data, Agustin was focused only on technology. The team found it very difficult to connect what Agustin was seeing on his computer and the evidence Corey was collecting in the field.

The team consequently adjusted its way of considering the data-processing artifacts in the investigative process: designing a database, or building a Web application, had to be viewed as a "reporting process." Instead of seeing the database in itself as encapsulating a truth, the journalists considered it rather as a fragile construction that needed ongoing adjustments to get it to correspond to the "real-life evidence" collected on the ground. Kendall Taggart, who was hired in August 2010 as an intern and then as a "data reporter," described to us how challenging it had been to match the database to the qualitative information collected on the ground:

> Two weeks before it went up, one of the schools that we'd written about that was in Corey's story was, in the state database it was called like high school number 2. And then in real life it was called Southeast Middle. So when you went to the website for Southeast Middle it showed no problems and we'd just spent months writing a print story about some of the problems at that school and Corey saw that. You can see why from a data perspective someone who's not embedded and doesn't know that high school number 2 is Southeast Middle is going to miss it. It does happen a lot if you don't figure out ways to make sure that everything, including building an app, is a reporting process. (Taggart, interview, September 6, 2012)

Until October 2010, the journalists continuously adjusted the database to the "real-life evidence" that was collected on the ground. Such a shift entailed a substantial increase in the human resources dedicated to the investigation—starting with two journalists, the team ended up with 11 journalists. It also resulted in the definition of a new job assignment as "data reporters" were hired to check systematically a large part of all the data stored in the database.

The making of algorithms was also viewed as having to stick to the epistemological standards of an investigation. It implied the integration of ethical considerations into the algorithms, concerning what journalists considered as their professional duty towards their audience. As noted above, the team was particularly concerned about the faulty location of schools and the unfounded reactions this might cause. Agustin therefore decided to integrate a "buffer" into the algorithm, to increase the size of the zone taken into account by it:

What I did is that once you stitch together a map of the seismic hazards in California, and you put the schools in proximity to those, can I lay a buffer, a half-mile buffer, around that point at which they say the school is at and see if there are features, you know, hazards that fall within it. (Armendariz, interview, September 12, 2012)

Throughout the process, the data-processing artifacts involved were adjusted to the established standards of an investigation. The idea that the database could encapsulate a hidden truth had not been envisioned at all in the investigative process. On the contrary, the team reacted by sticking more firmly to the established epistemological standards.

Emergence of Confidence in the Data

Adjusting the artifacts to the established epistemologies was a demanding process for the organization. The total cost has been estimated at $550,000, most of that in staff expenses (Doctor 2011). But it ended up producing collective confidence in the data. In late September 2010, after almost a full year of collective work on the data, Agustin gave Corey a list of more than a hundred schools that had failed to comply with safety standards; and Corey found a good match between the data and the qualitative evidence collected on the ground:

As Corey went out, down this target list I gave him, he wasn't able to disprove in real life any of the things that I was finding in the technology. So as he came back and as I understood that he was seeing the same things I was seeing, you know, the same things I was seeing in the data, he was seeing in the documents, he was seeing at the campuses, he was seeing in interviews. (Armendariz, interview, September 12, 2012)

From then on the team's confidence in the data never wavered. The team finally managed to produce a collective confidence in the artifacts, reducing the tensions that had arisen from the will to comply with the established epistemologies. This successful adjustment resulted from a long and costly process in which the building of a shared epistemic culture within the team was crucial.

Producing Justified Beliefs with Data-processing Artifacts

The process of a journalistic investigation fundamentally consists in the collective production of justified beliefs about the world. Accordingly, news organizations, like scientific institutions (Knorr-Cetina 1999), rely on epistemic cultures that frame the valid ways of justifying a knowledge claim. In the last decade, new connections between the journalism community and the computer worlds have partly renewed these epistemic cultures in the United States (Parasie and Dagiral 2013). This has led to the emergence of another tension regarding the way data-processing artifacts support the making of a journalistic revelation. More specifically, the "On Shaky Ground" investigation provides evidence of two opposite ways of justifying beliefs with data-processing artifacts: a "hypothesis-driven approach" and a "data-driven approach."

Testing Hypotheses

Among the assertions at the core of the revelation, the following two have been inherently based on the use of data-processing artifacts:

(1) State regulators have routinely failed to enforce California's landmark earthquake safety law for public schools.
(2) Regulators have approved for jobs most of the inspectors accused of falsification and absence.

Throughout the investigation, the team's dominant approach was to formulate hypotheses first and subsequently to perform statistical processing in order to confirm or discard these hypotheses. In this hypothesis-driven approach, statistical sampling appears to be a major tool—much more important than the completeness of the data.

One key operation was to evaluate the size of the regulatory crisis. As mentioned above, the lead reporter, Corey Johnson, began his investigation with a total of almost 9000 schools that did not comply with safety standards. The hypothesis was therefore that many public schools failed to comply with legal standards. But the team quickly realized this number could not be taken for granted, given the poor quality of regulators' records. In particular, many of the school names were misspelled, were assigned to the wrong district, or did not even correspond to existing schools. In order to find a conservative number of unsafe schools, Agustin extracted a random sample of 370 schools so that the team's reporters could manually check which ones actually corresponded to an existing school. They found that 30 percent of the schools listed by the DSA could not be matched to official schools. They concluded that 6 schools out of 10 in California had at least one uncertified building project.

The claim that state regulators were guilty of supporting inefficient and/or dishonest inspectors relied on the same approach. From interviews, the team found that some inspectors did not show up during the buildings' construction, and that others agreed to certify projects that obviously could not comply with legal standards. The hypothesis was that state regulators had failed to control inspectors and may even have encouraged them to behave badly. In order to prove that claim, Agustin designed a second database concerning the inspectors' evaluation. The team obtained 17,000 inspector-rating forms corresponding to nearly 1800 inspectors over 30 years, and the reporters entered the information into this database. Agustin extracted a list of 300 inspectors who had received poor ratings, and found that 66 percent of them were approved for additional jobs. Here again, making a hypothesis and performing statistical sampling appeared to be a decisive way to produce a justified belief.

The database of school seismic safety was thus occasionally used in the investigation to point out some "examples" of unsafe schools on which reporters could then investigate further. The processing of the data relied here on explicit hypotheses made by the journalist. The application developer involved in the project recalls many instances when reporters came to Agustin for such "examples":

> The reporters did come back to Agustin multiple times and be like, "I need an example of X, can you find one?" And he did a lot of that. Once the data was in a structure, he was great for being able to find specific examples. Because we would, for example, hear that, "Whether these schools that are on the AB300 list of school buildings that have the most structural problems, can you find me one of those that are really close

to a fault?" And so that was the kind of thing that the dataset was great for. So he could then give her 10 examples and she'd go check it out. (Michael Corey, interview, August 24, 2012)

Although prevalent in the "On Shaky Ground" project, this hypothesis-driven approach has been challenged by another approach.

Letting the Data Speak

The collective design of a comprehensive database of every public school in California also gave reporters the opportunity to distance themselves from a strictly hypothesis-driven view. In October 2010, after almost a year of checking the accuracy of the data, Agustin extracted a list of schools from the cross-tabulation of each school's safety status and its proximity to the fault. Here again, a hypothesis was made, but less to prove a precise claim than to organize the joint collection of facts. Kendall recalls how she used the "hit list" of unsafe schools to collect new evidence on the ground:

[We were] using the data to identify what schools we thought were the worst, what schools clearly had safety problems, and really drilling down on what was happening there by talking to the structural engineers and the inspectors, all the people involved in that project. (Taggart, interview, September 6, 2012)

As a result, the database was used in the process as a means of disseminating the team's resources more efficiently. It allowed the reporters to collect more facts on the ground, and made it easier for them to cross-compare single cases of unsafe schools.

The reporters also relied on the database to gain more information from sources. As Corey recalls it, he showed the map of schools' seismic safety to geological experts in order to elicit additional information from them:

Once we had a chance to talk to another earthquake engineer … She knew which areas were somewhat hot zones for geological fault activity. So by seeing our map, she was able to help us to better understand threats—threats to some of the schools in a way that we just didn't have the technical understanding and knowledge of. So in that way, the mapping has helped because other people were able to put other information on top of those maps and really bring the issue to life for us so we could help the public understand why this is a big deal. (Johnson, interview, August 31, 2012)

More critically, the database was used to monitor the inconsistent accounts of state regulators. As mentioned above, the reporters strongly suspected the DSA of manipulating its records. In order to check their claims about the crisis, the team decided to regularly add in their general database the updated datasets from state regulators. This regular update allowed the team to hold regulators more accountable for the situation:

Often times for fact-checking the state's own claims about how many schools still had problems, having our own data that we'd gotten from them, every two months we were re-upping it, made it possible to know what kinds of changes they were making and whether or not they made sense. (Taggart, interview, September 6, 2012)

Although they relied mostly on a hypothesis-driven approach, other aspects of the investigation suggest that the data-processing artifacts were also used as means of organizing the collection of facts by reporters and obtaining supplementary and even unintentional accounts from sources. This approach strongly differs from the previous one. Instead of formulating strong hypotheses that are subsequently proven or discarded on the basis of data processing, reporters instead expect from data processing the identification of new and unexpected stories.

Two Paths to Produce Justified Beliefs

Throughout the investigation, the production of justified beliefs with data-processing artifacts followed two opposite paths. From an analytical perspective, it would be impossible to assert that one path was more valid than the other; each of them provided specific norms to produce shared beliefs, relying on specific epistemological grounds (Table 1).

The first path has its roots in the computer-assisted reporting tradition in the United States (Parasie and Dagiral 2013). According to this model, a journalist becomes interested in a dataset only because he or she has some leads regarding a particular issue. From this perspective, data-processing artifacts allow reporters to confirm or invalidate a lead they may have found in interviews or documentation. Statistical sampling is viewed here as an appropriate tool to prove or disprove the lead. The completeness of the data as well as the possibility for the reporter to access granular data (e.g., the safety status of a school) is not a major concern. What is much more important here is the possibility to grasp social groups (e.g., inspectors) through data analysis, and to identify unfair situations or wrongdoings.

The second path has its roots in the new connections that have developed between the computer worlds and journalism since the mid-2000s (Lewis and Usher 2013). It values highly the completeness of the data as well as the possibility to access granular data. Taking the lead as a starting point for the data processing does not appear here to be compulsory for the reporter. The completeness of the data allows him or her to explore the data and be open to a new and unexpected story.

Within the team, the epistemological tension between the two paths did not give rise to a major controversy. The two paths were made compatible, but their

TABLE 1

Two paths to produce justified beliefs

	The hypothesis-driven path	The data-driven path
Database's most valued feature	Its availability for sampling	Its completeness
Starting assumptions	A strong hypothesis	A light hypothesis
What makes the data interesting for reporters	It allows reporters to confirm or invalidate a lead	It allows journalists to explore the information, and eventually to find new leads
Level of investigation	Aggregates and social groups	Granular or incident-level
Connection to the collection of qualitative information	Qualitative information helps to formulate the hypothesis, and to illustrate the related claim	The processing of the data helps to collect supplementary information
Ways of making governments accountable	By identifying unfair situations or faulty actions from data sampling	By identifying inconsistencies in the tracking of government actions over time

coexistence fed the discussion about the possibility to explore the data by relying on lighter hypotheses. The journalists connected to computer innovators of the San Francisco Bay area, in particular, supported this claim against the rest of the team. As a "news applications developer" involved in the "data science community," Michael Corey embodied that position:

> It's funny sometimes because reporters or editors, when we tell them about a project, one of the first things they'll say is, "Okay, well, what's the lead?" And we're like, "Well, there's not really a lead. That's not really the point." And sort of the idea of data not as an end into itself, because I think it's wrong. But there's just not having to do the traditional news lead or there's kind of a gotcha moment or there's a problem or highlighting. It's like, "No, we want to use the data as a vehicle to tell a story." (Corey, interview, August 24, 2012)

During the "On Shaky Ground" investigation, the team experienced two opposite ways of justifying beliefs with data-processing artifacts. On the one hand, this resulted in an epistemological tension between reporters with different backgrounds; on the other, these opposite ways were made compatible in the investigative process, as the same artifacts paradoxically helped to reduce the potential conflicts and to better organize collective work within the organization.

Conclusion

This article aims at contributing to the analysis of how technology affects the epistemologies of journalism. Because of the specificity of the case examined, the study does not bring to light a coherent epistemological framework that could apply to every investigative project involving a relation to data-processing artifacts, conducted in the United States or abroad. Instead, it points out the existence of epistemological tensions in the making of journalistic revelations through the processing of huge quantities of data. Because the "On Shaky Ground" project is the result of a collective organization consisting of journalists with different epistemological backgrounds, the tensions made visible here may be more broadly shared across other newsrooms.

This paper makes contributions to two streams of scholarship. The first deals with the future of investigative reporting and the role of technology therein. Noting the decline of investigative journalism in the United States in recent years, several scholars have emphasized the impact of the financial crisis and online technologies (Schudson 2010; Siles and Boczkowski 2012). Other scholars have nevertheless shown great expectations about how technology—especially data-processing artifacts—could facilitate investigation by lowering its cost (Cohen, Hamilton, and Turner 2011). The present study provides ambivalent arguments in this debate. On the one hand, it shows that the adjustment of artifacts to the established epistemologies of investigation has been a long and costly process. Mobilizing such resources may appear particularly problematic as most news organizations experience economic difficulties. But on the other hand, the analysis shows how one organization has succeeded in building the elements of a shared epistemic culture—which may reduce the cost of future projects. It thus suggests that data-processing artifacts can be used to enhance the collective organization of an investigation.

The second contribution of this paper concerns the study of journalistic knowledge. The notion of news as a form of knowledge is a well-established tradition in sociology, but analyzing the knowledge claims held by reporters is still rare in research (Ettema and Glasser 1998; Godler and Reich 2013), and usually poorly connected to technological matters. The present study suggests that it is crucial to study how journalists make such claims in relation to artifacts. Because of new connections with the computer worlds, news organizations experience alternative ways of producing justified beliefs from data (Parasie and Dagiral 2013).

Two limitations in this study should be addressed by further research. First, the organization that conducted the "On Shaky Ground" project is strongly committed to the established epistemologies of investigative reporting. Further research should study the making of investigative projects by organizations that are less respectful of established epistemologies. It could eventually point out distinct material and moral processes whereby they collectively make justified beliefs in relation to artifacts. Second, the case analyzed here is US-specific. Because news organizations based in other countries regularly conduct comparable projects, it seems crucial to understand whether they encounter similar tensions. The limited diffusion of a "computer-assisted reporting" tradition outside the United States, however, may profoundly shape the way news organizations globally deal with the processing of vast amounts of data.

ACKNOWLEDGEMENTS

This article has greatly benefited from close readings by Eric Dagiral. I also thank the special issue editor, Seth Lewis, and two anonymous reviewers for their most helpful suggestions.

FUNDING

The French Ministry of Culture and Communication supported this work.

NOTES

1. This series reached 7 million people in three days (Rosenthal 2011).
2. Introduced in March 2012, the bill was finally dropped in September 2012, officially for financial reasons.
3. This earthquake caused the death of 63 people in the San Francisco Bay area on October 17, 1989.

REFERENCES

Anderson, Chris. 2008. "The End of Theory: The Data Deluge Makes the Scientific Method Obsolete." *Wired*, June 23. http://www.wired.com/science/discoveries/magazine/16-07/pb_theory.

Cohen, Sarah, James T. Hamilton, and Fred Turner. 2011. "Computational Journalism." *Communications of the ACM* 54 (10): 66–71.

Cox, Melisma. 2000. "The Development of Computer-assisted Reporting." Paper presented to the newspaper division, association for Education in Journalism and Mass Communication, southeast colloquium, University of North Carolina, Chapel Hill, NC, March 17–18.

Doctor, Ken. 2011. "The Newsonomics of a Single Investigative Story." *Nieman Journalism Lab*, April 21. http://www.niemanlab.org/2011/04/the-newsonomics-of-a-single-investigative-story/.

Ettema, James S., and Theodore L. Glasser. 1998. *Custodians of Conscience. Investigative Journalism and Public Virtue*. New York: Columbia University Press.

Ettema, James S., and Theodore L. Glasser. 2005. "On the Epistemology of Investigative Journalism." In *Journalism: The Democratic Craft*, edited by Stuart G. Adam and Roy P. Clark, 126–140. New York: Oxford University Press.

Garrison, Bruce. 1998. *Computer-assisted Reporting*. Mahwah, NJ: Lawrence Erlbaum Associates.

Godler, Yigal, and Zvi Reich. 2013. "How Journalists Think About Facts. Theorizing the Social Conditions Behind Epistemological Beliefs." *Journalism Studies* 14 (1): 94–112.

Gray, Jonathan, Liliana Bounegru, and Lucy Chambers. 2012. *The Data Journalism Handbook*. Sebastopol, CA: O'Reilly Media.

Hallin, Daniel C. 2005. *We Keep America on Top of the World: Television Journalism and the Public Sphere*. London: Routledge.

Houston, Brant, Len Bruzzese, and Steve Weinberg. 2002. *The Investigative Reporter's Handbook: A Guide to Documents, Databases and Techniques*. New York: Bedford/St. Martin's Press.

Keating, Peter, and Alberto Cambrosio. 2012. "Too Many Numbers: Microarrays in Clinical Cancer Research." *Studies in History and Philosophy of Biological and Biomedical Sciences* 43 (1): 37–51.

Knorr-Cetina, Karin. 1999. *Epistemic Cultures: How the Sciences Make Knowledge*. Cambridge, MA: Harvard University Press.

Latour, Bruno and Steve Woolgar. 1979. *Laboratory Life. The Construction of Scientific Facts*. Princeton, NJ: Princeton University Press.

Lewis, Seth C. 2011. "Journalism Innovation and Participation: An Analysis of the Knight News Challenge." *International Journal of Communication* 5: 1623–1648.

Lewis, Seth C., and Nikki Usher. 2013. "Open Source and Journalism: Toward New Frameworks for Imagining News Innovation." *Media, Culture & Society* 35 (5): 602–619.

Mayer-Schönberger, Viktor, and Kenneth Cukier. 2013. *Big Data: A Revolution That Will Transform How We Live, Work and Think*. Boston, MA: Houghton Mifflin Harcourt.

Parasie, Sylvain, and Éric Dagiral. 2013. "Data-driven Journalism and the Public Good. Computer-assisted Reporters and Programmer-journalists in Chicago." *New Media and Society* 15 (6): 853–871.

Rosenthal, Robert J. 2011. "Reinventing Journalism. An Unexpected Personal Journey from Journalist to Publisher." *California Watch*, October 4. http://californiawatch.org/project/reinventing-journalism.

Schudson, Michael. 1978. *Discovering the News*. A Social History of American Newspapers. New York: Basic Books.

Schudson, Michael. 2001. "The Objectivity Norm in American Journalism." *Journalism* 2 (2): 149–170.

Schudson, Michael. 2010. "News in Crisis in the United States: Panic—And beyond." In *The Changing Business of Journalism and Its Implications for Democracy*, edited by David A. L. Levy, and Rasmus K. Nielsen, 95–106. Oxford: Reuters Institute for the Study of Journalism.

Siles, Ignacio, and Pablo J. Boczkowski. 2012. "Making Sense of the Newspaper Crisis: A Critical Assessment of Existing Research and an Agenda for Future Work." *New Media and Society* 14 (8): 1375–1394.

Strasser, Bruno. 2012. "Data-driven Sciences: From Wonder Cabinets to Electronic Databases." *Studies in History and Philosophy of Biological and Biomedical Sciences* 43 (1): 85–87.

Tuchman, Gaye. 1972. "Objectivity as Strategic Ritual: An Examination of Newsmen's Notions of Objectivity." *American Journal of Sociology* 77 (4): 660–679.

FROM MR. AND MRS. OUTLIER TO CENTRAL TENDENCIES
Computational journalism and crime reporting at the *Los Angeles Times*

Mary Lynn Young and **Alfred Hermida**

This study examines the impact of computational journalism on the creation and dissemination of crime news. Computational journalism refers to forms of algorithmic, social scientific, and mathematical processes and systems for the production of news. It is one of a series of technological developments that have shaped journalistic work and builds on techniques of computer-assisted reporting and the use of social science tools in journalism. This paper uses the Los Angeles Times' Homicide Report and its Data Desk as a case study to explore how technological adaptation occurred in this newsroom in the early twenty-first century. Our findings suggest that computational thinking and techniques emerged in a (dis)continuous evolution of organizational norms, practices, content, identities, and technologies that interdependently led to new products. Computational journalism emerges from an earlier and still ongoing turn to digital within broader organizational, technological, and social contexts. We place this finding in the local, situated context of the Homicide Report, one of the first crime news blogs to adopt computational journalism in North America.

Introduction

Computational journalism tends to be represented as one of a series of digital antidotes to the challenges facing mainstream journalism. Its proponents find possibility in the form's promise, from investigative depth, innovation, and increased audience engagement, to its ability to reinvent journalism for the twenty-first century in a way that empowers journalists for a more complicated information environment (Flew et al. 2012; Gynnild 2013; Karlsen and Stavelin 2013; Powers 2012). While many have examined the potential of computational journalism, a more site-specific and local understanding of how it is developing within specialized news genres is an important and underdeveloped area of study. Boczkowski's (2004) research on the transition of print to online newspapers convincingly focused on daily newspapers in the 1980s and 1990s in order to understand the complexity of how technological change combines with and emerges out of existing norms, routines, relationships, and social and material contexts. By approaching newsroom technological change through an understanding of the adoption process in specific local contexts, scholars can discern how digital media both constitute and are constituted by practice and innovation.

This paper examines how the Homicide Report, part of the Data Desk at the *Los Angeles Times*, adapted new technologies and different approaches to computational journalism as one of the first interactive mainstream media database/map of homicides in North America. The Data Desk is a team of reporters and Web developers at the *L.A. Times'* headquarters in downtown Los Angeles. We argue that the database and map were the result of newsroom practices combined with a new technology that started a relatively (dis)continuous evolution of organizational practices, content, identities, and tools that interdependently led to a new product. Paradoxically, this new product differs materially in its construction of the role of the crime journalist originally envisioned by the Homicide Report's founder. The study offers generalizable tendencies for understanding the technological adoption of computational thinking and techniques in journalism. Computational journalism at the *L.A. Times* can be understood as part of a much earlier and yet-ongoing turn to *digital* within journalism, framed within broader organizational, technological, and social contexts.

Literature Review

The emerging computational journalism literature largely frames its contribution within the potential for news production and journalism as a competitive and transformational tool for the industry. This approach is not a surprise, given the tendency of journalism professors and scholars to have originated from and/or be linked to the profession. Zelizer (2004) identified a similar bias towards pro industry-centric analyses of journalism education in her study of how journalism educators approach curriculum development. She suggests that they tend to focus on reinvention of the profession as opposed to critical analysis of the educational and journalism context. Similarly, Anderson (2013, 1007) critiques the technological "rise and fall narrative" emerging from the computational literature as related to its early stage of development, noting what he calls the "internalist" bent of the genre in general. He argues that the computer science literature on computational journalism, too, is focused on prescription, such that it is largely about "building things" through technology as opposed to analysis of larger structural, cultural, and sociological questions (1008).

Anderson's analysis of the literature includes prescriptions for future conceptual frameworks to explore computational journalism. This analysis provides a useful starting place for an assessment of the contribution of computational journalism to news production (see also Lewis and Usher 2013). He isolates six frameworks that could be used to approach technological change in news work. Specifically, Anderson (2013, 1009) draws from Schudson's sociology of news, suggesting that scholars apply "political, economic, organizational and cultural frames" to analyses of computational journalism, adding "technological and institutional or 'field' perspectives" to that list. In this way, analyses will move beyond a quick fix to understanding the interrelated forces underlying news work and technological adaptation.

We take on Anderson's exhortation to examine these new initiatives critically and apply Schudson's (1989, 2005) organizational approach to news by examining how news practices and organizational routines had an impact on the launch and growth of the Homicide Report from a blog to one of the first mainstream media entrants in computational crime journalism in North America. We also draw from Boczkowski's (2004) comprehensive socio-material approach that promotes the idea of "mutual shaping" to understand the relationship between new technology and news production. For Boczkowski, as referenced in Anderson, "organizational factors, work routines, and representations of users shape adoption processes, which are themselves afforded by technological changes. Only at the end of this far more complex process do distinct editorial products begin to emerge" (Anderson 2013, 1014).

Within this larger conceptual context, we define computational journalism using Diakopoulos (2011, 1, emphasis in original) as "the application of computing and computational thinking to the activities of journalism including *information gathering, organization and sensemaking, communication and presentation*, and *dissemination and public response* to news information." Similar to Coddington, we also draw from Wing (2006), who asserts the importance of "abstraction and automation" in understanding the contribution of computational thinking to journalism norms and practices (Coddington 2014).

Algorithm as Journalist

Other concepts relevant to our discussion include the algorithm as journalist. Algorithms are invisible agents that sort and filter online information to shape interactions on social networking sites or highlight what is popular online often through automation. Initial research focused on search technology and the information biases built into the algorithms used to highlight particular online content (Hindman, Tsioutsiouliklis, and Johnson 2003; Introna and Nissenbaum 2000). As algorithms have played an increasingly important role in society (Mayer-Schonberger and Cukier 2013; Steiner 2012), there has been a growth in literature on how algorithms structure ways of knowing and require interrogation (Anderson 2011; Beer 2009). Gillespie (2014) argues that algorithms have become a communication technology, locating them as the latest response to the processing, management, and delivery of information in a complex society.

Algorithms are already being used in sports and financial journalism to automatically generate and publish thousands of news stories without human intervention and at little or no cost (van Dalen 2012). Machine-written news has led to claims that a robo-story will win a Pulitzer Prize within five years to speculation of an apocalypse for the news industry (Marshall 2013). How far the audience realizes or notices robo-stories is unclear, with one small-scale test finding no significant differences in the perception of human or robo-written copy (Clerwall 2014).

To understand the development and application of algorithms in journalism requires both a technological and sociological lens. Algorithm providers contend the neutrality and objectivity of such systems. Yet algorithms are the product of individual and institutional norms and practices. Gillespie (2014) draws a parallel between the assertion of algorithmic objectivity by technology providers and the journalistic norm of objectivity. In both cases, objectivity comes through practices and decisions hidden from the public that lend legitimacy to the production of knowledge.

The algorithm as journalist raises questions about how decisions of inclusion and exclusion are made, what styles of reasoning are employed, whose values are embedded into the technology, and how they affect public understanding of complex issues. As with other technologies, they are the result of a mix of professional, technical, economic, and political factors. Unraveling the choices embedded in the code presents challenges when, as Anderson (2011) notes, algorithms promiscuously combine human and non-human judgment to a degree where it becomes hard to discern between them. "Data-crunching algorithms and other increasingly invisible information ordering devices are neither entirely material, nor are they entirely human—they are hybrid, composed of both human intentionality and material obduracy," writes Anderson (2013, 1016).

Much debated is how algorithmic journalism fits in with the normative notion of journalism as vital to democratic life. In their report on a 2009 workshop on computational journalism, Hamilton and Turner (2009) write of the potential for the algorithm to sustain the watchdog function of journalism, identify story leads, or shape how a story is constructed and presented to readers. Flew et al. (2012, 168) cite the example of *The Guardian* using a combination of crowdsourcing and computational methods to investigate Members of Parliaments' expenses, concluding that computational journalism can "add real value to journalistic knowledge production." van Dalen (2012) suggests that there is a degree of recognition in the profession about the potential benefits of using algorithms to produce basic commodity news, allowing journalists to focus on more creative, analytical, and in-depth stories, rather than routine news.

Yet there is also an acknowledgement that technology is neither good nor bad (nor neutral). Anderson (2011, 541) suggests that algorithmic journalism "might represent the most recent, and thus most unsettling, model for both communication and democracy." He argues that algorithmic journalism contains various normative assumptions: it embraces big data, blurs divisions between humans and non-human data, is inclined towards gathering more information rather than better information, and "contains at least *the seeds* of an internal bias towards prediction" (542, emphasis in original). Indeed, Rieder (2014) points to the development of algorithms as engines of order that combine data collection, analysis, decision-making, and execution all in one.

The use of algorithms for media production contains an editorial logic based on the socially situated choices of media professionals. The algorithm as journalist can be considered an expression of the ideology of journalism that includes "the general process of the production of meanings and ideas" (Deuze 2005, 445). Studying the practices around the use of algorithms in journalism can help to illuminate how these technologies reproduce, embody, or alter norms of professional ideology.

Online Crime News

As this article is largely focused on the development of the Homicide Report, the final section of the literature review will assess scholarly analyses of crime news content in a digital media environment. Interest in and research on digital media in this domain has largely been concerned with police communications innovations, not mainstream media technology adoption. Scholars have tended to be interested in questions of how police use social media or other forms of digital media to reach out directly to the public, as opposed to the traditional media–police relationship, which is seen as contested and negotiated (Crump 2011; Heverin and Zach 2010; Mawby 2010).

A final conceptual area that is relevant to this paper is the definition of crime news. In a well-known historical account of crime content, Barnhurst and Mutz (1997) examined news about crime, accidents, and jobs over a 100-year period from 1884 to 1994 in three respected US regional mainstream daily newspapers. They found that crime content shifted from largely event-centered accounts to longer stories with more analysis and context. They noted that crime stories changed from stories about highly specific local places early in the period to encompassing a larger geographic focus. They conclude: "crime remained a local denotative event until becoming identified with social problems after the 1960s. The reporting of crime analyses, interpretations and themes surged by 1974" (Barnhurst and Mutz 1997, 44).

They situate the development of crime news as a "more interpretive form of reporting" in shifts in journalism culture, such as an increase in journalism-school graduates trained in the social sciences and emerging definitions of news that identified the importance of context (Barnhurst and Mutz 1997, 49). In addition, they suggest that an increase in the availability of data and computers facilitated media interest in an area long held to be the domain of academics.

Methods and Context

This study examined the launch of the Homicide Report as part of the growth of the *L.A. Times'* Data Desk using qualitative interviews and textual analysis of journalism, industry, and public realm accounts of the Report. Specifically, our research question is how computational journalism thinking and practices emerged in relationship to organizational norms, practices, structures, and technologies at the *L.A. Times*. We used long-form, semi-structured interviews with seven employees[1] of the *L.A. Times* Data Desk and Homicide Report to gain insights into their individualistic perceptions (Arksey and Knight 1999; McCraken 1988). The interviews were supplemented with a textual analysis of the material written (11 articles in total) about its deployment in industry and professional publications, including the transcript of a radio interview with Homicide Report founding journalist Jill Leovy. We also attended a news meeting of the Data Desk team in August 2013.

Of the respondent interviews, we talked to five subjects in person. The interview length ranged from 45 to 90 minutes each. We interviewed an additional two respondents by phone for between 40 and 50 minutes. The respondents held a range of key professional positions from reporter to editor, researcher, and data journalist, varying in expertise from early to mid- and late-career. Only one journalist had explicitly studied as a data journalist, first at university and later in a non-legacy journalism organization. The questions focused on how the Data Desk and Homicide Report developed historically, how *L.A. Times* journalists defined crime journalism and data/computational journalism, the roles identified for these journalists, skills of those hired to work in this area, workflows on the Homicide Report, allocation of resources, journalistic practices, and the impact of computational methods on crime coverage. We completed a textual analysis of the transcripts to identify key themes and ideas related to a set of core issues of interest to the researchers. These included the evolution of computational journalism at the *L.A. Times*, how it was framed to improve quality and economics of news, and how approaches to and understandings of the role of technology affected adoption in newsroom interactions, rationales for the Homicide Report, and overall perceptions of the role of the Data Desk and computational journalism.

The Homicide Report Launches in 2007

The Homicide Report launched as a blog in January 2007 under the authorship of journalist Jill Leovy, whose goal was to cover each of the almost 1000 homicides in Los Angeles County for a year. At the time, the newspaper typically reported on 10 percent of the annual homicides (Leovy 2008). The format included "uniform information" about each homicide, including "race, gender, location of killing or where the body was found" (Gahran 2007; Leovy 2008). A map was added some months later as initially the Web team lacked the ability and expertise to create it (Ulken 2008). The blog was described in early media coverage as a "compilation" of postings and "dispatches" (Gahran 2007). In a radio interview, Leovy said her goal was to respond to racism and structural bias in the news media's coverage of homicide:

> There's sort of an upside-down logic of press coverage in homicide where the nature of news is to cover the man-bites-dog story, and what you end up doing is you cover the statistical fringe of homicide. You cover the very unlikely cases that don't represent what's really happening most days in Los Angeles County. It creates, I think, a false view of who's safe and who's not and where homicide is concentrated. And *The Times* wanted to give an accurate view of what homicide looks like, both from afar and close up. (Leovy, quoted in *On the Media* 2007)

Leovy managed the blog for approximately a year before she was asked by the *L.A. Times* to hand it over to a colleague (Leovy 2008). She noted publicly that the blog was not able to cover every homicide because of a variety of technical and data issues, adding that "the relentless demands of this beat have at times exceeded the abilities of this reporter" (Leovy 2007). A number of junior Metro journalists filled in on the blog after Leovy left (Roderick 2013), and in November 2008, readers were told that the Homicide Report was going on hiatus (*Los Angeles Times* 2008). The break lasted 14 months until it was relaunched in January 2010 to include a searchable database and mapping tool (Garvey and Pesce 2010). The database information largely originated from the coroner's office in Los Angeles County. At the time of the relaunch, the *L.A. Times* introduced algorithmic reporting tools to produce short posts for the Homicide blog. The posts are automatically written and published, and later can be expanded by a reporter. The robo-post includes the date, incident location, time, race or ethnicity, age, jurisdiction and neighborhood. Finally, in 2013, the Report was renewed once again when a full-time reporter was hired for the first time to manage what *L.A. Times* assistant managing editor Megan Garvey called one of the paper's "marquee online public service projects" (quoted in Roderick 2013).

Findings

We found that the adoption of computational journalism thinking and technologies in the Homicide Report was uneven and (dis)continuous. It emerged out of existing norms and practices, was unrecognized in its genesis, and marked by early failures, ultimately evolving interdependently out of relationships with other journalism technologies and grounded in new journalistic identities. In this mutual shaping of technology and journalism practices we identified "stages of innovative energy" supported by various actors and their networks, and application of existing "know-how" to problems that were both defined through existing norms, practices, and economic contexts, as well as re-interpreted through computational thinking (Bijker, Hughes, and Pinch 1989, 4).

The Homicide Report's first iteration as a blog in which all homicides in Los Angeles County were to be reported for a year used the Web to enable already evolving definitions of crime news content. Leovy's goal of identifying the racialized structure of homicide in Los Angeles through a blog format can be understood as shaped by historical changes in the definition of crime news identified by Barnhurst and Mutz as emerging during the previous century. They include a shift towards journalism as populist social science, with both different and larger interpretative goals, conceptually and geographically. In an email cited by *LA Observed*, Leovy noted:

> This is my way of throwing a stone at the monster, and I hope people at least glance at it. At the very least, seeing all the homicides arrayed in a list like this will give readers a much more real view of who is dying, and how often. And for me, it means no longer having to confront weeping mothers who say their sons' deaths were never covered by the press. (quoted in Roderick 2007)

Leovy's mission rearticulates the role of journalist as gatekeeper in an online environment, in that her overarching goal was to explicitly set the news agenda *vis-à-vis* representations of homicide, despite legitimate critique about her decision to identify race using signifiers grounded in a racialized social history. Indeed, she clearly advocates for what some scholars have labeled a public health approach to crime news content in that the Homicide Report approaches violence as "epidemic," with certain groups more at risk than others. A public health reporting model for crime news content was launched in 1995 by a group of journalists and journalism scholars as educational outreach to a number of US mainstream daily newspapers, including the *L.A. Times* (Stevens 1998). Part of its mission was to educate journalists on the biases inherent in traditional crime news content in which: "Readers and viewers are rarely given enough information to put reported violent incidents into context to know what violence is 'usual' and able to be prevented, and what is unusual and thus unlikely to be preventable" (Stevens 1998, 38).

This approach is reflected in Leovy's blog, in which she stressed that "I wanted readers to see all the killings—roughly 1,000 violent deaths each year, mostly of young Latinos and, most disproportionately, of young black men" (Leovy 2008). While the Report's first iteration was grounded in contemporary definitions of crime news and the role of the crime journalist, Leovy's motivations included the seeds of a more systematic computational thinking as defined by Diakopoulos (2011). She was attempting to make sense of the nature of homicide in Los Angeles through aggregation in a way that previous, more episodic journalism genres were unable to articulate. The Homicide Report was successful in this respect, in that it was singled out by non-journalists and advocates as having a positive impact as "a tool for prevention and public awareness" of "non-killing journalism initiatives" by scholars such as Pim (2013, 25).

Leovy's blog and her contribution to journalism at the *L.A. Times* were constructed as both innovative and experimental but not in the sense that there was an explicit path to its role in launching computational journalism at the *L.A. Times*. That sensibility emerged later, resulting in one of its next iterations. Megan Garvey, an editor recognized for her leadership in journalism and technology innovation, recalled:

> She was definitely an early innovator. I don't think she even had an editor. So it's almost like, if you look at the very early blog, it's almost like a stream of consciousness ... It's just kind of what she's seeing and thinking. (Garvey, interview, December 6, 2013)

From Blog to Database and Algorithm

The Homicide Report's first phase as a blog ended after Leovy finished her year. The blog was sporadically updated and eventually put on hiatus, reemerging in a new form three years after Leovy had founded the report. Garvey said the project stumbled and was "almost killed several times" after Leovy left, adding that she stepped up to take it over because she "thought it was valuable" and that "we could turn it into a database" (interview, December 6 2013). She said she and a number of others worked to "restore" the Homicide Report, eventually relaunching in January 2010 as an "interactive map and searchable database." "It was sort of like the volunteer army ... people who just felt like it was important and spent time doing it" (interview, December 6, 2013). This "volunteer army" included two individuals specifically hired to work in computational and data journalism: Ben Welsh, who had experience in computer-assisted reporting (CAR) and considers himself a data journalist, and Ken Schwencke, a programmer/journalist. The innovations in this version conform to Diakopoulos' (2011) and Wing's (2006) definitions of computational journalism in that the newspaper used abstraction and automation to extend computational thinking and practices to a number of areas of journalism such as: research and information gathering, sensemaking, presentation, and dissemination.

The 2010 re-launch of the Homicide Report included a structured database with "the atomic pieces of a homicide" (Ken Schwencke, interview, December 17, 2013), including the date, location, time, race or ethnicity, age, gender, and jurisdiction. Blog posts from before the re-launch in January 2010 were downloaded and the relevant information extracted and added to the database. Schwencke, who wrote the algorithm, described it as "embarrassingly simple". He added:

> It is a simple sort of innovation, a simple sort of tool that has strong impact. It does a lot with very little. It is not a complicated piece of code, it is not a complicated theory, it is not a complicated algorithm. It is this simple thing that we built that has impact disproportionate to the amount of time that we actually spend on it. (Schwencke, interview, December 17, 2013)

The algorithm writes the first paragraph of a post, which contains facts about the homicide. For Schwencke, the robo-post is "about what a normal reporter would write. When you don't have a lot of information, you write to the information you have." A journalist can later add more information to the entry. The basic post, though, for Nicole Santa Cruz, "doesn't have the human touch to it" (interview, August 16, 2013).

For the initial facts, the algorithm relies on the same sources used by human reporters: law enforcement or related sources. The starting point for the Homicide Report is the coroner's office. If the coroner lists a death as a homicide, it will automatically be written up as a robo-post. Details about the homicide are based on the information from the Los Angeles County coroner's office. Given that the information is complex and subject to change, the journalist can also amend the details. Thus, the algorithm and its "development of intelligent systems" to "process meanings in contextually relative ways" (Flew et al. 2012, 158) allowed the Homicide Report to extend beyond its early iteration as a blog of every homicide in Los Angeles. This extension initially supplants "humanistic perspectives" and approaches to thinking about crime such as curiosity as a possible motivation for exploring one homicide in more detail than another with abstract thinking and processing (158; see also Wing 2006; Coddington 2014). Journalists at the *L.A. Times* understood the algorithm as enhancing the role of crime reporters rather than replacing them.

For example, the *L.A. Times* also uses algorithms to alert the newsroom to levels of crime that exceed the norm for an area in another neighborhood crime project, not the Homicide Report. "There's an algorithm we developed that identifies neighborhoods that relative to their own history are having an unusual amount of crime in the last week" (Ben Welsh, interview, August 16, 2013). There is a perception that by enabling the *L.A. Times* to be able to report every homicide, however rudimentary the initial post, algorithms reduce "the load on reporters and producers and pretty much everybody in getting the information out there as fast as possible" (Schwencke, interview, December 17, 2013). For Welsh, the algorithm also has a potential economic benefit:

> If through computer programming and data we're able to, at a lower cost, sort of scale out, even reporting just the fact that all these minor crimes happened, right, that is something that could be of interest to people who care about what happens near they live. (Welsh, interview, August 16, 2013)

The fact that the computer might be able to systematically report on all basic crimes better than the journalist did not emerge as a concern. Finally, Schwencke believes that the public appreciates the robo-posts and their presentation as a blog as a way of learning about every homicide in Los Angeles County. For example, adoption of computational journalism at the *L.A. Times* focused on organizing information geographically, and presenting the map interactively and visually. It provides an immediate overview of the current homicides across the city with circles proportionate to the number of deaths. Readers are able to interact with the data to focus in on neighborhoods, street locations, and individual homicides. Schwencke adds:

> They are good and they are useful as they get something into the general post stream that a person can come across … It gives you a familiar interface for the information. The Homicide Report could have just been a map and an interactive database, but giving it the blog sort of feel gives people a familiar starting place. (Schwencke, interview, December 17, 2013)

The *L.A. Times*' use of the blog format with an interactive map is broadly consistent with the adoption of digital communication technologies within journalism. Blogs, while initially resisted, have been assimilated by news outlets to offer short updates presented in a chronological manner online. Similarly, interactive maps allow newsrooms to incorporate the interactive capabilities of the Web in the visual presentation of information. Innovation at the Homicide Report comes from the use of computational and algorithmic approaches to the gathering, organization, and sensemaking of the crime data communicated and presented through the blog and interactive map.

"More Evergreen ... More Interactive"

Flew et al. (2012) suggest that three technological areas are pushing the growth of computational journalism: increased amount of accessible data, more and less expensive Web 2.0 applications, and greater online participation. They argue this context is supporting the development of computational journalism practices that may help news organizations balance quality and accuracy with speed and lower costs, while attracting audiences as online participants (Flew et al. 2012). Some of these motivations are more visible than others as the *L.A. Times* adopted and adapted to computational journalism techniques.

Garvey sees part of the shift to data and computational journalism as technology providing the ability to be transparent about journalistic research practices. According to Garvey, newspaper journalists have not been able to share their research information because of space constraints, thereby limiting the public's access to supporting evidence. On data journalism's contribution, she suggests: "The evolution really is in how the work is used and then it becomes in some cases with the databases more evergreen or more interactive in terms of exposing work that we've done for a long time." She adds that the new ability to take "unstructured information" and create a database will require journalists with a "more sophisticated" approach to journalism such that they can "compile this information in a way that can be used beyond ... what I can write fairly easily" (Garvey, interview, December 6, 2013).

For Doug Smith, the shift towards data journalism allows journalists to address a long-standing bias in the business toward "unusual events."

> I think that our track record too much has been one of generalizing from events, even if not explicitly, just sort of by implication ... I try to get in the middle and say, let's just be sure we know how this event fits into everything else. (Smith, interview, August 16, 2013)

Similarly, for Welsh, the Homicide Report's articulation of crime journalism widens the lens of interpretation, moving from journalism's general focus on "Mr. and Mrs. Outlier" to the "central tendency":

> Mr. and Mrs. Outlier get covered really well in crime news. And they drive tons of traffic, and we have full-time reporters who do that. But as you know that's an incredibly small fraction of the amount of crime that happens. And they probably reflect certain cultural predispositions ... But what data can bring us ... is to try to give some fuller sense of crime as a phenomenon in the city. (Welsh, interview, August 16, 2013)

The notion of systematic homicide coverage has defined the project since its inception. Welsh frames it in the context of an "idea of completeness" (interview, August 16, 2013). The current journalist assigned to the Homicide Report, Santa Cruz, noted that it defies "the traditional notion of news because news is the extraordinary, the unique" (interview, August 16, 2013). The affordances of an online venue are described as enabling a break from traditional norms of crime reporting by both Leovy (2008) and Santa Cruz.

Thus, similar to van Dalen's research, *L.A. Times* journalists on the Data Desk saw the incorporation of computational journalism as an opportunity to enhance existing practice and allow journalists to focus on more contextual reporting. In practice, however, the actual news work of the current crime reporter is relatively similar to past practices, focusing on relationships with law enforcement sources, verification, and finding the "human-interest" story, rather than going beyond the immediate context of an event. In this way, the rank-and-file crime reporter becomes part of a new professional hierarchy and labeling system for journalists. For example, Doug Smith referenced the emerging professional identity of the data journalist in relationship to the newsroom hierarchy: "Everybody thinks Ben [Welsh] works for me, which is ridiculous. Ben works for God" (Smith, interview, August 16, 2013). This identity reifies the data/computational journalist *vis-à-vis* the general reporter. Similarly, in our interview, Schwencke noted that he was offered a permanent position at the *L.A. Times* after receiving a competitive job offer from another news publication.

Mutating Technologies and New Identities

We found that the Homicide Report's various forms suggested a clear process of mutual adaptation with previous technologies, in this case data journalism projects, online projects, as well as the creation of a new professional identity for journalists. For example, a number of respondents identified the importance of previous projects and their success and subsequent learning as key to the generative process on the Data Desk. This is supported by research from Boczkowski (2004, 11), who suggests, "media innovation unfolds through the interrelated mutations in technology, in communication, and in organization."

For example, Garvey identifies two technological factors that shaped the emergence of the Data Desk and Homicide Report. She cites the role of the paper's CAR tradition and its first database project, California's War Dead. The project is an online record of service members born in or from the state who died during the wars in Iraq and Afghanistan. The War Dead was referenced by almost all interview subjects as a key moment that supported newsroom understanding of the possible role of databases. Welsh described it as

> one of the first examples of the print and Web coming together behind a project that wasn't seen as a Web baby or a print baby, but was kind of the Web hitching up with print on one of the high editorial priorities. (interview, August 16, 2013)

The project pointed to how data techniques could be applied in the future.

> The CAR tradition evolved into what we now call the Data Desk, which is people who can do both internal reporting work and turn around and then expose that work to the public in ways that are engaging. (Garvey, interview, December 6, 2013)

Similarly, the coding for the robo-posts for the Homicide Report was drawn from work done for another *L.A. Times* project, called Mapping LA. "I figured we could expand that idea into making an actual blog post," said Schwencke (interview, December 17, 2013). In a further indication of the iterative process of technological adaption, the algorithms behind the homicide robo-posts have since been tailored to write posts about earthquakes in California.

Finally, we found that the Homicide Report was only able to evolve because of a leadership change and its relationship with the "cool kids team" (Ulken 2008) on the Data Desk.

> Megan [Garvey], who was a, I think, assistant or deputy editor at the time, decided to come down and join us. And that was a terrific boost for the Data Desk ... Megan had a direct channel into the news operation. So it sort of kept us alive and engaged when we were down in limbo. (Smith, interview, August 16, 2013)

In 2010, Welsh, Schwencke and the CAR team sat side by side on the second floor of the L.A. Times' building, near the graphics department, but reported to different hierarchies – web and metro, respectively – in the newspaper. As a result, the skills and team emerged alongside existing CAR expertise. Further support from senior management followed when Ashley Dunn, a former science editor, became Metro editor in March 2011 (*Los Angeles Times* 2011). In his previous science role, Dunn got to know Smith. "We're good work friends because we know each other well. We always talk. Because his group in the old days was right across from science," recalled Dunn (interview, August 16, 2013). When he took over Metro, Dunn decided to move the team to the main newsroom in front of his office because he "wanted to make sure people were availing themselves to this" (interview, August 16, 2013). Smith noted: "He not only got me here. At the time there were three of us. But he's expanded." (interview, August 16, 2013). He added: There are now seven positions in two departments.

Discussion

The Homicide Report grew out of existing social, organizational, and material contexts, as well as mutually reinforcing access to new technologies, which exemplifies the importance of understanding specialized news genres in their local environment in examining technological innovation in journalism. The history of computational thinking and practices in the Homicide Report was uneven and (dis)continuous, to the extent that evidence of a systematic computational approach emerged unrecognized in its first iteration. Gynnild (2013) argues that the quality of computational journalism depends on a shift in mindset, with journalists learning to think more like computer scientists. We identify that mindset as existing in the Homicide Report—systematic coverage as a public service and related to the changing definition of crime news more generally—from its outset but not explicitly identified as such among journalists. Our interviews provide some evidence that there is an emerging professional class of data journalists but that the mindset suggested by Gynnild is still in process. As with the adoption of other technological innovations, such as blogging, journalists appropriated and adapted computational and algorithmic methods to suit the purposes of journalism. Similar to Royal's (2010) study of the *New York Times'* interactive desk, we also found the importance of leadership, self-taught skills, and collaboration in the Homicide Report's trajectory.

The discourse of the Data Desk also underplays the potential influences of algorithmic journalism. For example, data from our interviewees suggest that journalists framed the robo-posts as a tool to facilitate systematic coverage and freeing journalists to add more depth, context, and the human touch, as well as possibly decrease costs. van Dalen (2012) reached a similar conclusion about the downplaying of the impact of algorithmic journalism in his study of coverage of machine-written sports stories. He too found a belief that automated content could give journalists more time for research and in-depth reporting. The perspective of the Data Desk is not necessarily indicative of journalists at the *L.A. Times*. But it is indicative of the attitudes of early adopters and innovators within the newsroom. Journalists involved in the development of algorithmic journalism might be expected to be more open to the potential benefits of such technologies, seeing how abstraction and automation could enable more complete reporting. The automated content is not perceived as a threat as it is not replacing a human member of the data team but rather assisting the *L.A. Times* to advance its stated editorial goal of reporting on every homicide.

The robo-posts present a challenge to the emergent role of the crime journalist as envisioned by Leovy in that now homicides are initially reported by a non-human actor, the algorithm, while the rank and file crime journalist supplies the "human touch" (Santa Cruz, interview, August 16, 2013), such as details about the victim's life and family. In this way, a problem, how to generate consistent and comprehensive homicide data in a context of inadequate and inconsistent ability to staff the blog was solved through computational innovation and automation. The result addresses the comprehensiveness and economic problem, and could, potentially, free up journalists from routine newswork to focus on applying expertise, judgment, and insight in the pursuit of wisdom journalism (Mitchell 2010). But our findings indicate that journalists returned to familiar, historic, and gendered practices associated with sensational crime stories, the "sob sister," whose role was to supply the emotional and human-interest context to news. In this new workplace context, the programmer and the algorithm assume *a priori* roles with respect to who gets to define the "real" homicide news. This new professional labeling and power relationship is complicated by the fact that the robo-posts, while they extend professional expertise in journalism to include the identities of the programmer and non-human actor, are themselves an expression of basic norms and practices with respect to reporting homicide, albeit with greater completeness. These entail the production of crime news as a routine task, with a standard format with basic facts as defined by official sources. This finding is also in contrast to the generally lower-status role of journalists who are connected to distinct technologies (Powers 2012). In closing, the evolution of the Homicide Report at the *L.A. Times* involved the emergence of a new class of computational journalist and non-human journalist, repositioning the "human" crime reporter in a more historic and less powerful job classification

Conclusion

The Homicide Report could be said to illustrate a central tendency in understanding innovation in computational journalism, which has implications for how we assess technology adaptation in legacy media institutions. In taking on Anderson's suggestion to apply a more critical sociological approach to the emergence of computational journalism, this study's findings show an uneven process of technology adoption/adaptation that builds on changing crime news norms and practices, and interdependencies with other technologies to somewhat paradoxical ends, focusing on a neutral or positive understanding of computational journalism's contributions to the industry despite potential evidence of more systematic impacts on the nature and identity of the journalist.

The Homicide Report began using blog technology to support a more systematic approach to crime journalism with a public health agenda. Its first iteration emerged out of contemporary changes in the definition of crime news and contained early traces of computational thinking, which shaped subsequent innovation. A later adaptation was more explicit in its adoption of computational journalism thinking and techniques, as a new class of journalist was hired with specific expertise, extending the professional to both non-human crime journalists. As newsroom resources for the Homicide Report diminished and new technologies emerged, its focus shifted to computational approaches to crime journalism. This iteration built on existing newsroom organizational structures and the *L.A. Times'* history with CAR, including two early high-profile data journalism projects. The data team applied and re-interpreted its previous learning, resulting in a new form, the Homicide Report, as an interactive database and map. In the later period, journalists approached the adaptation process with an industry-centric lens, focusing on the competitive possibilities for systemic coverage, transparency, and audience engagement offered by computational journalism. Ultimately, however, it can be argued that the approach masked a paradoxical shift in the professional role of the crime journalist, while, at the same time, nurturing the emergence of new and powerful identities of computational journalist in both its human and non-human forms.

ACKNOWLEDGEMENTS

We would like to thank our anonymous reviewers for incisive feedback on an earlier version of this article, Candis Callison for her insight and Elizabeth Hames for her research assistance.

FUNDING

This research was funded by the GRAND NCE as part of the NEWS project.

NOTE

1. List of interviewees: Nicole Santa Cruz, staff writer (Homicide Report); Ashley Dunn, assistant managing editor; Megan Garvey, assistant managing editor; Maloy Moore, data team production coordinator; Ken Schwencke, digital editor; Doug Smith, database editor; Ben Welsh, senior digital editor.

REFERENCES

Anderson, C. W. 2011. "Deliberative, Agonistic, and Algorithmic Audiences: Journalism's Vision of Its Public in an Age of Audience." *Journal of Communication* 5: 529–547.

Anderson, C. W. 2013. "Toward a Sociology of Computational and Algorithmic Journalism." *New Media & Society* 15 (7): 1005–1021. doi:10.1177/1461444812465137.

Arksey, Hilary, and Peter Knight. 1999. *Interviewing for Social Scientists: An Introductory Resource with Examples*. Thousand Oaks, CA: Sage.

Barnhurst, Kevin, and Diana Mutz. 1997. "American Journalism and the Decline of Event-centered Reporting." *Journal of Communication* 47 (4) Autumn: 27–53.

Beer, David. 2009. "Power through the Algorithm? Participatory Web Cultures and the Technological Unconscious." *New Media and Society* 11 (6): 985–1002.

Bijker, Wiebe, Thomas Hughes, and Trevor Pinch, eds. 1989. *New Directions in the Sociology and History of Technology*. Cambridge: MIT Press.

Boczkowski, Pablo J. 2004. *Digitizing the News: Innovation in Online Newspapers*. New Baskerville: First MIT Press.

Clerwall, Christer. 2014. "Enter the Robot Journalist." *Journalism Practice*. February 25. doi: 10.1080/17512786.2014.883116.

Coddington, Mark. 2014. "Clarifying Journalism's Quantitative Turn: A Typology for Evaluating Data Journalism, Computational Journalism, and Computer-assisted Reporting." *Digital Journalism*. doi: 10.1080/21670811.2014.976400.

Crump, Jeremy. 2011. "What Are the Police Doing on Twitter? Social Media, the Police and the Public." *Policy & Internet* 3 (4): 1–27. doi:10.2202/1944-2866.1130.

van Dalen, Arjen. 2012. "The Algorithms behind the Headlines: How Machine-written News Redefines the Core Skills of Human Journalists." *Journalism Practice* 6 (5-6): 648–658. doi:10.1080/17512786.2012.667268.

Deuze, Mark. 2005. "What is Journalism?: Professional Identity and Ideology of Journalists Reconsidered." *Journalism* 6 (4): 442–464. doi:10.1177/1464884905056815.

Diakopoulos, Nicholas. 2011. "A Functional Roadmap for Innovation in Computational Journalism." http://www.nickdiakopoulos.com/2011/04/22/a-functional-roadmap-for-innovation-in-computational-journalism/.

Flew, Terry, Christina Spurgeon, Anna Daniels, and Adam Swift. 2012. "The Promise of Computational Journalism." *Journalism Practice* 6 (2): 157–171. doi:10.1080/17512786.2011.61665.

Gahran, Amy. 2007. "Homicide Report: Traditional Journalism, Delivered via Blog." *Poynter*, February 28. http://www.poynter.org/how-tos/digital-strategies/e-media-tidbits/81019/homicide-report-traditional-journalism-delivered-via-blog/.

Garvey, Megan, and Anthony Pesce. 2010. *"Please Visit the Homicide Report at Its New Location."* The Homicide Report, *Los Angeles times*. January 25. http://latimesblogs.latimes.com/homicidereport/2010/01/new-blog-location.html.

Gillespie, Tarleton. 2014. "The Relevance of Algorithms." In *Media Technologies: Essays on Communication, Materiality, and Society*, edited by Tarleton Gillespie, Pablo Boczkowski and Kirsten Foot, 167–194. Cambridge: MIT Press.

Gynnild, Astrid. 2013. "Journalism Innovation Leads to Innovation Journalism: The Impact of Computational Exploration on Changing Mindsets." *Journalism* 15 (6): 713–730.

Hamilton, James T., and Fred Turner. 2009. "Accountability through Algorithm: Developing the Field of Computational Journalism." Report from summer workshop Developing the Field of Computational Journalism at the Center For Advanced Study in the Behavioral Sciences, Stanford, July 27-31. http://www.stanford.edu/~fturner/Hamilton%20Turner%20Acc%20by%20Alg%20Final.pdf.

Heverin, Thomas, and Lisl Zach. 2010. "Twitter for City Police Department Information Sharing." *Proceedings of the American Society of Information Science and Technology* 47 (1): 1–7. http://www.asis.org/asist2010/proceedings/proceedings/ASIST_AM10/submissions/277_Final_Submission.pdf.

Hindman Matthew, Kostas Tsioutsiouliklis, and Judy A. Johnson. 2003. "Googlearchy: How a Few Heavily-Linked Sites Dominate Politics on the Web", in Proceedings of the Annual Meeting of the Midwest Political Science Association.

Introna, Lucas, and Helen Nissenbaum. 2000. "Sustaining the Public Good Vision of the Internet: The Politics of Search Engines." *Preferred Placement: Knowledge Politics on the Web, Edited by Richard Rogers, Jan Van Eyck Akademy.* 25–47.

Karlsen, Joakim, and Eirik Stavelin. 2013. "Computational Journalism in Norwegian Newsrooms." *Journalism Practice* 8 (1): 34–48.

Leovy Jill. 2007. "Notes on 2007: Missing Cases." The Homicide Report, *Los Angeles* Times. December 31. http://latimesblogs.latimes.com/homicidereport/2007/12/notes-on-2007-m.html.

Leovy Jill. 2008. "Unlimited Space for Untold Sorrow." *Los Angeles times*, February 4. http://articles.latimes.com/2008/feb/04/local/me-homicide4.

Lewis, Seth C., and Nikki Usher. 2013. "Open Source and Journalism: Toward New Frameworks for Imagining News Innovation." *Media, Culture and Society* 35 (5): 602–619. doi:10.1177/0163443713485494.

Los Angeles Times. 2008. " A Note to Our Readers." The Homocide Report, November 13. http://latimesblogs.latimes.com/homicidereport/2008/11/a-note-to-our-r.html.

Los Angeles Times. 2011. "Ashley Dunn named Times California editor." Readers' Representative Journal, March 28. http://latimesblogs.latimes.com/readers/2011/03/ashley-dunn-named-times-california-editor.html.

Marshall Sarah. 2013. "Robot Reporters: A Look at the Computers Writing the News." *Journalism.Co.Uk*, March 12. http://www.journalism.co.uk/news/robot-reporters-how-computers-are-writing-la-times-articles/s2/a552359/.

Mawby, Rob C. 2010. "Police Corporate Communications, Crime Reporting and the Shaping of Policing News." *Policing & Society* 20 (1): 124–139.

Mayer-Schonberger, Viktor, and Kenneth Cukier. 2013. *Big Data: A Revolution That Will Transform How We Live, Work, and Think.* New York: Houghton Mifflin Harcourt.

McCracken, Grant. 1988. *The Long Interview*. Newbury Park: Sage.

Mitchell Stephens. 2010. "The Case for Wisdom Journalism–And for Journalists Surrendering the Pursuit of News." *Daedalus* 139 (2): 76–90.

On the Media. 2007. "Murder Ink Transcript." http://www.onthemedia.org/story/129146-murder-ink/transcript/.

Pim Joám Evans. 2013. "When the Messenger is the Killer … the Possibility and Need for Nonkilling Media." In *Nonkilling Media*, edited by Joám Evans Pim, 23–34. Centre for Nonkilling Media and Creighton University. http://www.nonkilling.org/pdf/nkmedia.pdf#page=23.

Powers, Matthew. 2012. "In Forms That Are Familiar and Yet-to-be Invented: American Journalism and the Discourse of Technologically Specific Work." *Journal of Communication Inquiry* 36 (1): 24–43. doi:10.1177/0196859911426009.

Rieder Bernhard. 2014. "Engines of Order: Social Media and the Rise of Algorithmic Knowing." Papre presented at the Social Media and the Transformation of Public Space conference, University of Amsterdam, June 18–20.

Roderick Kevin. 2007. "L.a. Gets a Homicide Blog." *LA Observed*, February 5. http://www.laobserved.com/archive/2007/02/la_gets_a_homicide_blog.php.

Roderick Kevin. 2013. "Homicide Report Gets New Life at the LA times." *LA Observed*, March 18. http://www.laobserved.com/archive/2013/03/homicide_report_gets_new.php.

Royal Cindy. 2010. "The Journalist as Programmer: A Case Study of *the New York times* Interactive News Technology Department." Paper presented at the *International Symposium on Online Journalism*, Austin, April. https://online.journalism.utexas.edu/2010/papers/Royal10.pdf.

Steiner, Christopher. 2012. *Automate This: How Algorithms Came to Rule Our World*. New York: Portfolio.

Stevens, Jane. 1998. "The Violence Reporting Project: A New Approach to Covering Crime". *Nieman Reports* Winter: 37–40. http://www.nieman.harvard.edu/reports/article/100533/The-Violence-Reporting-Project.aspx.

Ulken, Eric. 2008. "Building the Data Desk: Lessons from the L.a. times." Online *Journalism Review* 21: 2008.

Wing, Janette M. 2006. "Computational Thinking." *Communcations of the ACM*, March, 49 (3): 33–35.

Zelizer, Barbie. 2004. *Taking Journalism Seriously: News and the Academy*. Thousand Oaks: Sage Publications.

ALGORITHMIC ACCOUNTABILITY
Journalistic investigation of computational power structures

Nicholas Diakopoulos

Every day automated algorithms make decisions that can amplify the power of businesses and governments. Yet as algorithms come to regulate more aspects of our lives, the contours of their power can remain difficult to grasp. This paper studies the notion of algorithmic accountability reporting as a mechanism for elucidating and articulating the power structures, biases, and influences that computational artifacts exercise in society. A framework for algorithmic power based on autonomous decision-making is proffered and motivates specific questions about algorithmic influence. Five cases of algorithmic accountability reporting involving the use of reverse engineering methods in journalism are then studied and analyzed to provide insight into the method and its application in a journalism context. The applicability of transparency policies for algorithms is discussed alongside challenges to implementing algorithmic accountability as a broadly viable investigative method.

Introduction

We are now living in a world where algorithms, and the data that feed them, adjudicate a large array of decisions in our lives: not just search engines and personalized online news systems, but educational evaluations, the operation of markets and political campaigns, the design of urban public spaces, and even how social services like welfare and public safety are managed. But algorithms can arguably make mistakes and operate with biases. The opacity of technically complex algorithms operating at scale make them difficult to scrutinize, leading to a lack of clarity for the public in terms of how they exercise their power and influence.

Journalists are beginning to adapt their traditional watchdogging and accountability functions to this new wellspring of power in society. They are investigating algorithms in order to characterize their power and delineate their mistakes and biases in a process of what I call "algorithmic accountability reporting." Examples span everything from relatively straightforward comparisons and visualizations of statistical models of unemployment correction (Ingraham 2014), to sophisticated reverse engineering investigations of price discrimination online (Valentino-DeVries, Singer-Vine, and Soltani 2012).

In this paper, I study the broad question of how algorithms exert their power and are worthy of scrutiny by computational journalists. I explore approaches such as transparency and reverse engineering and how they may be useful for articulating algorithmic power. I analyze five case studies of journalistic investigations of algorithms and describe the challenges and opportunities they illustrate for doing algorithmic accountability work, including identifying newsworthy algorithms, sampling the input–output relationships of those algorithms to study correlations, and ultimately finding a story. This work contributes both (1) a theoretical lens positing various atomic algorithmic decisions which suggest a number of leading questions that can inform the investigation of algorithms and the development of transparency policies for algorithms, and (2) an initial assessment and analysis of how algorithmic accountability is being employed in practice, including its various limitations. I further discuss challenges to employing this mode of reporting, including human resources, legality, and ethics, and also look ahead to how journalists themselves may employ transparency in their own use of algorithms.

Related Work

Here I discuss relevant research in computational journalism, the study of the bias of algorithms, and attempts to investigate algorithms in the literature.

Computational journalism was initially conceived as the application of computing technology to enable journalism across information tasks such as information gathering, organization and sensemaking, storytelling, and dissemination (Diakopoulos 2010), as well as activities relating to data-driven investigations (Cohen, Hamilton, and Turner 2011). Computational journalism is often presented as tool-oriented (Lewis and Usher 2013), with literature describing the development of new tools and techniques in application areas like social media (Diakopoulos, De Choudhury, and Naaman 2012; Diakopoulos, Naaman, and Kivran-Swaine 2010; Schifferes et al. 2014; Stavelin 2013; Zubiaga, Ji, and Knight 2013), data visualization (Gao et al. 2014; Hullman, Diakopoulos, and Adar 2013), and audience understanding (Diakopoulos and Zubiaga 2014; Lee, Lewis, and Powers 2014). A parallel track of research on computational journalism has looked at the sociology of computing in the newsroom and how work practices are adapting (Anderson 2012; Karlsen and Stavelin 2013). In this paper, I proffer a new branch of research in computational journalism that inverts the typical tool-orientation and foregrounds journalism by making computation its *object*. Algorithmic accountability reporting thus seeks to articulate the power structures, biases, and influences that computational artifacts play in society.

Researchers have been aware of and have critiqued the biases embedded in computational systems for many years (Friedman and Nissenbaum 1996). More recent research has considered how values (Fleischmann and Wallace 2010) or even ideologies (Mager 2012) manifest themselves in computational models, as well as how such biases are observed in media systems (Bozdag 2013; Gillespie 2014). This paper explores and studies a diffusion and adaptation of such critiques of algorithms into journalism, including the use of reverse engineering techniques.

Reverse engineering has long been used in domains as diverse as archeology, architecture, forensics, and the military, not to mention software (Eilam 2005; Mancas 2013).

More recently there have been a number of studies in the computing literature that take a reverse engineering approach toward understanding "big data" systems and algorithms, such as in online reviews (Mukherjee et al. 2013), autocomplete systems (Baker and Potts 2013), online pricing systems (Mikians et al. 2012), search personalization (Hannak et al. 2013), online advertising (Guha, Cheng, and Franci 2010), and public health prediction (Lazer et al. 2014), which inform my understanding of the method and its limitations for journalistic investigations. This paper studies a number of examples of the technique in journalism and delineates the challenges and opportunities of employing the method as a broader strategy to enable algorithmic accountability reporting.

Algorithmic Power

An algorithm can be defined as a series of steps undertaken in order to solve a particular problem or accomplish a defined outcome. Here I consider algorithms that operate via digital computers due to their prevalence and ability to effect large numbers of people through scale.

There are myriad ways in which algorithms interact with and potentially problematize public life, including how they necessitate the datafication of the world, create complex feedback loops with social data, or encourage the creation of calculated publics (Gillespie 2014). Here I focus on the underlying and perhaps intrinsic crux of algorithmic power: autonomous decision-making. Algorithmic decisions can be based on heuristics and rules, or calculations over massive amounts of data. Rules may be articulated directly by programmers, or be dynamic and flexible based on machine learning of data. Sometimes a human operator maintains agency and makes the final decision in a process, but even in this case the algorithm biases the operator's attention toward a subset of information.

We can begin to assess algorithmic power by analyzing the atomic decisions that algorithms make, including *prioritization*, *classification*, *association*, and *filtering*. Sometimes these decisions are chained in order to form higher-level decisions and information transformations, such as summarization, which uses prioritization and then filtering operations to consolidate information while maintaining the interpretability of that information.

Prioritization

Prioritization serves to emphasize or bring attention to certain things at the expense of others, such as when a search engine prioritizes and ranks the most relevant search results. Among other uses, prioritization algorithms can enable more efficient management of many social services, such as fire-code inspections, policing and recidivism, immigration enforcement, or welfare management (Flowers 2013; Kalhan 2013; Perry and McInnis 2013), where assigning risk and orienting official attention can provide efficiency gains. But such risk ranking raises interesting questions: is that risk being assigned fairly and with freedom from malice, abuse, or discrimination?

Embedded in every prioritization algorithm are criteria that are computed and used to define a ranking through a sorting procedure. These criteria embed a set of choices and value-propositions, which may be political or otherwise biased, that determine what gets pushed to the top. Sometimes these criteria are not public, making it difficult to understand the weight of different factors contributing to the ranking.

Classification

Classification decisions involve categorizing a particular entity as a constituent of a given class by looking at any number of that entity's features. Google's Content ID is an example of an algorithm that makes classification decisions that feed into filtering decisions ("How Content ID Works" 2013). It scans all videos uploaded to YouTube and classifies them according to whether they have any copyrighted music playing during the video. If the algorithm classifies a video as an infringer it can automatically remove (i.e., filter) that video from the site as well as trigger other types of responses from the uploader or copyright holder.

In addition to the potential for uncertainty and mistakes, classification algorithms can also have biases. In a supervised machine-learning algorithm, training data is used to teach the algorithm how to separate classes. That training data is often gathered from people who inspect thousands of examples and tag each instance according to its category. The algorithm learns how to classify based on the definitions and criteria humans used to produce the training data, thus potentially introducing human bias into the classifier.

In general, there are two kinds of mistakes a classification algorithm can make— *false positives* and *false negatives*. For Content ID, a false positive is a video classified as "infringing" when it is actually "fair use." A false negative, is a video classified as "fair use" when it is in fact "infringing." Classification algorithms can be tuned to make fewer of either of those mistakes, but as false positives are tuned down, false negatives will increase, and vice versa. Tuned all the way toward false positives, the algorithm will mark a lot of fair use videos as infringing; tuned the other way it will miss a lot of infringing videos altogether. Tuning can privilege different stakeholders in a decision, implying an essential value judgment by the designer of such an algorithm in terms of how false positive and false negative errors are balanced (Kraemer, van Overveld, and Peterson 2011).

Association

Association decisions mark relationships between entities and draw their power through both semantics and connotative ability. For example, IBM's InfoSphere Identity Insight is a system that builds up context around people (the entities in this example) and then associates them. It is used by various governmental social service management agencies to reduce fraud and help make decisions about resource allocation. An IBM use-case for the system highlights the power of associative algorithms ("Outsmarting the Social Services Fraudster" 2013). The scenario involves the assessment of a potential foster parent, Johnson Smith. InfoSphere associates him, through a shared address and phone number, with his brother, a convicted felon. The report then renders judgment: "Based on this investigation, approving Johnson Smith as a foster parent is not recommended." In this scenario the social worker might deny a person the chance to be a foster parent because he or she was associated with a felon in the family via the algorithm.

Association algorithms are also built on criteria that define the association, including the similarity definition of how precisely two things must match to be considered associated with each other. When the similarity reaches a particular threshold value, the two things are said to have that association. Association decisions thus also suffer the same kinds of false positive and false negative mistakes as classification decisions.

Filtering

Filtering involves including or excluding information according to various rules or criteria. Inputs to filtering algorithms often take prioritizing, classification, or association decisions into account. In news personalization apps like Flipboard, news is filtered in and out according to how that news has been categorized, associated to the person's interests, and prioritized for that person.

Filtering decisions exert their power by either over-emphasizing or censoring certain information. The notion of a "filter bubble" is largely predicated on the idea that by only exposing people to information that they already agree with (by overemphasizing it) it amplifies biases and hampers people's development of diverse and healthy perspectives (Pariser 2011). Outright censorship is also an issue in some online information regimes such as the Chinese social network Weibo, which uses computer systems to constantly scan, read, and remove any objectionable content on the platform.

Algorithmic Accountability

Above I have articulated several ways that algorithms exert power though decisions they make in prioritizing, classifying, associating, and filtering information. Through these descriptions, it should also be clear that there are a number of human influences embedded into algorithms, such as criteria choices, training data, semantics, and interpretation. Algorithmic accountability must therefore consider algorithms as objects of human creation and take into account *intent*, including that of any group or institutional processes that may have influenced their design, as well as the *agency* of human actors in interpreting the output of algorithms in the course of making higher-level decisions. In the next section, I turn to an examination of transparency and how it may be useful for algorithmic accountability. Understanding the weaknesses of a transparency approach then motivates this paper's study of algorithmic accountability by journalists using reverse engineering methods.

Transparency

Transparency has recently gained purchase among journalists seeking to build public trust, becoming a new pillar of journalism ethics identified by McBride and

Rosenstiel (2013). Transparency can be a useful lever to bring to bear on algorithmic power when there is sufficient motive on the part of the algorithm's creator to disclose information and reduce information asymmetry.

Public relations concerns or competitive dynamics can incentivize the release of information to the public. Google, for instance, publishes a biannual transparency report showing how often it removes information or discloses it to governments. In other cases, the government imposes targeted transparency policies that compel disclosure (Fung, Graham, and Weil 2009). Such policies can improve public safety, the quality of services provided to the public, or have bearing on issues of discrimination or corruption that might persist if the information were not public. Transparency policies like restaurant inspection scores or automobile safety tests have been quite effective, for instance.

In other cases, algorithm operators may have ulterior goals which conflict with a desire for transparency. Oftentimes corporations limit how transparent they are, since exposing too many details (trade secrets) of their proprietary systems may undermine their competitive advantage, hurt their reputation and ability to do business, or leave the system open to gaming and manipulation. Trade secrets are a core impediment to understanding automated authority like algorithms since they, by definition, seek to hide information for competitive advantage (Pasquale 2011). Moreover, corporations are unlikely to be transparent about their systems if that information hurts their reputation or ability to do business. Finally, gaming and manipulation are issues that can undermine the efficacy of a system.

In the case of governmental use of algorithms, there is often a tension between transparency and national security. Despite policy such as the Federal Agency Data Mining Reporting Act of 2007 (42 USC § 2000ee–3. Federal Agency Data Mining Reporting 2007), which compels disclosure about a range of data-mining activities in the federal government, the leaked documents from Edward Snowden reveal that such policy is not effective when pitted against national security concerns. Furthermore, even in cases where national security is not an issue, the corporate concern for trade secrecy can bleed into the government's use of algorithms. Exemption 4 to the US federal Freedom of Information Act (FOIA) covers trade secrets and allows the federal government to deny requests for transparency concerning any third-party software integrated into its systems.

Transparency is far from a complete solution to balancing algorithmic power. When corporations or governments are not legally or otherwise incentivized to disclose information about their algorithms, we might consider a different, more adversarial approach employing reverse engineering.

A Study of Algorithmic Accountability Through Reverse Engineering

While transparency faces a number of challenges as an effective check on algorithmic power, an alternative approach is emerging based on the idea of reverse engineering. In this section, I first explain the method of reverse engineering, describe a study of the journalistic use of the technique, delineate five case studies where journalists have reverse engineered an algorithm, and synthesize the processes used by journalists in such investigations.

Reverse Engineering

Reverse engineering is the process of articulating the specifications of a system through a rigorous examination drawing on domain knowledge, observation, and deduction to unearth a model of how that system works. It is "the process of extracting the knowledge or design blueprints from anything man-made" (Eilam 2005, 3).

Some algorithmic power may be exerted intentionally, while other aspects might be incidental. The inadvertent variety benefits from reverse engineering's ability to characterize unintended side effects. Because the process focuses on the system's performance in-use, it can tease out consequences that might not be apparent even if you spoke directly to the designers of the algorithm. On the other hand, talking to a system's designers can also uncover useful information: design decisions, descriptions of the objectives, constraints, and business rules embedded in the system, major changes that have happened over time, as well as implementation details that might be relevant (Chikofsky 1990; Singh 2013). Thus, the journalistic adaptation of reverse engineering will naturally include reporting methods such as interviews or document reviews in conjunction with reverse engineering analysis.

Algorithms are often described as black boxes, their complexity and technical opacity hiding and obfuscating their inner workings. At the same time, algorithms must always have an input and output, two openings that can be manipulated to help shed light on the algorithm's functioning. It is not essential to understand the code of an algorithm to begin surmising something about how the algorithm operates in practice.

Study Methodology

The overall goal of this study was to understand the opportunities and limitations of a reverse engineering approach to investigating algorithms. In-depth interviews were conducted with four journalists who had worked on or edited stories involving the reverse engineering of algorithms in a news context, including Michael Keller (*The Daily Beast*), Scott Klein (ProPublica), Jeremy Singer-Vine (*Wall Street Journal*), and Rob Barry (*Wall Street Journal*). The author also engaged in participant observation and gained first-hand experience of developing a news story using reverse engineering. The five journalistic stories are presented in the next section as a series of case studies that inform the findings. Three additional investigative journalists (Sheila Coronel, Chase Davis, and Alyssa Katz) were then interviewed to better contextualize the findings in terms of investigative journalism. The interview protocol was semi-structured and covered questions regarding the genesis of the reverse engineering stories they were involved with, other stories where they had considered using the method, what the biggest challenges were, and how the method related to more traditional forms of investigative journalism. Interviews were analyzed qualitatively and in context with the journalistic output, including primary articles as well as any extant methodological articles explaining how the story was accomplished. The sample for the study is small as a result of the novelty of the technique and its narrow adoption, but even an analysis of these few cases begins to provide valuable insight into the challenges and opportunities of the method.

Case Studies in Reverse Engineering

Autocompletions on Google and Bing.. The Google autocomplete FAQ reads, "We exclude a narrow class of search queries related to pornography, violence, hate speech, and copyright infringement." Bing makes similar claims about filtering spam and detecting adult or offensive content. Such editorial choices set the stage for broadly specifying censorship criteria. But what exactly are the boundaries of that censorship, and how do they differ among search engines?

To assess these questions, I gathered autosuggest results from hundreds of queries related to sex and violence in an effort to find those that were blocked (Diakopoulos 2013b). A list of 110 sex-related keywords was drawn from carefully crafted academic sources as well as the slang Urban Dictionary as inputs to the algorithm (Diakopoulos 2013a). I then looked to see which inputs resulted in zero output—suggesting a blocked word. While many of the most obvious words were outright blocked—like "ass" and "tits"—a number of the search terms were not.

In this case some transparency by the services through their FAQs and blogs suggested a hypothesis and tip as to what types of input the algorithm might be sensitive to (i.e., pornography and violence). Moreover, the algorithms themselves, both their inputs and outputs, were observable and accessible through application programming interfaces (APIs), which made it straightforward to collect a range of observations about the input–output relationship.

Autocorrections on the iPhone. Another example of surfacing editorial criteria in algorithms comes from Michael Keller, who at *The Daily Beast* dove into the iPhone spelling correction feature to see which words, like "abortion" or "rape," the phone would not correct if they were typed incorrectly (Keller 2013).

Michael's first attempt to sample this phenomenon was an API on the iPhone, which he used to identify words from a large dictionary that were not getting corrected, essentially pruning down the space of inputs to see what the algorithm "paid attention" to. He noticed that some of the words the API did not correct *were* getting corrected when they were typed directly on an iPhone. In order to mimic the real user experience he had to run an iPhone simulator on a number of computers, scripting it to act like a human typing in the word and then clicking the word to see if spelling corrections were presented.

Sometimes algorithms expose inputs and make it possible to record outputs, but those outputs are then further transformed and edited by downstream algorithms used to produce the user interface. What really matters to the end-user is the composition of these algorithms, not just the algorithm accessible via an API, but also how the user-interface algorithm interacts with that API to render the output that a user actually experiences. Understanding the context of how an algorithm's output is transformed for human consumption is thus an important aspect to reporting on an algorithm's consequences.

Targeting political emails. ProPublica's Message Machine tried to reverse engineer how the Obama campaign in 2012 was using targeting information to adapt and personalize email messages for different recipients (Larson and Shaw 2012). In addition to collecting the emails from end-users, ProPublica asked participants to fill out a survey with basic demographic information, where they lived, and their campaign donation and volunteer history. These survey answers then served as a stand-in for the input to the algorithm they were trying to dissect. In this case, the output was observable—crowdsourced from thousands of people—but the types of inputs used by the targeting algorithm were hidden behind the campaign wall. Instead, ProPublica tried to determine what types of inputs the campaign's targeting algorithm was paying attention to based only on the outputs collected and a crowdsourced proxy for the inputs.

In one instance the analysis was wrong, as Scott Klein, an editor on the project explained to me: "We slipped and we said that 'in such and such an example they are targeting by age.'" After the campaign was over they found out that in fact the campaign was not targeting by age, but by donation history, a correlated variable. But correlation does not imply causation, nor intent on the part of the algorithm designer. Relying on correlation to make claims about what inputs an algorithm is using is thus error prone and demands additional reporting to help answer the question of "why?"

Price discrimination in online commerce. In 2012, the *Wall Street Journal* began probing e-commerce platforms to identify instances of potential price discrimination—the provision of different prices to different people (Valentino-DeVries, Singer-Vine, and Soltani 2012). By polling different websites it was able to spot several vendors, such as Staples, Home Depot, Rosetta Stone, and Orbitz, that were adjusting prices dynamically based on different factors like user geography, browser history, or mobile-browser use. In the case of Staples, it found that the input most strongly correlated to price was the distance to a rival's store, explaining about 90 percent of the pricing pattern.

To get the story the *Wall Street Journal* had to simulate visiting the various sites from different computers and browsers in different geographies (Singer-Vine, Valentino-DeVries, and Soltani 2012). Various archetype users and user profiles were built using cookies to see how those user profiles might impact the prices recorded. The journalists had to painstakingly construct those profiles to simulate inputs to the algorithm, and then looked to see if any of the variables in the profiles led to significant differences in output (prices).

Using reverse engineering on the scale of the Web surfaces several challenges, underscored both by the *Wall Street Journal* story and by academic efforts to reverse engineer personalization in Web search (Hannak et al. 2013). One of the issues is that sites like Staples might be using A/B testing to assess different tweaks to their interface. In other words, they are already running experiments on their sites, and to a reverse engineer it might look like noise, or just confusing irregularities. "While we try to experiment on algorithms, they are experimenting on us," observes Nick Seaver (2013, 6). Algorithms may be unstable and change over time, or have randomness built in to them, which makes understanding patterns in their input–output relationship much more challenging. Other tactics such as parallelization or analysis of temporal drift may be necessary in order to control for a highly dynamic algorithm.

Executive stock trading plans. Executives and corporate leaders sometimes use preset trading plans to avoid accusations of insider trading. The algorithmic plans can be triggered by any number of different parameters, like specific dates, stock prices, or announcements from competitors. The only catch is that the plans cannot be based on inside information. When an executive makes a trade, he or she files a form with the US Securities and Exchange Commission (SEC). The *Wall Street Journal* collected millions of these forms in an attempt to use reverse engineering to see if any of the plans were "opportunistic"—if they appeared to be taking advantage of market timing to increase profits (Pulliam and Rob 2012).

In this case, the output was observable since the prices of all trades were known. What the *Wall Street Journal* was interested in was reverse engineering how timing information was being used by different plans as an input. Essentially the *Wall Street Journal* had a sampled input–output relationship for each executive's plan specified by the documents filed with the SEC. However, what it did not know was any of the other inputs that could have also been feeding into these plans. Even though trade forms must be filed, the details of the plans themselves are hidden, leaving the reverse engineer to guess what inputs the algorithm was likely using. Perhaps competitor or sector prices are also inputs to some plans, requiring consideration of each variable in turn to assess whether there were correlations suggesting a connection. This case underscores the challenge with trying to understand *which* inputs an algorithm pays attention to. There is a huge space of potential inputs, some of which are observable and some of which are not.

Analysis of Cases: Toward a Theory and Methodology

I analyzed the cases presented above, together with the interviews of key informants and a review of algorithm reverse engineering in the literature (Baker and Potts 2013; Guha, Cheng, and Franci 2010; Lazer et al. 2014; Mikians et al. 2012; Mukherjee et al. 2013; Hannak et al. 2013; Sweeney 2013). I first present a model of different reverse engineering scenarios based on the visibility and accessibility of the algorithm. Then I identify processes and challenges to investigating algorithms which can be broadly characterized as identifying a newsworthy target, sampling the algorithm, and finding the story.

Theory. Figure 1 depicts two idealized black-box scenarios of interest to journalists reverse engineering algorithms by examining the input–output relationship. Each represents an extreme on a spectrum of observability of inputs and outputs to the algorithm. The first scenario, in Figure 1A, corresponds to an ability to fully observe all of an algorithm's inputs and outputs. This is the case for algorithms accessible via an online API. The cases of autocompletion, autocorrection, and price discrimination exemplify this scenario, though with varying degrees of difficulty in constructing and recording the inputs and outputs.

Figure 1B depicts a different scenario in which only the outputs of the algorithm are visible. The message machine case is a good example of this scenario in which the inputs are crowdsourced. This is a common case that data journalists encounter: a large

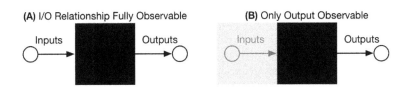

FIGURE 1
Two black-box scenarios with varying levels of observability

output dataset is available but there is limited information about how that data was transformed algorithmically. Interviews and document investigation can be especially important here and crowdsourcing is a way to cope with this issue by collecting data that might be used as inputs to the algorithm.

Sometimes inputs can be partially observable but not controllable; for instance, when an algorithm is driven off public data but it is unclear exactly what aspects of that data serve as inputs into the algorithm, such as in the cases of the executive stock trading plans or message machine. In general, the variable observability of the inputs and outputs is a limitation and challenge to the use of reverse engineering in practice. There are many algorithms that are used behind an organizational barrier that makes them difficult to prod. In such cases, partial observability (e.g., of inputs or outputs) through FOIA, document leaks, scraping, or crowdsourcing can still lead to some interesting results.

Identification. The interviews elucidated a number of questions relating to the newsworthiness of algorithm stories. "You need to ID algorithms that are very much non-hypothetical and direct in their impact," Alyssa Katz told me. Identifying algorithms to scrutinize thus involves asking questions like: What are the consequences and impact of that algorithm for the public, how significant are those consequences, and how many people might be affected by or perceive an effect by the algorithm? Does the algorithm have the potential for discrimination? Do errors from the algorithm create risks that negatively impact the public or individuals? While newsworthiness criteria for algorithms are still not well-defined, these are but a few examples of questions that might lead to newsworthy investigations of algorithms.

Sampling. A challenge in the process of reverse engineering is to choose how to sample the input–output relationship of the algorithm in some meaningful way. Sometimes the algorithm is out in the open and there are APIs that can be sampled, whereas other times inputs are obfuscated. Figuring out how to observe or simulate those inputs is a key part of a practical investigation involving reverse engineering. Reporting techniques and talking to sources can help uncover what inputs are being fed into an algorithm, but when trade secrets obscure the process we can be reduced to guessing, such as in the Message Machine or executive stock trading plans examples. Figuring out *what* the algorithm pays attention to as input becomes as intriguing a question as how the algorithm transforms input into output.

Given a vast potential sampling space, sampling decisions are often driven by hypotheses or potentially newsworthy outcomes. For the autocomplete story, the sampling strategy followed from a question of legality that might lead to a newsworthy story. If sex-related queries with "child" led to child pornography this would be a legal violation and a newsworthy story. There are, of course, tradeoffs between what you *can* sample and what you *would like* to sample in order to answer your question. Sampling an algorithm is not just about getting *any* valid sample either. The sample must simulate the reality of importance to your audience. This was a key difficulty for the autocorrection story, which eventually used a simulation of the iPhone with scripts that mimic how a human uses the phone. My experience analyzing autocompletions had a similar issue —the API results did not perfectly line up with what the user experiences. The Google API returns 20 results, but only shows 4 or 10 in the user interface (UI) depending on how preferences are set. Data returned from the API but that never appears in the UI is less significant since users will never encounter it in their daily usage.

In some cases, a dataset may be "found" in which someone else has already sampled an input–output relationship. Or you may not have any control of inputs because those inputs are actually individual people that you are unable or not ethically willing to simulate. Such datasets can still be useful, but the method is more powerful when the sampling strategy can be defined in a way to help directly answer the question at hand.

Finding the story. Once the input–output relationship of a black box is mapped out, the challenge becomes a data-driven expedition to find a news story. Has the algorithm made a bad decision or broken an expectation for how we think it should be operating? If there is a break with expectation, what is driving that—a bug, an incidental programming decision, or a deep-seated design intent? Expectations may be statistically based, or built on an understanding of social and legal norms. Looking at the false positives and false negatives can provide ideas about how and where the algorithm is failing, and lead to interesting stories.

In the price discrimination case, the first filter used for narrowing in on e-commerce sites was a statistical one: the variance of prices returned from a site for a given item across a variety of geographies. If any non-random variance was observed the site was marked for a more rigorous and in-depth analysis. Similarly, for the executive trading plans story, a sophisticated data-mining technique involving clustering and Monte Carlo simulation was used to find newsworthy cases and identify trading plans that fell outside of the norms of expectation.

In the autocompletions story, I used social and legal norms to help zero in on stories inside the collected data. Both Google and Bing had publicly expressed a desire to filter suggestions relating to pornography. Taking that a step further, child pornography is indeed a violation of the legal code, so searching for instances of that became a starting point for filtering the data I had collected. Knowing where the algorithm violates the designers' expectations (e.g., it lets through child pornography when the stated intent is not to do so), or where it may have unintended side effects can both make for interesting stories.

Reporting is still a key part of finding a story in a reverse engineering analysis. For every site that was flagged as a statistical hit, the price discrimination team did a much more comprehensive and custom analysis. Knowing what makes something a story is perhaps less about a filter for statistical, social, or legal deviance than it is about understanding the context of the phenomenon, including historical, cultural, and social expectations related to the issue—all things with which traditional reporting and investigation can help. Reaching out for interviews can still be valuable since information about the larger goals and objectives of the algorithms can help better situate a reverse engineering analysis.

Discussion

The study of algorithmic accountability reporting and reverse engineering described above exposes a number of challenges to incorporating the method into practice, including issues of human resources, legality, ethics, and the role that transparency might still effectively play.

Challenges in Human Resources, Legality, and Ethics

Developing the human resources to do algorithmic accountability reporting will take dedicated efforts to teach the computational thinking, programming, and technical skills needed to make sense of algorithmic decisions. The number of computational journalists with the technical skills to do a deep investigation of algorithms is still limited. Teaming computationally literate reporters with tech-savvy computer scientists in interdisciplinary "trading zones" (Lewis and Usher 2014) might be one method for doing more algorithmic accountability reporting. Another way would be to train journalists in more computational techniques. More applied experience with the technique is essential. "It's a lot of testing or trial and error, and it's hard to teach in any uniform way," noted Jeremy Singer-Vine in his interview.

More work is also needed to explore the legal ramifications of algorithmic accountability through reverse engineering by journalists. In the United States the Digital Millennium Copyright Act is one statute that poses issues, in addition to the anti-reverse engineering clauses that corporations typically add to their End User License Agreements (Eilam 2005). Even more severe is a law like the Computer Fraud and Abuse Act (18 USC § 1030. Fraud and Related Activity in Connection with Computers 2011). The need for qualified legal advice and potential for harsh sanctions for reverse engineering online sites suggests that non-professional journalists may find it more difficult to do algorithmic accountability investigations.

There are ethical questions that arise in the context of studying algorithms which also demand more research. In particular, we need to ask about the possible ramifications of publishing details of how certain algorithms work. Would publishing such information negatively affect any individuals? By publishing details of how an algorithm functions, specifically information about what inputs it pays attention to, how it uses various criteria in a ranking, or what criteria it uses to censor, how might that allow the algorithm to be manipulated or circumvented? And who stands to benefit or suffer disadvantage from that manipulation?

Transparency and the Journalistic Use of Algorithms

As previously noted, transparency as a mechanism for algorithmic accountability suffers from the issues of trade secrecy and manipulation. This creates a tension with journalism since, on the one hand, journalistic organizations are competitive corporations like any other, but on the other hand, have newly emerging ethical ideals promoting transparency (McBride and Rosenstiel 2013). As news organizations also come to employ algorithms in the shaping of the news they report, whether that be in finding new stories in massive datasets or presenting stories interactively, journalistic standards for transparency of algorithms will need to be developed. Well-trodden transparency policies in other domains do offer some opportunity to reflect on how such policy might be adapted for algorithms (Fung, Graham, and Weil 2009). For instance, targeted transparency policies might indicate the boundaries of disclosure (e.g., the factors or metrics of the algorithm), the frequency of their disclosure, and the user experience for communicating that information.

The case studies and their analysis above suggest several informational dimensions that might be disclosed in a standard transparency policy for algorithms, possibly for use by newsrooms themselves as well. These might include: the (1) the criteria used to prioritize, rank, emphasize, or editorialize things in the algorithm, including their definitions, operationalizations, and possibly even alternatives; (2) what data act as inputs to the algorithm—what it "pays attention" to, and what other parameters are used to initiate the algorithm; (3) the accuracy including the false positive and false negative rate of errors made in classification (with respect to some agreed-upon ground truth), including the rationale for how the balance point is set between those errors; (4) descriptions of training data and its potential bias, including the evolution and dynamics of the algorithm as it learns from data; and (5) the definitions, operationalizations, or thresholds used by similarity or classification algorithms. The legal and ethical perspectives alluded to above provide an overarching context for how these dimensions might variably be implemented or meet with resistance.

Another challenge to a transparency policy is to develop an effective user experience for transparency information. Ideally, the disclosed information needs to integrate into the decisions that the end-user would like to make based on such information. Some have argued for source code transparency in algorithms (O'Neil 2014), and while that may be helpful for specialists, it does not provide for an effective user experience for the public since they may not have adequate technical expertise to make meaningful choices based on such information. Furthermore, examining source code introduces a complication related to versioning: is the source code in operation the same that you are looking at and have access to, or could there be differences?

Journalistic innovation in algorithmic transparency is already emerging. Take, for instance, the *New York Times* 4th Down Bot, which is exemplary in its transparency (Burke and Quealy 2013). The bot uses a model built on data collected from NFL games going back to the year 2000. For every fourth down in a game, it uses that model to decide whether the coach should ideally "go for it," "punt," or "go for a field goal." How the bot sees the world is clearly articulated (Burke and Quealy 2013). It pays attention to the yard line on the fourth down as well as how many minutes are left in the game. Those are the inputs to the algorithm. It also defines two criteria that inform its predictions: expected points and win percentage. The model's limitations are clearly delineated—it cannot do overtime properly, for instance. And the bias of the bot is explained too: it is less conservative than the average NFL coach.

Two things that the bot could be more transparent about are its uncertainty—how *sure* it is in its recommendations—and its accuracy. Moreover, the information is "buried" in an article format, but might be made more salient to the end-user through innovations in information design (e.g., an information box that clearly answers the key questions above). Nonetheless, the 4th Down Bot already represents a fairly robust example of journalistic norms adapting to algorithmic technologies.

Conclusions

This paper has identified algorithmic power as something worthy of scrutiny by computational journalists interested in accountability reporting. I have offered a basis for understanding algorithmic power in terms of the types of decisions algorithms make in prioritizing, classifying, associating, and filtering information. Furthermore, I have presented five case studies, which contribute to delineating algorithmic account-ability methods in practice, including challenges and considerations about the variable observability of input–output relationships as well as identifying, sampling, and finding newsworthy stories about algorithms. The case studies show that reverse engineering the input–output relationship of an algorithm can elucidate significant aspects of algorithms such as censorship. Finally, I have discussed challenges to the further application of algorithmic accountability reporting, and shown how transparency might be used to effectively adhere to journalistic norms in the use of newsroom algorithms.

ACKNOWLEDGEMENTS

A number of people have been generous with their time in providing critical feedback on this work, including the anonymous reviewers of this article. Scott Klein, Cathy O'Neil, and Cliff Stein deserve special praise for publicly critiquing the work on a panel at Columbia University. I am also grateful to those whom I interviewed about their experience (Rob Barry, Michael Keller, Scott Klein, and Jeremy Singer-Vine) and who helped me contextualize the findings (Sheila Coronel, Chase Davis, and Alyssa Katz). The Tow Center for Digital Journalism was also very supportive of the work.

REFERENCES

Anderson, C. W. 2012. "Towards a Sociology of Computational and Algorithmic Journalism." *New Media & Society*, December. doi:10.1177/1461444812465137. http://nms.sagepub.com/cgi/doi/10.1177/1461444812465137.

Baker, Paul, and Amanda Potts. 2013. "'Why Do White People Have Thin Lips?' Google and the Perpetuation of Stereotypes via Auto-complete Search Forms." *Critical Discourse Studies* 10 (2): 187–204.

Bozdag, Engin. 2013. "Bias in Algorithmic Filtering and Personalization." *Ethics and Information Technology* 15 (3): 209–227.

Burke, Brian, and Kevin Quealy. 2013. "How Coaches and the NYT 4th down Bot Compare." *New York Times.* http://www.nytimes.com/newsgraphics/2013/11/28/fourth-downs/post.html

Chikofsky, Elliot. 1990. "Reverse Engineering and Design Recovery: A Taxonomy." *IEEE Software* 7 (1): 13–17.

Cohen, Sarah, James T. Hamilton, and Fred Turner. 2011. "Computational Journalism." *Communications of the ACM* 54 (10): 66–71.

Diakopoulos, Nicholas. 2010. "A Functional Roadmap for Innovation in Computational Journalism." http://www.nickdiakopoulos.com/wp-content/uploads/2007/05/CJ_Whitepaper_Diakopoulos.pdf.

Diakopoulos, Nicholas. 2013a. "Sex, Violence, and Autocomplete Algorithms: Methods and Context." http://www.nickdiakopoulos.com/2013/08/01/sex-violence-and-autocomplete-algorithms-methods-and-context/.

Diakopoulos, Nicholas. 2013b. "Sex, Violence, and Autocomplete Algorithms." *Slate*, August. http://www.slate.com/articles/technology/future_tense/2013/08/words_banned_from_bing_and_google_s_autocomplete_algorithms.html

Diakopoulos, Nicholas, and Arkaitz Zubiaga. 2014. "Newsworthiness and Network Gatekeeping on Twitter: The Role of Social Deviance." *International Conference on Weblogs and Social Media (ICWSM)*, Ann Arbor, MI.

Diakopoulos, Nicholas, Mor Naaman, and Funda Kivran-Swaine. 2010. "Diamonds in the Rough: Social Media Visual Analytics for Journalistic Inquiry." In *Proceedings of the Symposium on Visual Analytics Science and Technology (VAST)*, 115–122. Salt Lake City, UT. http://ieeexplore.ieee.org/xpl/login.jsp?tp=&arnumber=5652922&url=http%3A%2F%2Fieeexplore.ieee.org%2Fxpls%2Fabs_all.jsp%3Farnumber%3D5652922.

Diakopoulos, Nicholas, Munmun De Choudhury, and Mor Naaman. 2012. "Finding and Assessing Social Media Information Sources in the Context of Journalism." *Conference on Human Factors in Computing Systems (CHI)*, Austin, TX.

Eilam, Eldad. 2005. *Reversing: Secrets of Reverse Engineering*. Indianapolis, IN: Wiley.

Fleischmann, Kenneth R., and William A. Wallace. 2010. "Value Conflicts in Computational Modeling." *Computer* 43 (7): 57–63.

Flowers, Michael. 2013. "Beyond Open Data: The Data-driven City." In *Beyond Transparency: Open Data and the Future of Civic Innovation*, edited by Brett Goldstein. Code for America Press. http://beyondtransparency.org/chapters/part-4/beyond-open-data-the-data-driven-city/.

Friedman, Batya, and Helen Nissenbaum. 1996. "Bias in Computer Systems." *ACM Transactions on Information Systems* 14 (3): 330–347.

Fung, Archon, Mary Graham, and David Weil. 2009. *Full Disclosure: The Perils and Promise of Transparency*. New York: Cambridge University Press.

Gao Tong, Jessica Hullman, Eytan Adar, Brent Hecht, and Nicholas Diakopoulos. 2014. "NewsViews: An Automated Pipeline for Creating Custom Geovisualizations for News." *Proceeding of Conference on Human Factors in Computing Systems (CHI)*, Toronto.

Gillespie, Tarleton. 2014. "The Relevance of Algorithms." In *Media Technologies: Essays on Communication, Materiality, and Society*, edited by Tarleton Gillespie, Pablo Boczkowski, and Kirsten Foot. Cambridge, MA: MIT Press.

Guha, Saikat, Bin Cheng, and Paul Franci. 2010. "Challenges in Measuring Online Advertising Systems." Internet Measurement Conference (IMC), Melbourne.

Hannak, Aniko, Piotr Sapiezynski, Arash Molavi Kakhki, Balachander Krishnamurthy, David Lazer, Alan Mislove, and Christo Wilson. 2013. "Measuring Personalization of Web Search." Proceeding of World Wide Web Conference (WWW), Rio de Janeiro.

"How Content ID Works." 2013. https://support.google.com/youtube/answer/2797370?hl=en.

Hullman, Jessica, Nicholas Diakopoulos, and Eytan Adar. 2013. "Contextifier: Automatic Generation of Annotated Stock Visualizations." *Conference on Human Factors in Computing Systems (CHI)*, Paris.

Ingraham, Christopher. 2014. "Jobs Preview: Pay Less Attention to the Sausage, and More to How It's Made." *Washington Post*, April. http://www.washingtonpost.com/blogs/wonkblog/wp/2014/04/03/jobs-preview-pay-less-attention-to-the-sausage-and-more-to-how-its-made/.

Kalhan, Anil. 2013. "Immigration Policing and Federalism through the Lens of Technology, Surveillance, and Privacy." *Ohio State Law Journal* 74: 1105–1165.

Karlsen, Joakim, and Eirik Stavelin. 2013. "Computational Journalism in Norwegian Newsrooms." *Journalism Practice* 8 (1): 34–48.

Keller, Michael. 2013. "The Apple 'Kill List': What Your IPhone Doesn't Want You to Type." *The Daily Beast*, July.

Kraemer, Felicitas, Kees van Overveld, and Martin Peterson. 2011. "Is There an Ethics of Algorithms?" *Ethics and Information Technology* 13 (3): 251–260.

Larson, Jeff, and Al Shaw. 2012. "Message Machine: Reverse Engineering the 2012 Campaign." *ProPublica*, July.

Lazer, David, Ryan Kennedy, Gary King, and Alessandro Vespignani. 2014. "The Parable of Google Flu: Traps in Big Data Analysis." *Science* 343 (6176): 1203–1205.

Lee, Angela, Seth Lewis, and Matthew Powers. 2014. "Audience Clicks and News Placement: A Study of Time-lagged Influence in Online Journalism." *Communication Research* 41 (4): 505–530.

Lewis, Seth C, and Nikki Usher. 2013. "Open Source and Journalism: Toward New Frameworks for Imagining News Innovation." *Media, Culture and Society* 35 (5): 602–619.

Lewis, Seth C, and Nikki Usher. 2014. "Code, Collaboration, and the Future of Journalism: A Case Study of the Hacks/Hackers Global Network." *Digital Journalism* 2 (3): 383–393. doi:10.1080/21670811.2014.895504.

Mager, Astrid. 2012. "Algorithmic Ideology: How Capitalist Society Shapes Search Engines." *Information, Communication & Society* 15 (5): 769–787.

Mancas, Christian. 2013. "Should Reverse Engineering Remain a Computer Science Cinderella?" *Information Technology & Software Engineering.* http://omicsgroup.org/journals/should-reverse-engineering-remain-a-computer-science-cinderella-2165-7866.S5-e001.php?aid=12682.

McBride, Kelly, and Tom Rosenstiel, eds. 2013. *The New Ethics of Journalism*. Thousand Oaks, CA: CQ Press.

Mikians, Jakub, László Gyarmati, Vijay Erramilli, and Nikolaos Laoutaris. 2012. "Detecting Price and Search Discrimination on the Internet." *Workshop on Hot Topics in Networks*: 79–84. http://dl.acm.org/citation.cfm?id=2390245.

Mukherjee, Arjun, Vivek Venkataraman, Bing Liu, and Natalie Glance. 2013. "What Yelp Fake Review Filter Might Be Doing?" *International Conference on Weblogs and Social Media (ICWSM)*, Boston, MA.

O'Neil, Cathy. 2014. "An Attempt to FOIL Request the Source Code of the Value-added Model." http://mathbabe.org/2014/03/07/an-attempt-to-foil-request-the-source-code-of-the-value-added-model/.

"Outsmarting the Social Services Fraudster." 2013. IBM White Paper.

Pariser, Eli. 2011. *The Filter Bubble: How the New Personalized Web is Changing What We Read and How We Think*. New York: Penguin Press.

Pasquale, Frank. 2011. "Restoring Transparency to Automated Authority." *Journal on Telecommunications & High Technology Law* 9: 235–256.

Perry, Walter, and Brian McInnis. 2013. *Predictive Policing: The Role of Crime Forecasting in Law Enforcement Operations*. Santa Monica, CA: RAND.

Pulliam, Susan, and Barry Rob. 2012. "Executives' Good Luck in Trading Own Stock." *Wall Street Journal*, November. http://online.wsj.com/news/articles/SB10000872396390444100404577641463717344.17.

Schifferes, Steve, Nic Newman, Neil Thurman, David Corney, Ayse Göker, and Carlos Martin. 2014. "Identifying and Verifying News through Social Media: Developing a User-Centred Tool for Professional Journalists." *Digital Journalism* 2 (3): 406–418.

Seaver, Nick. 2013. "Knowing Algorithms." *Media in Transition* 8: 1–12.

Singer-Vine, Jeremy, Jennifer Valentino-DeVries, and Ashkan Soltani. 2012. "How the Journal Tested Prices and Deals Online." *Wall Street Journal*. http://blogs.wsj.com/digits/2012/12/23/how-the-journal-tested-prices-and-deals-online/.

Singh, Ramandeep. 2013. "A Review of Reverse Engineering Theories and Tools." *International Journal of Engineering Science Invention* 2 (1): 35–38.

Stavelin, Eirik. 2013. "The Pursuit of Newsworthiness on Twitter." *Norsk Informatikkonferance (NIK)*: 1–12.

Sweeney, Latanya. 2013. "Discrimination in Online Ad Delivery." *Communications of the ACM (CACM)* 56 (5): 44–54.

18 USC § 1030. Fraud and Related Activity in Connection with Computers. 2011. http://www.law.cornell.edu/uscode/text/18/1030.

42 USC § 2000ee–3. Federal Agency Data Mining Reporting. 2007. http://www.law.cornell.edu/uscode/text/42/2000ee-3.

Valentino-DeVries, Jennifer, Jeremy Singer-Vine, and Ashkan Soltani. 2012. "Websites Vary Prices, Deals Based on Users' Information." *Wall Street Journal*. http://online.wsj.com/news/articles/SB10001424127887323777204578189391813881534.

Zubiaga, Arkaitz, Heng Ji, and Kevin Knight. 2013. "Curating and Contextualizing Twitter Stories to Assist with Social Newsgathering." *International Conference on Intelligent User Interfaces (IUI)*, Santa Monica, CA.

THE ROBOTIC REPORTER
Automated journalism and the redefinition of labor, compositional forms, and journalistic authority

Matt Carlson

Among the emergent data-centric practices of journalism, none appear to be as potentially disruptive as "automated journalism." The term denotes algorithmic processes that convert data into narrative news texts with limited to no human intervention beyond the initial programming choices. The growing ability of machine-written news texts portends new possibilities for an expansive terrain of news content far exceeding the production capabilities of human journalists. A case study analysis of the pioneering automated journalism provider Narrative Science and journalists' published reactions to its services reveals intense competition both to imagine an emergent journalism landscape in which most news content is automated and to define how this situation creates new challenges for journalists. What emerges is a technological drama over the potentials of this emerging news technology concerning issues of the future of journalistic labor, the rigid conformity of news compositional forms, and the normative foundation of journalistic authority. In these ways, this study contends with the emergent practice of automated news content creation both in how it alters the working practices of journalists and how it affects larger understandings of what journalism is and how it ought to operate.

Introduction

On the morning of March 17, 2014, a 4.7 magnitude earthquake struck Los Angeles. Three minutes after the rumbling stopped, one of the first news accounts appeared on the website of the *Los Angeles Times*. Although short and factual in tone, the speedy article was notable for its author: a computer program dubbed Quakebot (*Slate*, March 17, 2014). This was an example of automated journalism in which a program turns data into a news narrative, made possible with limited—or even zero—human input. Various examples of automated journalism have begun to emerge: the *Los Angeles Times* uses another program to report on homicide, the *Washington Post* has developed TruthTeller to automatically fact-check political speeches in real time, and two companies—Automated Insights and Narrative Science—market automated news content products to a growing number of news outlets.

Automated news content creators are an outgrowth of the intersection between journalism and the growing emphasis on data analysis known popularly as "big data" (Mayer-Schönberger and Cukier 2013). Much of the discourse around this confluence has explored new data tools available to journalists, including partnerships between journalists and computer programmers—or hacks and hackers (Lewis and Usher 2013) —as well as skills journalists need going forward (Gray, Chambers, and Bounegru 2012). This study suggests that the movement of big data from newsgathering aid to the production of news itself requires careful analysis not only of emergent practices and technological capabilities, but also to related discourses regarding issues of labor, compositional forms, and journalistic authority.

This article uses a case study of the technology start-up company Narrative Science to explore issues related to "automated journalism," conceptualized as algorithmic processes that convert data into narrative news texts with limited to no human intervention beyond the initial programming. The term denotes a split from data analysis as a tool for reporters encompassed in writings about "computational and algorithmic journalism" (Anderson 2013) to indicate wholly computer-written news stories emulating the compositional and framing practices of human journalism. Interpretations of automated journalism are analyzed through two interlinked data points: public statements by Narrative Science's management and mediated reactions from journalists. What emerges through this discourse is a "technological drama" (Pfaffenberger 1992) in which journalists and technologists compete to define the place of automated journalism within the larger context of news. While still nascent, early understandings matter as they often crystallize with the maturation of communication technology (Williams 1974, 152). An analysis of the design choices and potential uses articulated by Narrative Science helps avoid a technological deterministic reading of automated journalism to instead question how Narrative Science positions its technology within a vision of what journalism should be as well as how journalists react to this innovation. At issue at the outset of the development of automatic journalism is how these opposing discourses structure understandings of acceptable norms and practices, all of which bears on the role of computer-authored news within the social practice of journalism.

Big Data Meets Journalism

In his classic study on newsrooms' adoption of online technologies, Boczkowski (2004) demonstrates how non-technological organizational and professional factors complicate journalism's relationship with technology. Journalists react to technological innovation in complex ways, from fear of discontinuity to reinvention (Carlson 2007a, 2007b; Powers 2012). The same dynamics carry over with the adoption of practices associated with big data. Anderson (2013) calls for the need to look beyond shallow questions of usability to larger questions of how the turn toward computational and algorithmic journalism reshapes the cultural practice of news creation. Amid optimistic rhetoric and rapid adoption, wider analytical frames should situate emergent data-driven practices within the context of their creation and use. To this point, Anderson argues for closely examining algorithmic journalism's material and nonmaterial elements: "Data-crunching algorithms and other increasingly invisible information ordering devices are neither entirely material, nor are they entirely human—they are hybrid, composed of both human intentionality and material obduracy" (1016). The tools of computational journalism have technological affordances, but they are also shaped through use. Flew et al. (2012, 159) emphasize this dynamic by connecting news products to the assumptions underlying their creation: "the information that is generated from data cannot be separated from the social relationships and cultural references which give it meaning and value." Automated journalism is no exception.

Scant scholarly attention has been paid to the specific topic of automated journalism. Clerwall (2014) found through an experiment that news audiences could not distinguish between automated and human journalism—a finding supporting journalists' assessments recounted below. Anderson, Bell, and Shirky (2012, 27) included automated journalism within "post-industrial journalism" and raised the issue of transparency into its workings. To date, the only empirical investigation of discourse surrounding automated journalism is van Dalen's (2012) study of the automated news creator Statsheet Network after its 2010 launch. His skills-based perspective interrogated journalists' reactions, finding concerns over labor as well as efforts at skills differentiation through the emphasis of human qualities. The present study deepens analysis into public discourse around automated journalism by focusing on how actors connect the emergent practice to new ways of imagining journalism.

To examine discourse around automated journalism, this study employs Pfaffenberger's (1992, 285) concept of "technological drama," defined as "a discourse of technological 'statements' and 'counterstatements'" through which social definitions of new technologies develop (see also Braun 2013). As a drama, this concept accentuates conflict among competing claims offered by "impact constituencies" or actors occupying different social locations with deeply held axiomatic commitments (286). When faced with new technologies that threaten core understandings, an impact constituency may engage in "countersignification" to develop meanings that provide "a way to live within the system without suffering unhealthy losses of self-esteem" (301). Within journalism, the question becomes not only how technological changes alter news practice, but more importantly how they alter the ways in which practice is imagined by the actors involved (Gynnild, 2014). Attitudes within the profession are hardly homogenous, which gives rise to potential conflict between journalists with different backgrounds (Parasie and Dagiral 2013). Automated journalism complicates this dynamic through intervention from non-journalistic actors—in this case the firm Narrative Science.

The benefit of the technological drama approach is how it augments technological questions with sensitivity to social and professional issues. Within the study of journalism, this perspectival broadening provides a link to larger questions of journalistic authority. The core concern with authority is how a particular set of discursive practices sustains itself as an accepted way of knowing about the world (Zelizer 1992). The conditions of authority cannot be wholly regulated by practitioners, as the legitimacy of journalism rests on the wider cultural acceptance of these practices as worthy of being listened to. More specifically, defining news to be a form of knowledge specifies journalists' need for "epistemic authority," which Gieryn (1999, 1) defines as the "the legitimate power to define, describe, and explain bounded domains of reality" (see Carlson and Lewis, 2015). This definition underscores the contextual nature of journalistic authority—its validity is circumscribed within a particular domain and through certain epistemological commitments (Ekström 2002). This authority is mediated rather than interpersonal, as audiences normally encounter news texts through the use of a technology, be it a printing press, broadcast transmission, or the internet. But while technology is at the core of journalistic authority, so too is the assumption of human agency. Emphasizing journalistic professionalism as the backbone for epistemic authority (Waisbord 2013) conjures trained professionals with particular expertise (Anderson 2008; Reich 2012). Professional journalists not only write and report, but also designate newsworthiness by selecting and ordering the news out of the mess of occurrences happening on any given day.

This study of the public discourse of automatic journalism utilizes a conceptual framework informed by the technological drama perspective to engage larger questions concerning the changing conditions of journalistic authority. This occurs through inquiry guided by several core questions: How does the discourse surrounding automated journalism indicate changing conceptions about news content and news production practices in a changing news industry? In what ways do actors envision automated journalism as collaborative with existing journalistic modes and in what ways is it presented as antagonistic? And finally, how does the specter of automated journalism lead to reconsiderations of the characteristics underlying journalistic authority? As the role of big data in journalism shifts from reporting tool to the generation of news content, these questions become vital for understanding emergent news forms.

Method

While automated journalism involves a range of actors, this study takes a case study approach by focusing on Narrative Science. The Chicago company grew out of a partnership at Northwestern University between computer scientists and the Medill School of Journalism that produced the automated sports writing program StatsMonkey. In 2010, the project morphed into the independent company Narrative Science, and began attracting investors, clients, and—pertinent to this study—attention from journalists. This analysis follows the lead of van Dalen's (2012) earlier study on reactions to automated news. To look at the meaning-formation around automated journalists, news stories were collected that detailed Narrative Science's technology and considered its impact on journalism. A three-part method was used to locate texts for analysis. First, articles were found through the Lexis-Nexis database using the terms "Narrative Science" and "news" or "journalism" for articles and blog posts in English published between January 1, 2010 and March 1, 2014. Second, further searches through Google, Google News, and the Narrative Science website's "press" section helped locate online items that were not captured in the Lexis-Nexis database. Finally, hyperlinks within captured stories were used to identify additional stories not captured through the first two searches. After false hits and repeats were removed, the final sample contained 63 texts including traditional media stories, the business and journalism trade press, online news sites, and blogs. The website of Narrative Science was also added to the sample.

The texts in the sample were analyzed using qualitative textual analysis. This method emphasizes the role of news texts in creating and circulating meaning about social phenomena, including journalism itself. Thus, the analysis is concerned both with modes of expression within texts and the larger structures that shape—and are shaped by—such texts (Fairclough 2003). For example, the sample includes a diversity of journalistic genres, from long-form magazine stories examining the issue at length to business stories regarding the economic significance of Narrative Science to opinion pieces commenting on the emergence of automated journalism. Each genre carries its own inbuilt assumptions regarding appropriate representational forms and imagined audiences. To make sense of emergent meanings across this range of texts, the stories were examined using open coding methods associated with grounded theory (Corbin and Strauss 2008). Multiple close readings of the text helped the researcher to identify recurrent themes across the sample. Individual themes were then amassed into broader category constructs to organize interpretive patterns. As with qualitative research generally, this study does not aim to account for the total range of voices and interpretations present in the sample, but it does highlight dominant threads appearing throughout the sample.

Findings

The sections below trace the technological drama over automated journalism playing out in public through news texts covering the technology developed by Narrative Science. As an emergent practice within an established field of practices, automated journalism inevitably runs up against existing journalistic practices and meanings. Conversely, its introduction forces journalists to confront assumptions regarding their work practices and their arguments for authority. In both these ways, automated journalism's implementation—whether realized or potential—impels impact constituencies to formulate competing definitions of core understandings of journalism. To trace these reactions, the following sections begin with Narrative Science's efforts to define how its technology will alter journalism. Subsequent sections divide reactions to automated news into three different domains: journalistic labor, compositional form, and the question of authority.

Imagining Automated Journalism

Like any new technology start-up seeking a market, Narrative Science sought to define the problem its services solve. Beyond business strategy, this is a cultural process of characterizing the future state of an affected industry, which, in this case, is journalism. In the particular case of Narrative Science, public statements made by its management reported in news about the company reveal two commonly expressed beliefs about how its technology will improve journalism: automation will augment—rather than displace—human journalists, and it will greatly expand journalistic output. The former argument was made by CEO Stuart Frankel who told the *Wall Street Journal* (September 10, 2013): "It's less about replacing people, and more about leveraging those folks that are already there." Elsewhere, Frankel described an emerging hybrid form in which "a reporter is off researching his or her story, getting information that's not captured in some database somewhere, really understanding the story in total, and writing part of that story, but also including a portion of the story that in fact is written by a piece of technology". (*Globe and Mail*, May 9, 2012). Kristian Hammond, one of the key scientists behind the technology, similarly dismissed fear of displacement with the language of cooperation: "No one should be worried about automated writing systems … [T]hey are designed for writing into spaces where no one else is writing and working in co-ordination with other writers and analysts" (*South China Morning Post*, January 18, 2013). The vision here of partnership was meant to allay fears that automated news would prolong the wave of layoffs shrinking the news industry during the past half-decade.

The case for hybridity corresponds to a second argument that Narrative Science's ability to turn data into narratives will greatly expand the news universe. Hammond told the *American Journalism Review* (November 25, 2013) that its technology is being used for "writing stories in spaces where no one is writing stories." This argument both inoculates Narrative Science against fears of displacing human journalism while defining a niche area for its services. In a company profile in *Wired* (April, 24, 2012), Steve Levy predicted that "the universe of newswriting will expand dramatically, as computers mine vast troves of data to produce ultracheap, totally readable accounts of events, trends, and developments that no journalist is currently covering." But Levy also notes the ambition of Narrative Science: "I asked Hammond to predict what percentage of news would be written by computers in 15 years. At first he tried to duck the question, but with some prodding he sighed and gave in: 'More than 90 percent.'" Behind the boldness of this prediction lies a more important vision of automated journalism. The narrativization of data through sophisticated artificial intelligence programs vastly expands the terrain of news. Automated journalism becomes a normalized component of the news experience. Moreover, Narrative Science has tailored its promotional discourse to reflect the economic uncertainty of online journalism business models by suggesting that its technology will create a virtuous circle in which increased news revenue supports more journalists. Hammond argued for this relationship in a *Columbia Journalism Review* (October 27, 2010) interview: "We're providing a possible set of solutions that will help an industry, and if you help an industry, it will create more jobs." This statement, while self-serving for Narrative Science, indicates larger assumptions about online journalism. Print and broadcast journalism long operated within a news landscape marked by scarcity. Only so many news outlets could exist, and only a finite number of news stories could fit into any news product—a 30-minute broadcast or 24-page newspaper issue. Hierarchical arrangement doubled as a statement about salience (Schudson 1995, 21). With online news, a lack of space constraints coupled with labor limitations provide conditions for automated news to thrive. But this also transforms news from a delimited selection of importance to an expansive terrain in which the economic logic of the long tail dominates (Anderson 2006)—with implication for journalistic authority (see below).

Narrative Science's claims to both augment human journalists and greatly extend news content should be understood within the context of what Narrative Science is. The company does not consider itself a journalistic organization or its technology as journalism-specific. Rather, its focus on journalistic narratives stems not from an interest in news, but from a belief this area would garner public attention. Frankel admitted as much: "We always knew that this technology would be able to be applied to lots of business problems," but journalism "has really helped us, because journalists can't seem to resist writing about journalism and things that are potentially disrupting journalism" (*Investor's Business Daily*, August 22, 2012). In *Forbes* (September 5, 2013), Frankel advocated for the breadth of Narrative Science's automated writing: "It is a horizontal platform, it can take just about any data from any industry and create any kind of narrative content." Its entry into journalism is not driven by normative commitments, but because of public attention and its technology's ability to produce simple news stories. As Narrative Science has extended its technology to other industries, news becomes less important to its identity. On its site, journalism is folded into the abstract "Research & Information Services" sector.

Given Narrative Science's lack of a journalism identity and its ambition to transform the news sector, the automated news stories it produces should be understood as a boundary object (Star and Griesemer 1989)—a particular material object serving as a common symbol with multiple meanings for the different communities it brings together. Hammond has noted that Narrative Science's technology is "a synthesis of data analytics, artificial intelligence and editorial expertise" (*South China Morning Post*, January 18, 2013) that derives from "two-thirds engineering and one-third journalism" (*Phys.org*, July 11, 2012). The automated news story thus works as a boundary object connecting different communities. For scientists, it provides a testing ground to hone algorithms capable of producing automated narratives. For journalists, the technology facilitates a vast array of inexpensive data-driven news stories. And for the company's management, it supplies a ready market for the technology. This perspective highlights the competing forces shaping how Narrative Science approaches journalism, including motives falling outside of journalism.

In sum, core assumptions expressed publicly by Narrative Science's management reveal a non-normative view of journalism as a type of narrative output based on data input. In terms of technological drama, the company extols the value of expanding the terrain of news through automation. But, crucially, it will be a particular sort of data set-driven journalism—a point not lost on journalists. But more immediate concerns arose around questions of labor and narrative.

Redefining Labor

Automated journalism's ability to generate news accounts without intervention from humans raises questions about the future of journalistic labor. Foremost was whether the technology threatened the employment of human journalists (van Dalen 2012). This anxiety was made palpable in news headlines about Narrative Science explicitly questioning the viability of automated journalism to displace journalists: "Can an Algorithm Write a Better News Story Than a Human Reporter?" (*Wired*), "Can Robots Run the News?" (*Mashable*), "Will Robots Steal Your Job?" (*Slate*), "Could a Computer Write This Story?" (CNN), "The Robot Journalist: Heralding an Apocalypse for the News Industry?" (*Guardian*), "What Jobs Will the Robots Take?" (*Atlantic*), "Could Robots Be the Journalists of the Future?" (*Guardian*), "Are Sportswriters Really Necessary?" (*BusinessWeek*), and "Are Robots and Content Farms the Future of the News?" (*GigaOm*). The popularity of this convention indicates sensitivity surrounding journalistic labor. For example, the *American Journalism Review* (November 25, 2013) invoked the larger historical context of news production to question coming changes to journalism: "The printing press put a generation of scribes out of a job, and the telegraph sent couriers scurrying to find new employment. Could software robots do the same for reporters?" Much of this fear equated improvements to Narrative Science's automation technology with more news industry layoffs. On *PandoDaily* (January 28, 2013), David Holmes noted: "Using the terms 'robots' and 'journalism' in the same sentence doesn't always inspire good vibes among a tribe that's seen more than its share of cut-backs and lay-offs over the past decade." The sensitivity here stems from ongoing reductions in news staffing due to difficulties in generating both online and offline revenues from news content. This context led many journalists to question Narrative Science's prediction that its service would free up or augment journalists, including Mathew Ingram (*GigaOm*, April 25, 2012): "That's a powerful argument, but it presumes that the journalists who are 'freed up' because of Narrative Science ... can actually find somewhere else that will pay them to do the really valuable work that machines can't do. If they can't, then they will simply be unemployed journalists." This view challenges the virtuous circle suggested above to instead argue that some degree of displacement is inevitable. After quoting Hammond's claim—"Nobody has lost a single job because of us"—in his *Wired* profile, Levy added ominously, "At least not yet." To many, automated journalism entailed future staff reductions.

Journalists fearing displacement invoked larger narratives of automation superseding human labor. Viewed within this context, Narrative Science portends the encroachment of automation into knowledge production domains previously considered impervious to replacement. For example, the *Guardian* (May 13, 2011) considered the wider outlook for labor: "Until now it has been assumed that job growth will be in the information economy ... However, an increasing number of technology analysts believe recent developments in computing may mean that some white-collar jobs are more vulnerable to technological change than those of manual workers. Even highly skilled professions, such as law, may not be immune." Professional knowledge producers now face displacement through automation due to what the *Atlantic* (January 23, 2014) called "the edge of a breakthrough moment in robotics and artificial intelligence," with uncertainty over what these processes would mean for job security. The *New York Times*'s Steve Lohr (September 10, 2011) also invoked automation to contextualize Narrative Science's impact on journalism: "The innovative work at Narrative Science raises the broader issue of whether such applications of artificial intelligence will mainly assist human workers or replace them. Technology is already undermining the economics of traditional journalism. Online advertising, while on the rise, has not offset the decline in print advertising. But will 'robot journalists' replace flesh-and-blood journalists in newsrooms?" The interrogatory form of this statement, already seen in the headlines above, suggests the potential for the drastic upheaval of journalistic labor.

Beyond questions of augmentation or elimination, Narrative Science's vision of automated journalism requires the transformation of journalistic labor to include such new positions as "meta-writer" or "metajournalist" to facilitate automated stories. For example, Narrative Science's technology can only automate sports stories after journalists preprogram it with possible frames for sports stories (e.g., comeback, blowout, nail-biter, etc.) as well as appropriate descriptive language. After this initial programming, automated journalism requires ongoing data management. Beyond the newsroom, automated journalism also redefines roles for non-journalists who participate in generating data. One popular application of Narrative Science—automated recounts of Little League baseball games—already relies on voluntarily data input.

Automated journalism will unquestionably raise concerns about journalistic labor. Whether it leads to further layoffs as online publishers look to save costs, augmentation that better empowers journalists, the transformation of work roles, or some combination remains to be seen. Reactions to automated journalism need to be considered within the larger context of automation. In this sense, automated journalism harkens to the recurring technological drama between automation and labor present since the earliest days of industrialization. The long-running trope of human versus machine is now complicated by developments in artificial intelligence regarding the mimicking of human storytelling—at least in a rough approximation, as we see in the next section.

Redefining Compositional Forms of News

While Narrative Science flaunts the transformative potential of automated journalism to alter both the landscape of available news and the work practices of journalists, its goal when it comes to compositional form is conformity with existing modes of human writing. The relationship here is telling: the more the non-human origin of its stories is undetectable, the more it promises to disrupt news production. But even in emulating human writing, the application of Narrative Science's automation technology to news prompts reconsiderations of the core qualities underpinning news composition. The attention to the quality and character of Narrative Science's automated news stories reflects deep concern both with existing news narratives and with how automated journalistic writing commoditizes news stories.

To begin with, it is imperative to grasp how Narrative Science articulates the epistemic importance of compositional form. Amid the optimism surrounding big data, the company promises to lessen the emphasis on quantitative data by heightening narrative as a way of knowing. In interviews, the company's management equates the reliance on human interpretation with wasted data because humans can only generate a limited number of reports. Hammond argued that a data set is "not valuable as a spreadsheet of numbers. It's valuable based on the insights that you can glean from it" (*The Atlantic*, April 12, 2012). Similarly, Frankel supported the link between narrative and understanding: "People are used to consuming and retaining information by reading it in narrative form" (*Crain's Chicago Business*, October 31, 2011). This should not be dismissed as mere promotional rhetoric. Although the technology to create narratives is still developing, these arguments indicate beliefs about knowledge production advocating for narrative above other forms of displaying data. It provides insight into the intentions of the creators behind automated journalism.

With Narrative Science's emphasis on the cognitive strengths of narrative as backdrop, journalists consistently judged the quality of its automated stories to be passably human but entirely generic. The stories drew qualified praise, including: "it might not be riveting, but it is perfectly readable" (*The Sunday Times*, May 20, 2012). Peter Kafka (*All Things D*, February 16, 2012) added: "The result isn't elegant, but it gets the job done, in a brute force sort of way." Other assessments made clear that the stories lacked the quality of the best writing, but were still serviceable as news accounts: "Though these pieces lack the verve of, say, Chuck Klosterman's sportswriting, the highly customizable platform does adopt a sports fan's idiomatic shorthand" (*The Atlantic*, April 12, 2012). *Fast Company* (June 19, 2012) added, "The phrase 'convincingly human' has probably never been used by the Pulitzer Prize committee, but it's good enough when it comes to analyzing large data sets, or the earnings reports that Narrative Science files for Forbes.com." The phrase "good enough" in the last quote usefully captures the recurring sentiment that automated journalism is capable of meeting minimum expectations that news writing provide clear and accurate information. But it also invokes what Robert Capps (2009) labeled the "good enough revolution"—the emergence of technology whose success is not due to high quality but in being functionally adequate and inexpensive. The potential for "good enough" news invokes the specter of disruption as theorized by Christensen (1997). In this respect, news automation commoditizes news discourse by allowing for the mass production of interchangeable content. Past scholars have warned against commoditization (see McNair 2000, 7; also McManus 1992), but automated journalism has the potential to drastically alter the conditions of news production and reception.

Scholars have long documented the formulaic nature underlying compositional forms of news exposed by the arrival of automated news. New narratives have evolved over time (Schudson 1982), taking on conventional generic forms (Allan 2004, 90). Journalists follow preexisting templates to fit facts to story forms (Darnton 1975). The ability of a program to emulate this form exposes this sameness, as Farhad Manjoo wrote in *Slate* (September 26, 2011): "Whether we admit it or not, many writers loosely follow a script when they work. How do you write a wire-service-style news story? You start by noting the most important thing that happened—what the jury found, who got killed, which team won. Then you get into the particulars. Structural rules even dominate more high-minded genres." News writing tends to coalesce around set forms. Moreover, mastering formal conventions remains an integral part of professionalization (Soloski 1989), and occurs when orientating new writers:

> Imagine an organization has just hired a new writer. Her boss discusses the topic of coverage with her and passes along a style guide. She writes a bunch of samples. She gets feedback. She writes some more. At some point the feedback stops because she knows what she's doing. According to Kris Hammond, Narrative Science's technology head, that's exactly how his company's technology, called Quill, works. "It just happens to be the case that it's a machine," he says. (*Quartz*, October 9, 2013)

Hammond's collapse of human and computer learning speaks to the sophistication of Narrative Science's technology, but it also underscores how much journalistic writing is standardized to exclude individual voice. This characteristic makes at least a portion of journalistic output susceptible to automation. In addition, Narrative Science can adapt its automated writing to different tones. One executive told *Wired* (April 24, 2012): "We could cover the stock market in the style of [legendary newspaper columnist] Mike Royko." In this way, Narrative Science can even commoditize particular styles, depending on client needs. The emulative capacity of automated journalism raises further questions about the uniqueness of human writing for journalists to confront when espousing their irreplaceability.

Another way Narrative Science prompts a rethinking of news compositional forms is its ability to scale and personalize news stories. Without automated journalism, the limited availability of both news personnel and space causes news organizations to base coverage decisions on ideas of newsworthiness to attract its desired audience both maximally and efficiently. Automated news alters this equation in two ways. First, its lowered cost allows for a greater quantity of news. Frankel touted the scalability of the technology: "It starts with the data and whatever the system gleans from the data it will generate in a document for the audience, *even an audience of one*" (*The Wire*, April 25, 2013, emphasis added). Rather than considering a small audience as a negative, Narrative Science redefines it as a positive. Business news outlets like *Forbes* use Narrative Science to write stories about earnings reports for many more companies than human reporters do. Any one report may receive very few hits, but in aggregate they add up to increased Web traffic. This accretion of audiences emerges in Narrative Science's stories about Little League games, of which the company creates two million stories a year (*Globe and Mail*, May 9, 2012).

Finally, the future of automated news suggests the ability to create multiple customized versions of the same story for individual audience members. Hammond told the *Columbia Journalism Review* (October 27, 2010) that the company focuses on "who's the audience and what's important to them." Coupling this audience-centric vision of automated journalism with the data collection abilities of online media could result in mass personalization at the reader level. Evgeny Morozov questioned this development on *Slate* (March 19, 2012): "What if we click on the same link that, in theory, leads to the same article but end up reading very different texts?" While customization connects to larger discourses of online personalization, human labor costs have made alternative narratives impossible. The newfound plausibility of customization through automated news leads Morozov to warn that mass customization would result in "a world that advertisers—along with Google, Facebook, and Amazon—can't wait to inhabit, but it's also a world where critical, erudite and unconventional thinking may become harder to nurture and preserve." That this is a possibility necessitates engaging with the social consequences of the shift of news from a collective statement about the relative importance of events meant for wide audiences to personalized accounts.

Until now, considerations of big data within journalism have sidestepped compositional form so long as journalists still mediated between data and text. But automated journalism's removal of the human element behind the generation of texts highlights the role of stylistic elements and formulas within news texts. It also leads to concerns that the scalability of news for an audience of one, or multiple stories for multiple ones, redefines journalism from a collective statement to individualized information. Thus, beyond narrative deeper questions pertain to the state of journalistic authority in the age of automated news.

Redefining Authority

Automated journalism's increasing presence—someday generating up to 90 percent of the news, Narrative Science predicts—necessitates rethinking the arguments supporting journalistic authority. As "human journalism" becomes a meaningful retronym offset from newer forms of automated journalism, it would be a mistake to merely map the authoritative strategies of the latter onto the former. Instead, the ability of Narrative Science and other competing applications to automatically generate news narratives fundamentally alters the authority relation, which requires conceptualizing what kind of journalistic authority automated journalism possesses. A useful place to start is Shirky's (2009) concept of "algorithmic authority." In a blog post, Shirky separates traditional modes of journalistic authority vested in institutions from new forms including both "unmanaged" algorithmic processes and aggregation as a means of filtering information. *Fast Company* (June 19, 2012) cited Shirky's argument bifurcating traditional and emergent forms of journalistic authority, before claiming: "Good journalism isn't about writing like a human. It's about trust. And as trust in conventionally authoritative sources continues to erode, Narrative Science's robots may be lying in wait to pick up the slack." By acknowledging the context of widespread criticism directed at journalists, this particular argument elucidates the division between human and machine intervention necessary to conceptualizing a particular perspective of journalistic authority for automated news. With Narrative Science in mind, this essay proposes modifying the definition of "algorithmic authority" to address the particular case of data-driven automated stories. By removing humans, the authority of automated news becomes that of the thinking machine capable of objectively sorting through data. Gillespie (2014, 180) notes that what he terms "algorithmic objectivity" has become an essential characteristic in arguments upholding the legitimacy of algorithms as a means of generating knowledge. Meanwhile, the cognitive shortcomings of human journalists have long been recognized—including Lippmann's critique a century ago (see Schudson 2010)—but novel attempts at automated solutions deserve study.

The utility of automated news to overcome the limitations of traditional human journalism was observed by *PandoDaily* (January 29, 2013): "now that bloviating TV pundits have come to dominate so many of the places we used to look to for journalistic authority, algorithmic authority looks more appealing than ever." Automated news may lack the stylistic flavor of the best news writing, but it substitutes a meticulous commitment to factuality possible precisely because it is not human. *Mashable* (July 9, 2010) expanded on the functionality of automated news: "Computers can more accurately and efficiently find patterns in data. They can alert journalists to what's new, create visualizations and timelines, track sources, and interact with readers." These quotes show the outlines of algorithmic authority and the development of arguments for automated news that transcend cost savings to tout what may be called its epistemic purity in generating news accounts.

The link between automated news and algorithmic authority rests on a view of Narrative Science as producing a "smart" technology capable of exacting judgment over data when crafting news narratives. The management of Narrative Science explicitly states that its stories are not pre-written templates but individually composed accounts capable of identifying "correlations that you did not expect." Hammond went on to predict to the *New York Times* (September 10, 2011) that within five years "a computer program will win a Pulitzer Prize—and I'll be damned if it's not our technology." This boast stems from the program's ability to identify patterns or trends from data sets too complicated for humans, as a business press article noted: "It can, for instance, scan stock data and pinpoint a company that is doing remarkably well, a company not in the public eye and, therefore, easy to miss by a human researcher" (*Financial Express*, February 9, 2014). This praise treats automated journalism as a new form of knowledge creation exceeding human capabilities. The utility of algorithmic authority was succinctly expressed by Hammond, who stated that society "can understand more because the system knows more" (*PandoDaily*, September 10, 2013). The social value necessary for any conception of authority derives from both an automation process removing human biases and analytical prowess to generate meaning from complex data.

In contrast to praise for the algorithmic authority of automated news, journalists defended human qualities supporting a non-automated view of journalistic authority. Like van Dalen's (2012) earlier study on reactions to automated news, journalists accentuated qualities of news writing that could not be emulated by algorithmic writing. These tactics recall Pfaggenberger's notion of "countersignification" in which an "impact constituency" affected by technological change develops "a way to live within the system without suffering unhealthy losses of self-esteem" (Pfaggenberger 1992, 301). This can be seen in the words of a critic who lashed out at automated news with its "imitation honesty" by writing: "Journalists don't just bundle data together. They bring a human presence to reporting" (*Canwest News Service*, September 18, 2011). The writer continued, "Good writing embodies human characteristics, like imagination and humour and critical thinking. Whether these qualities can be reduced to a mathematical formula is not at all clear." Such passionate defenses of creativity in crafting news point to deeper conflicts within journalism than simply delimiting human from automated news. Efforts to articulate the value of human storytelling often resorted to qualities outside traits commonly associated with journalism's normative commitment to objectivity (Carlson 2012). Qualities like emotion or empathy often fall outside of discussions of news, despite the centrality of storytelling for news discourse (Bird and Dardenne 1988).

Appeals to journalism as a creative activity also differentiated human from automated news. Rebecca Greenfield (*The Wire*, April 25, 2012) even questioned if what Narrative Science produced could even be considered journalism: "There are whole businesses built on the idea of producing massive quantities of news stories, quality controlled by machine-like formulas. Narrative Science may one day put a lot of these journalists out of work. But when most people talk about journalism, they're not thinking about rote earnings reports or baseball game recaps." Proper journalism was conceptualized as something deeper. *Deadspin* (May 1, 2010) wrote, "Writing has color, and it has characters, and it has life. It gives people a reason to read and re-read; it is affecting." Elsewhere, Matt Waite (*Reporters' Lab*, April 22, 2012), a journalist-turned-professor who pioneered technology-enabled computer-assisted reporting methods, defended essential human elements of journalism not reproducible by automated news: "You know what there isn't an algorithm for? Humanity. … Great journalism, I believe, reflects us as human beings: flawed, complicated, emotional. It is precisely the things that can't be defined in a programming language that makes us human." In establishing values outside the reach of algorithms, this explanation suggested an expanded view of journalism beyond its objectivity norms to acknowledge other elements of storytelling that contribute to journalistic authority.

The discourse around Narrative Science reveals competition over the foundation of journalistic authority. Support for algorithmic authority associated with automated news trumpets the speed and breadth of non-human processing while attributing its epistemic authority precisely to the lack of human intervention. By contrast, reconsiderations of what makes human-produced news unique suggest that journalistic authority derives from something more than delivering objective information about the world; it thrives on dissecting the drama of public life and the emotionality of quality news writing. Gillespie (2014, 192) expressed this distinction as the competing knowledge logics of "editorial" and "algorithmic." Editorial knowledge logics stress the expertise of subjective actors accumulating authority through their institutionalization. By contrast, algorithmic knowledge logics rest on the concretization of procedures of automation encoded by human operators. To fulfill their aim of providing knowledge to the public, both systems must seek recognition as legitimate knowledge producers. As the technology improves and the umbrella of automated journalism grows, these two logics will be put into conversation with one another in ways bound to raise larger questions about what constitutes quality public knowledge and how it should be created.

Conclusion

This study contends with the emergent practice of automated news content creation both in how it alters the working practices of journalists and how it affects larger understandings of what journalism is and how it ought to operate. A range of outcomes has been suggested above. At the positive end of the spectrum, the growth of automated journalism greatly expands the amount of available news and frees up journalists to pursue less mechanical stories. The technology also aids journalism as a smart system capable of finding patterns easily missed by human perception. Conversely, negative predictions include increased layoffs, polarizing personalization, and the commoditization of news writing. These are largely empirical questions to be answered in due time as the technology continues to improve.

Beyond these outcomes, automated journalism raises questions striking at the core of how journalism should be understood. The ability for automated journalism to pass for human writing forces a reexamination of newswriting as caught between a reliance on learned formulas and the need for individualized style. Viewed in terms of its output, journalism provides not only information but also a way of knowing the world that has accrued the epistemic authority to be considered legitimate. The adherence to formal patterns, while not always imaginative, rests on an argument that this style of conveying news should be respected. For journalists reacting to the automated writing of Narrative Science, quality newswriting involves something more than what is encompassed in normative ideas of news discourse. Journalists identifying what cannot be automated touted the dramatic possibilities of news and the power of stories, which suggests a broader understanding of journalistic authority to better account for these elements.

In many ways, this study raises more questions than can be answered at this early point in the development of automated journalism. Nonetheless it is imperative at this stage to formulate critical questions for future research agendas. If automated journalism is to occupy a central role in the news landscape, will an overreliance on the quantifiable push out other stories that cannot be rendered from analyzing data? Even as systems get smarter, the terrain of automated journalism will likely be constrained by both available data and narrative-creating abilities. What is needed is research into how newsrooms are utilizing automated news technologies and how this alters production practices and labor definitions. This will involve how different sets of actors treat the automated news story as a boundary object spanning technological and journalistic practices. On an epistemological level, questions need to be asked regarding whether an increase in algorithmic judgment will lead to a decline in the authority of human judgment. This is perhaps the central question at stake with the technological drama surrounding automated journalism. Another necessary area of research on automated journalism is attention to how news audiences—another impact constituency—make sense of and interact with news produced by algorithms. After all, the economic and authoritative underpinnings of automated journalism rest on its acceptance outside the newsroom. A final concern is the need to place automated journalism within larger discussions of automation and the future of knowledge labor. In this regard, the issues explored above expose the entrenched cultural conflict between equating technological development with progress and deep distrust of machines as dehumanizing forces. The progress of artificial intelligence extends this conflict into new terrains of knowledge and expertise that warrant much more investigation.

REFERENCES

Allan, Stuart. 2004. *News Culture*. Maidenhead: Open University Press.

Anderson, Chris. 2006. *The Long Tail*. New York: Random House.

Anderson, C. W. 2008. "Journalism: Expertise, Authority, and Power in Democratic Life." In *The Media and Social Theory*, edited by David Hesmondhalgh and Jason Toynbee, 248–264. New York: Routledge.

Anderson, C. W. 2013. "Towards a Sociology of Computational and Algorithmic Journalism." *New Media & Society* 15 (7): 1005–1021.

Anderson, C. W., Emily Bell, and Clay Shirky. 2012. *Post-industrial Journalism: Adapting to the Present*. New York: Tow Center for Digital Journalism.

Bird, Elizabeth S., and Robert W. Dardenne. 1988. "Myth, Chronicle, and Story, Exploring the Narrative Qualities of News." In *Mass Communication as Culture*, edited by James W. Carey, 67–87. Beverley Hills, CA: Sage.

Bockzkowsi, Pablo. 2004. *Digitizing the News*. Cambridge, MA: MIT Press.

Braun, Josh. 2013. "Going Over the Top: Online Television Distribution as Sociotechnical System." *Communication, Culture and Critique* 6 (3): 432–458.

Capps, Robert. 2009. "The Good Enough Revolution." *Wired*, September. http://archive.wired.com/gadgets/miscellaneous/magazine/17-09/ff_goodenough.

Carlson, Matt. 2007a. "Order versus Access: News Search Engines and the Challenge to Traditional Journalistic Roles." *Media, Culture and Society* 29 (6): 1014–1030.

Carlson, Matt. 2007b. "Blogs and Journalistic Authority: The Role of Blogs in US Election Day 2004 Coverage." *Journalism Studies* 8 (2): 264–279.

Carlson, Matt. 2012. "Rethinking Journalistic Authority: Walter Cronkite and Ritual in Television News." *Journalism Studies* 13 (4): 483–498.

Carlson, Matt, and Seth C. Lewis, eds. 2015. *Boundaries of Journalism*. New York: Routledge.

Christensen, Clayton. 1997. *The Innovator's Dilemma*. Boston, MA: Harvard Business Review Press.

Clerwall, Christer. 2014. "Enter the Robot Journalist: Users' Perceptions of Automated Content." *Journalism Practice* 8 (5): 519–531.

Corbin, Juliet, and Anselm Strauss. 2008. *Basics of Qualitative Research*. Thousand Oaks, CA: Sage.

Darnton, Robert. 1975. "Writing News and Telling Stories." *Daedalus* 104 (2): 175–194.

Ekström, Mats. 2002. "Epistemologies of TV Journalism: A Theoretical Framework." *Journalism* 3 (3): 259–282.

Fairclough, Norman. 2003. *Analysing Discourse*. London: Routledge.

Flew, Terry, Christina Spurgeon, Anna Daniel, and Adam Swift. 2012. "The Promise of Computational Journalism." *Journalism Practice* 6 (2): 157–171.

Gieryn, Thomas. 1999. *Cultural Boundaries of Science*. Chicago: University of Chicago Press.

Gillespie, Tarleton. 2014. "The Relevance of Algorithms." In *Media Technologies: Essays on Communication, Materiality, and Society*, edited by Tarleton Gillespie, Pablo Boczkowski, and Kirsten Foot, 167–194. Cambridge, MA: MIT Press.

Gray, Jonathan, Lucy Chambers, and Liliana Bounegru. 2012. *The Data Journalism Handbook*. Sebastapol, CA: O'Reilly.

Gynnild, Astrid. 2014. "Journalism Innovation Leads to Innovation Journalism: The Impact of Computational Exploration on Changing Mindsets." *Journalism* 15 (6): 713–730.

Lewis, Seth C., and Nikki Usher. 2013. "Open Source and Journalism: Toward New Frameworks for Imagining News Innovation." *Media, Culture and Society* 35 (5): 602–619.

Mayer-Schönberger, Viktor, and Kenneth Cukier. 2013. *Big Data: A Revolution That Will Transform How We Live, Work, and Think*. New York: Houghton Mifflin Harcourt.

McManus, John. 1992. "What Kind of Commodity is News?" *Communication Research* 19 (6): 787–805.

McNair, Brian. 2000. *Journalism and Democracy*. London: Routledge.

Parasie, Sylvain, and Eric Dagiral. 2013. "Data-driven Journalism and the Public Good: 'Computer-assisted-reporters' and 'Programmer-journalists' in Chicago." *New Media and Society* 15 (6): 853–871.

Pfaffenberger, Bryan. 1992. "Technological Dramas." *Science, Technology and Human Values* 17 (3): 282–312.

Powers, Matthew. 2012. "In Forms That are Familiar and Yet-to-be Invented': American Journalism and the Discourse of Technologically Specific Work." *Journal of Communication Inquiry* 36 (1): 24–43.

Reich, Zvi. 2012. "Journalism as Bipolar Interactional Expertise." *Communication Theory* 22 (4): 339–358.

Schudson, Michael. 1982. "The Politics of Narrative Form: The Emergence of News Conventions in Print and Television." *Daedalus* 111 (4): 97–112.

Schudson, Michael. 1995. *The Power of News*. Cambridge, MA: Harvard University Press.

Schudson, Michael. 2010. "Political Observatories, Databases and News in the Emerging Ecology of Public Information." *Daedalus* 139 (2): 100–109.

Shirky, Clay. 2009. "A Speculative Post on the Idea of Algorithmic Authority." November 15. http://www.shirky.com/weblog/2009/11/a-speculative-post-on-the-idea-of-algorithmic-authority/.

Soloski, John. 1989. "News Reporting and Professionalism: Some Constraints on the Reporting of the News." *Media, Culture & Society* 11 (2): 207–228.

Star, Susan Leigh, and James R. Griesemer. 1989. "Institutional Ecology, Translations' and Boundary Objects: Amateurs and Professionals in Berkeley's Museum of Vertebrate Zoology, 1907–39." *Social Studies of Science* 19 (3): 387–420.

Van Dalen, Arjen. 2012. "The Algorithms Behind the Headlines: How Machine-written News Redefines the Core Skills of Human Journalists." *Journalism Practice* 6 (5–6): 648–658.

Waisbord, Silvio. 2013. *Reinventing Professionalism*. Cambridge: Polity.

Williams, Raymond. 1974. *Television: Technology and Cultural Form*. London: Fontana.

Zelizer, Barbie. 1992. *Covering the Body*. Chicago: University of Chicago Press.

WAITING FOR DATA JOURNALISM
A qualitative assessment of the anecdotal take-up of data journalism in French-speaking Belgium

Juliette De Maeyer, Manon Libert, David Domingo, François Heinderyckx, and **Florence Le Cam**

Data journalism has emerged as a trend worthy of attention in newsrooms the world over. Previous research has highlighted how elite media, journalism education institutions, and other interest groups take part in the emergence and evolution of data journalism. But has it equally gained momentum in smaller, less-scrutinized media markets? This paper looks at the ascent of data journalism in the French-speaking part of Belgium. It argues that journalism, and hence data journalism, can be understood as a socio-discursive practice: it is not only the production of (data-driven) journalistic artefacts that shapes the notion of (data) journalism, but also the discursive efforts of all the actors involved, in and out of the newsrooms. A set of qualitative inquiries allowed us to examine the phenomenon by first establishing a cartography of who and what counts as data journalism. It uncovers an overall reliance on a handful of passionate individuals, only partly backed up institutionally, and a limited amount of consensual references that could foster a shared interpretive community. A closer examination of the definitions reveal a sharp polyphony that is particularly polarized around the duality of the term itself, divided between a focus on data and a focus on journalism, and torn between the co-existing notions of "ordinary" and "thorough" data journalism. We also describe what is perceived as obstacles, which mostly pertain to broader traits that shape contemporary news-making; and explain why, if data journalism clearly exists as a matter of concern, it has not transformed in concrete undertakings.

Introduction

The Belgian chapter of the international grassroots group "Hacks/Hackers" was founded in 2010. As an organization, Hacks/Hackers (Lewis and Usher 2014) promotes collaborations between journalists and technologists. It is a loosely organized international network, with local informal groups—called "chapters"—free to join the organization by organizing meet-ups and other locally coordinated activities. The Belgian chapter first met in November 2010. It was an informal gathering of about 40 people in a Brussels cafe. The organizer of the meet-up, who was then the social media manager of the French-speaking public broadcaster, declared the event a success, attended by "mostly hackers but with a strong representation from national media." A short report on the event on the Hacks/Hackers website further announced two outcomes: a soon-to-be hackathon and the launch of an "open data effort," namely a shared list of "URLs of open databases in Belgium and Brussels."

The list was not updated after its ninth entry, and the hackathon never took place. In January 2011, the Hacks/Hackers chapter joined forces with another grassroots group, called HackDemocracy. Founded in December 2010 by Xavier Damman, the Belgian co-founder of Storify, this group stated its mission as follows: "Our motto is 'innovations for more democracy' and our aim is to get hackers and public officials to work together on the future of our democracies." The first joint meeting of HackDemocracy and Hacks/Hackers, in January 2011, attracted about 80 people. The theme was timely: the whole session was focused on WikiLeaks and guest speakers included journalists from OWNI, a French online news outlet that directly collaborated with WikiLeaks (and for whom the founder of the Belgian chapter of Hacks/Hackers was working at the time). Since then, what remains of Hacks/Hackers Brussels is its Twitter and Facebook feeds, sporadically updated with news about journalism and technology. "It was too early," reckons the founder of the chapter when asked about the demise of the group (T16).[1]

The Belgian chapter of Hacks/Hackers seems to embody the current state of data journalism in French-speaking Belgium: a couple of well-connected individuals generate enough enthusiasm to raise interest within the (small) media community, but the initial impetus fails to develop into a sustained momentum or any large-scale project. Yet, this is not to say that data journalism did not make it to Belgian newsrooms. This article seeks to assess the existence of data journalism in the French-speaking part of Belgium by tracing the nascent practices and discourses that a diversity of actors are articulating inside and outside the newsrooms. Results show that a collective, polyphonic discourse about data journalism is identifiable among journalists and media managers, but so far it has not developed into stable, systematic practices. Understanding the modes of discursive construction of data journalism (who is speaking about it, from what position, how it is conceptualized, and what activities are associated with it), sheds light on the modes of existence of this emerging news practice. Our analysis explores these dialectics between discourse and practice by tracing a small network of professionals, newsrooms, blogs, and training and funding institutions.

Gauging the Ascent of Data Journalism In and Out of Newsrooms

To document the fact that data journalism is a significant phenomenon, scholars have pointed to various signs denoting its importance and have argued that there is a convergence of indicators, both inside and outside news organizations. The first, most obvious indicator to look at is media organizations themselves: how much do they engage in the production of data journalism? Most studies supply evidence of the ascent of data journalism by relying on prestigious cases in point: that of "elite" newsrooms (Anderson 2013), such as *The New York Times* or *The Guardian*, that have produced widely discussed examples of data journalism. Beyond these prestigious examples, evidence that data journalism has become widespread across newsrooms is mixed, depending on the country and the context. Some witness a rather modest ascent, with signs that only a few newsrooms produce data journalism in Norway (Karlsen and Stavelin 2014) or that data journalism is still "fairly uncommon" in Sweden (Nygren and Appelgren 2013). Others seem to witness a more sustained trend, such as in the Netherlands, where several "prominent media organizations" produce some sort of data journalism artefacts (Smit, De Haan, and Buijs 2013).

Beyond the sheer description of how news organizations engage in the production of data journalism, scholars have also looked at the various aspects that could explain how this production is shaped. Many such inquiries are focused on the news organizations themselves but tackle the issue at different—interrelated and complementary—levels: from the broad economic issues to work dynamics and even individual-focused analyses. In his call for a "sociology of computational journalism," Anderson (2013) distinguishes different analytical lenses to approach the phenomenon, among which a focus on economic and organizational logics. Other studies similarly embrace the need to study the organizational level of newsrooms but also insist on understanding the "moving cause" (Karlsen and Stavelin 2014) of data journalism—that is, the people producing it. Empirical research has hence been carried out at an individual level, particularly addressing the skills, self-representations, or professional trajectories of news workers (Royal 2010; Smit, De Haan, and Buijs 2013; Parasie and Dagiral 2013). The question of the skills required to produce data journalism seems particularly crucial, with findings underlining the need to master skills at the intersection between journalism and technology (Royal 2010; Karlsen and Stavelin 2014). Trédan (2014) even suggests that there is no such thing as a data journalist—i.e., one person with a complete mastery of journalistic and technical skills—but rather a converging set of insights that allows newsworkers to take part in cooperation with professional actors from distinct worlds.

But relying solely on a newsroom-centric perspective falls short of accounting for all the actors potentially involved in the production of data journalism. Key actors outside of the newsrooms also play a role in the development of data journalism. Among them, at the intersection between the social worlds of technology and traditional journalism, we find, for example, actors such as the grassroots organization Hacks/Hackers or non-profit-making funding bodies such as the Knight Foundation that encourage projects mixing technologists and journalists and hence become instrumental in the emergence of a computational journalism culture (Lewis and Usher 2013).

Within the non-newsroom-centric perspective, we also find research that has focused on the *data* itself, or what Karlsen and Stavelin (2014) call the "material cause" of data journalism. The existence of data, as the raw material of data journalism, is not a given. On the contrary, data is at the core of political power struggles—illustrated by the importance played by open-data advocacy groups in how data journalism sometimes comes to the fore (Trédan 2014)—which emphasizes the necessity to study the "bureaucratic, policy-level initiatives that either allow computational journalism to thrive, or retard its growth" (Anderson 2013, 1011). Besides, data itself can be messy, forcing the journalists who work with databases to reconsider the epistemological ground on which they operate (Parasie 2014).

Finally, non-newsroom-centric perspectives also emphasize the role played by the wider cultural background in defining what counts as journalism. Along that line, the role of journalism education has been underlined as significant: the fact that a number of institutions active in journalism education have started to offer programmes in data journalism is pointed to by several authors as a significant sign that data journalism is gaining momentum (Anderson 2013; Lewis and Usher 2013; Trédan 2014)—and has been documented in the past to show how comparable trends, such as computer-assisted reporting, have been adopted both in newsrooms and in classrooms (Davenport, Fico, and DeFleur 2002).

Does Data Journalism Matter?

In order to assess whether data journalism exists in French-speaking Belgium, we adopt a perspective that rises above the dichotomy between discourse and materiality. In line with Cooren, Fairhurst and Huët (2012, 296), this perspective assumes that

> analysts do not actually need to keep turning in one direction or another, that is, choose between materiality and discourse, so to speak, but that they should rather focus on the multiple ways by which various forms of reality (more or less material) come to do things.

As such, our aim is to describe minutely the materiality of data journalism in a context where there is almost no data journalism that is actually produced—arguing that it is not because there are no artefacts that data journalism does not matter in Belgian newsrooms.

Journalism does not solely exist in the news that is produced, but also in discourse—discourse that is not just another symbolic layer placed on top of practices and news artefacts: practices and discourses exist in a mutually shaping relation. We consider journalism as a socio-discursive practice. As such, journalism has its own "conditions of possibility" that determine what constitutes the realm of possible speech, action, and performance. Such a perspective concurs with the conceptualization of journalism proposed by Zelizer (1993), as being an "interpretive community" that is discursively shaped.

The crucial question then becomes: where can we locate journalism as a discourse? Scholars have produced in-depth analyses of privileged loci of discursive production, drawing on discourses produced by institutions or organizations that are relatively stable, such as journalism unions (Ruellan 2014), the gradual constitution of professional organizations (Le Cam 2009), and metajournalistic discourses as they are expressed in trade journals (Powers 2012). Journalism as a socio-discursive practice has also been increasingly characterized as fundamentally "dispersed" (Ringoot and Utard 2005) and heteronomous. Hence, exploring the discursive production of journalism in a centralized, institutionalized space (such as a limited scope of traditional news organizations) is no longer satisfying: we need to "go beyond the usual suspects" (Fink and Anderson 2014) and trace "news networks" constituted by a variety of actors (Domingo, Masip, and Costera Meijer 2014).

That is exactly the approach that we use to unpack the notion of data journalism: not as a technology that needs to be adopted, or as a taken-for-granted existing practice (which is currently only relevant in a handful of elite news organizations)—but rather as something that materially and discursively exists in a fundamentally relational space, across organizations, outside of news organizations, and even probably across national contexts. In that regard, this study is an "inquiry," as conceptualized by Latour (2005, 2013), that traces the liaisons between humans and non-humans and seeks to account for the heterogeneous nature of the phenomenon.

In other words, the hypothesis we propose is that data journalism could exist as a discourse (re)appropriated by a range of actors, originating from different—and sometimes overlapping—social worlds. If we look beyond the output—i.e., the data journalism artefacts that are produced—we can argue that at least part of what is considered as forming the contemporary trend of data journalism mainly operates in the realm of discourse. Organizations such as Hacks/Hackers or the National Institute for Computer-Assisted Reporting, for instance, do not primarily produce data journalism artefacts (unless they engage in the organization of hackathons or similar events): they produce discourses promoting and legitimizing the idea of data journalism, thus encouraging and enabling data journalism initiatives. Conferences and meet-ups are not only an afterthought to the production of data journalism, but rather they are the discursive matter that makes it come into existence. As such, we argue that gauging the existence of data journalism by only looking at the actual production of artefacts falls short of understanding how the phenomenon is shaped. We also need to examine how it is appropriated, re-appropriated, and interpreted as a discourse. Our guiding research question is, therefore: how does the plurality of discourses and practices around data journalism mutually shape the concept and its development in French-speaking Belgium?

Method

Instead of taking the phenomenon for granted, we choose to assess its existence in discourse. Starting from a set of points of entry, suggested by the multiple indicators discussed above, we qualitatively track the existence and the nature of data journalism in the particular context of the French-speaking part of Belgium.

The core of our methodological strategy was 20 semi-structured interviews with a diversity of actors representing the different profiles involved in the adoption and development of data journalism, including journalists in newsroom managerial positions (editor-in-chief and similar); persons managing human resources in the media companies, in charge of organizing journalists' training; people in organizations that offer trainings in data journalism (among other professional or educational activities); trainers; and journalists practising data journalism (most of them involved in training workshops, either as trainees or as trainers). The interviewees were selected in a snowballing process: starting with a list of people who attended a training session on data journalism organized by the association of professional journalists in June 2013, we then added the people they named during the interviews. When we met journalists employed by news organizations, we also sought to meet people in managerial positions from the same organization.

The aim of the interviews was to assess the existence of data journalism from the point of view of our interviewees, to collect the diversity of definitions of data journalism, to understand how their discourses materialize the phenomenon, and how organizational and personal aspects motivate or constrain its development as a news practice. We analysed the interviews to find common themes, and systematically traced the references made by the interviewees to persons, institutions, and technological tools—in all, forming a landscape of 168 relevant actors connected through a network of 309 interdiscursive connections.

Beside this material, collected in 2013 and 2014, we also gathered and analysed 52 documents: detailed programmes of the trainings, blog posts about data journalism, as well as the occasional data journalism artefact. The authors of this article have also taken part as participants in some of the events of this history (e.g., Hacks/Hackers meetings and data journalism workshops), which provided an informal form of observation.

The French-speaking Belgian media market constitutes a stimulating case for the study of the adoption of innovations in journalism, avoiding the usual fascination of researchers for the early adopters and the best known outlets. The small size of this media market (4.5 million inhabitants) allowed the authors to reach most of the key actors (i.e., a census more than a sampling) and consider all the facets of the phenomenon.

What Data Journalism is Made Of

The interviews were rich in references to people, institutions, and tools involved in the development of data journalism in the francophone part of Belgium. These references indicate who or what populates the notion of data journalism for the people we met: their discourses call up a set of actors—be they technical tools, influential people, funding bodies, or famous examples. Tracing these references allowed us to determine who or what counts as a relevant actor, and subsequently to recompose the discursive landscape of data journalism in Belgium.

Even though our methodological choices (starting with journalists who followed training in data journalism) certainly imply a bias that might overemphasize the importance of the phenomenon—if there are trainings, data journalism must be something that exists—our interviewees were extremely cautious in assessing the actuality of data journalism in French-speaking Belgium, especially when trying to determine who could be considered a data journalist: "It's extremely limited … I wouldn't say there's nothing at all, because some people try to, but I'm thinking of three people. That's it" (J14). Another one insisted on this idea: "[W]e are talking about [data journalism], some of us are talking about it. But few really put that into practice. And it's mostly individual initiatives, emerging from the will of some journalists who decide to invest themselves in that" (J9).

In their description of who and what counts in the notion of data journalism, respondents also attributed authority and know-how. Most interviewees name the same two specific journalists (JT11, JT12) as the first (and only) professionals to produce data journalism stories in Belgium. They are seen as the only local experts in data journalism, and their expertise has led them to be asked to be instructors in data journalism trainings. Another sign of the vaporous existence of data journalism appears in the fact that other people are also designated as experts, even though—as they willingly admit (J13, T16)—they never really practised or produced data journalism. The founder of the local chapter of Hacks/Hackers and self-proclaimed "digital sherpa" as well as an "editorial webmaster" well known for his digital literacy, both involved in training sessions (as organizers or instructors), appear as key actors that have distributed and promoted the idea of data journalism in the past few years. At the other end of the spectrum, two journalists (J14, J15) who turned out to be extremely knowledgeable about data journalism (mobilizing many tools, actual experiences and references in their discourse) were only rarely mentioned.

While the handful of pioneers are self-trained, most of their colleagues fiddling with data journalism in Belgium have been initiated during training sessions, and deem them crucial to get to know the basics and the tools to practise it. Still, even those who organize trainings (X19, JX20) were cautious: "At our first initiation training, we had only six people. That shows that the interested audience, in Belgium, is extremely limited … There must be about 30 people in total, who are interested enough to follow training sessions, for now" (JX20).

Institutions also matter in the data journalism landscape, according to our respondents. Training sessions are, in some cases, initiated by media companies themselves—in a generic effort towards lifelong learning that goes beyond the sole practice of data journalism and embraces many other aspects of contemporary newsmaking—or by other stakeholders such as the organization of professional journalists (Association des Journalistes Professionnels, AJP) or by the trade association of newspaper publishers (Journaux Francophones Belges, JFB). Some journalism schools take part in the movement by acting as external contractors that deal with the logistics of the trainings (when solicited by the association of newspaper publishers, for example), but the topic does not seem to be part of the permanent curricula offered to journalism students so that schools often call on external instructors. Another example of institutional support is the fact that a foundation fostering investigative reporting in Belgium has received three applications for projects involving data journalism. However, the projects were subject to jurisdictional doubts, and the initiative's promoters (including the director of the foundation) had to struggle to convince the foundation that it was legitimate (JT12, X18). Ultimately, of three proposals that "contained some elements of data journalism" (X18), one was funded.

Data sources were also present among the institutional actors that matter, but they are mostly framed in a negative way: respondents complain of a lack of data sources (barely the National Institute of Statistics and its European counterpart). Strikingly, the diverse open-data initiatives showcased in the last few years by various governmental bodies (at the level of the European Union, the federal state of Belgium, the Walloon region, or the city of Brussels) are rarely mentioned (T16, J14). They do not seem to matter in the imagined landscape of data journalism. Journalists agree that the European Union (Eurostat in particular) is a much more accessible source of data than the national authorities, sometimes even for information produced by the latter, but with insufficient granularity to zero in on the local.

Some news organizations were also among the actors that count insofar as they constitute examples of good practices. Some Belgian cases related to fiscal scandals involving the bank sector are mentioned, but rarely. Foreign news organizations, however, appeared as exemplars: *The Guardian* and specifically its Datablog is a source of inspiration for many of the interviewees. Other big newsrooms like those of *Le Monde* or *The New York Times* are also mentioned, mainly to point out that the resources available in Belgian news media are no match.

Our overview of the network of actors that participate in the construction of the notion of data journalism, according to the interviewees, reveals that there is a handful of consensual actors which are often mentioned: the two journalists who are known for producing data journalism, the organization that hosted the trainings (our starting point), as well as the tools that were the topic of the said training session (Google Fusion), or foreign examples of news organizations successfully producing data journalism (*The Guardian*). Conversely, the majority of actors—people, tools, organizations—are only mentioned once: they populate the notion of data journalism for one of our interviewees, but these references are not necessarily shared. The "interpretative community" is, therefore, dispersed, fluid, and mostly unstructured, despite the efforts of some central actors.

The Vague Contours of the Definitions of Data Journalism

The very notion of data journalism shows a remarkably wide range of meanings among our respondents: despite the fact that there are themes that connect the diversity of discourses, there is no consensus on core issues regarding the definition of the phenomenon. Definitions stem from examples, experience, and discourses heard, appropriated and sometimes reinterpreted. Variations in the perception of data journalism seem unrelated to whether the respondent is a journalist, a manager, or a trainer but rather to how close they have come to the practice of data journalism. The extent to which respondents share representations of data journalism stems from the depth of their understanding of the corresponding practices or of the experience of seasoned data journalists. The participation of some of the interviewees in workshops seemed to foster closer points of view than with the other respondents.

Before any attempt to define the practice, to refer to examples, to try to incarnate the phenomenon, the idiom *data journalism* can be seen as concentrating a limited number of strong features. It appears to be orienting, if not dictating, the definitions that are offered. These meanings focus primarily on two main features: the data themselves and journalism. One journalist says it upfront:

> The way I see it, ultimately, is with both words: there is data, and there is journalism. Journalism is the daily job of the journalist, seek information, check it, possibly analyse it, criticise it if need be. The exact angle is the data, it's starting from the data, be they numbers or not. (J10)

This position highlights the extent to which respondents hang on to the very terms or how they distance themselves with their meanings. Along the same lines, a few respondents who emphasize the journalism component like to insist that data journalism is essentially just journalism.

> I see neither opposition nor real specificity between journalism and data journalism ... I really think it's something that has always existed and it has been thriving thanks to new technologies. (MJ2)

The term would be a new terminology used to designate a reality that pre-existed, a "return to the fundamentals in a modernized form" (MJ4). The practice would be pre-dating, journalists having consistently worked on the basis of data (J9, MJ4). Obviously, all focus narrowly on the term *data*. Doing data journalism implies to "process data" (JT12), to access it, to correlate it, and finally to present it, but also to do a form of data-seeking journalism (MJ4), or even a way to use databases (M6, MJ3, MJ1). Between journalism and data, the emphasis is often techno-determinist, with references to the tools and to modes of access to the data. Progress in tools and technologies would allow easier access and processing, and would make data journalism more natural in the context of euphoria associated with new technologies. Existing data are seen as easier to access (at least in the imaginary, not so much in practice), and the tools available are perceived as potentially facilitating a more complex form of journalism. But while some respondents frame data journalism in relation to pre-existing practices, others praise the explanatory power of the numbers, of the importance nowadays of data made available using new technologies (JT11, JT12, MJ3, J9). The emphasis on techniques is even present within expressions of scepticism: "What's new isn't so much data journalism, but rather the method that allows us to cross-tabulate data on a large scale" (MJ2). Computers and data processing are often mentioned either as progress or as an impediment when doing data journalism.

These perceptions are consistent with broader trends in the perceived effects of the internet on the media (Rebillard 2007). Respondents, however, often see opportunities in data journalism that, ultimately, would offer a potential to, in a way, improve journalism in general. This positive effect would result from an improved capacity to investigate. It encourages to "investigate by numbers" (JT11), it is now one of the forms of investigative journalism (MJ2), and it makes it possible to "reveal information that didn't exist … to reveal information from raw data" (J8). If many respondents underline the revelatory potential of data journalism, its capacity to show what is hidden, the emphasis is again either on the data or on the journalism end of the spectrum. Some argue that it is the data themselves that allow to "bring governments to their knees" (J15) and to gain independence from official channels (J10, MJ4); others argue that showing what is hidden and holding those in power accountable is what journalists have always done—with data being yet another instrument in the toolkit of investigative journalists (X18).

But these optimistic opinions are counterbalanced by views critical of desktop journalism, thus defending a model of journalism where journalists go into the field. An editor insists:

> Data journalism is nice, but it's not life. Yet, by doing our job as journalists, we must tell life as it happens. And it's not enough to stay behind one's desk with a computer, one must go out into the field. Check if the data that you have is for real. You will not tell people, on television for example, that life expectancy is 70 without going out to see old people. (MJ4)

Respondents are also swept along by their perception of the inevitability of technological change and the race for innovation within the media industry. Data journalism is clearly associated with innovation among some editors who then anchor their definition within the image of novelty associated with it (X18). Data journalism remains, for some, a way to make news more "sexy" (J8, M6, MJ2), to prefer forms of visualization that impress, intrigue, or entertain by their design, and so help explain complex stories or illustrate not very visual ones. But data journalism is one of many ways by which news organizations struggle to maintain their footing in a market in transformation. It is sometimes explicitly given a rather low rank among those priorities by editors who admit that "there is a billion other priorities" (MJ2), particularly when they feel that the return on investment for the training of journalists is debatable (MJ4, J9).

Ordinary Data Journalism

As respondents progressively come up with definitions, another division appears to shape what counts as data journalism in Belgium. There is, on the one hand, "ordinary" data journalism and, on the other hand, "thorough" data journalism. They are characterized by contrasting traits: the former is manageable by one individual, can be done on a daily basis, and can be included in the existing routines of news organizations if journalists master specific tools. The latter is eminently collective and requires the mobilization of a range of skills (journalism, computer science, statistics, graphic design), necessitate more time, primarily requires that news organizations completely rethink their workflow, and is more a question of "mind-set" than a question of mastering new tools.

In that regard, the notion of data visualization appears as strongly divisive and tends to shape prominently what counts as data journalism and what does not. Some dismiss the emphasis on visualization as a simulacrum of data journalism: "They think they do data journalism because they produced a graphic ... That is not data journalism. Data journalism means to retrieve data that are not given, and process them. Visualization comes at the very last stage" (J14). Others, however, argue that producing data visualizations is an integral part of the storytelling skills that are essential to good journalism (J6), and that the "ordinary" approach has merits: "People often seek extraordinary examples of data journalism. The glitter, the dream ... but I think data journalism can be banal ... Maybe to ultimately produce an unsophisticated graphic" (JX20).

Such distinction consequently complicates the question of the existence of data journalism in French-speaking Belgium, as respondents are very self-aware of the scale of what is produced: they, for example, acknowledge the know-how of the two local experts while admitting that what they do is "fairly basic" (MJ5, J13, JX20). As with the cacophony of definitions, every respondent's position on what really counts as data journalism depended on their knowledge, experience, and relative proximity to the practice rather than their role (editor, journalist, trainer). This increases the complexity of the collective discourse about data journalism and fosters the diversity of practices that are all labelled as data journalism, despite their disparity.

The Long Road to Data Journalism: Perceived Obstacles

When it comes to identifying obstacles to the practice of data journalism—or the transition from "ordinary" data journalism to "thorough" data journalism—respondents offer arguments that fall within three categories: obstacles within the news organization, obstacles outside the news organization, and obstacles that emerge at a more individual level.

The bulk of obstacles seem related to how news organizations function, with specific material constraints, be they in terms of time, resources, or workflow. Time, or the lack thereof, emerges as one of the main barriers to the practice of data journalism. Some respondents frame time as something that the organization refuses to give to journalists (M7) because it has other priorities, or admit that their practice of data journalism is confined to their free time (J9, J8). One journalist who has successfully engaged in the production of data journalism projects emphasizes that convincing his hierarchy to give him some time was a key enabler (JT11).

The question of time also ties in with that of the news cycle. Especially for those working in news organizations that primarily produce a daily issue, the work rhythm is such that taking the time to dig into a database is often impossible (J10, MJ1, M6): "The problem with producing a daily is that we are caught by the news, every day" (J9).

Data journalism projects are even further hindered by the fact that their return on investment seems feeble, uncertain, or plainly fruitless (M7, JT11, J10).

> We can spend days on it, without results … By cross-tabulating different databases, one might come up with a scoop. But it happens one time out of ten. It requires a lot of time, without immediate or systematic results. (M7)

A freelance journalist directly connects this issue with his conditions of employment and financial pressure: "If I stop for one day or two to analyse the data … It will bring nothing in, the work won't get paid for: only the article will get paid for" (J10). The financial resources available are also one of the organizational barriers. News organizations operate on a tight budget (J9); they do not devote enough resources to the hiring of skilled designers or developers or to the purchase of new tools that could produce better data visualizations (JT12).

Finally, the workflow and division of labour in traditional news organizations is also pointed out as an organizational impediment to the practice of data journalism. Here, the role of graphic designers and their collaboration with journalists comes forward as a major issue: either in terms of division of labour, or in terms of availability. Journalists who engage in the practice of data journalism worry that they are "doing the job" of the graphic designers when they produce data visualization (J10), or wonder if they really want to learn more design skills, as they primarily think of themselves as journalists and not designers (J9).

The availability of graphic designers to work on data journalism projects is also an issue (M6, JT12), especially when the development of data journalism is not encouraged by the organization: "If they [the graphic designers] are not personally excited by the project, they are not going to work on it. It is not a priority" (J9). In one of the newspapers, the role of graphic designers was explicitly linked to creating visualizations, which were considered as an "embryonic" form of data journalism, and explicitly promoted and channelled through the central desk coordinator in the newsroom.

Obstacles outside news organizations converge towards one shared concern: the availability and usability of data. All the interviewees agree that public institutions in Belgium still needed to fully embrace the policy of open data that they often claim to subscribe to. Overall, the access to public data is deemed extremely difficult (JT12, J9, MJ1). When datasets are available from public institutions, they are either out-dated (MJ4), they are not produced in a timely fashion (MJ1), they do not offer enough granularity to be useful (JT12, JT11), or are not available in a format that would be directly usable (J10). When explaining this situation, however, the interviewees did not blame public institutions for their blatant unwillingness, incompetence, or secrecy. Instead, they highlight structural problems—such as incompatibility between the different systems used by sub-parts of the administration and the transition from paper to digitized data (J10), an overall lack of a "culture of transparency" (J9), and the "old habits of the administration" (J8). "We're in the mediaeval age of statistics," one respondent (J10) summarizes.

Respondents seem aware—if vaguely—of the legal obligations that administrations have to publicize data, but to their knowledge, no journalist or media organization has ever attempted to use legal means to obtain data from a public administration. The only journalist (JT12) that ever considered doing so admits he quickly gave up because he felt too isolated, because his request for setting up structural support in his news organization never resulted in concrete measures, and because a lawyer told him that the data he was requesting were protected by privacy laws (and would therefore never be accessible).

Respondents also highlight obstacles at an individual level: they argue that most journalists are afraid of numbers (JT11, JT12, J9) and hence are deterred by the tools and raw material of data journalism. Journalists tend to display a literary sensitivity (J9); their personal taste implies that they prefer to write rather than process data and numbers (MJ2). This overall distaste is privileged over an explanation that would emphasize the technical difficulty as a main obstacle: most journalists who engaged in the practice of data journalism argue that the basic tools and techniques are rather easy to learn: "Any journalist could use these tools. They know how to use a computer, it's no more compli-cated than that" (J10). Even if they acknowledge that their skills can plateau out—with the most sophisticated tools requiring a lot more learning time and investment (J9, J10)—they argue that there is a mental block at play, rather than real technical impediments.

When it comes to assessing the flip side of the coin—i.e., the enablers that may facilitate the practice of data journalism—respondents mostly note one key aspect: the formation of an informal network of experts that constitutes both a supportive commu-nity and a source of technical support. Journalists who have followed training tend to say that they have difficulties applying their new skills in their newsrooms, but one of the outcomes of these sessions has been the formation of an informal network of Belgian French-speaking journalists interested in data journalism (J9, J10, JT12, JT11). They share tips on the use of tools and their advances in applying them, with the handful of experts taking a leading role in lifting doubts. The most intriguing aspect of this network is its inter-newsroom nature, jumping over competition barriers. Journalists admitted to being more akin to the colleagues they met in the trainings than the ones in their own newsrooms:

> Strangely, there are more walls falling between journalists from different newsrooms than within the newsroom itself. As of today, I have more contact with [two other journalists from different newsrooms], via e-mail or through their blogs … We exchange practical tips. It's interesting because it's a cooperative approach, we give each other a hand in learning the tools which would take a lot more time to discover by ourselves. (J9)

The human resources coordinator of one newspaper even underlines this ability to breach the newsroom walls as one of the strengths of the trainings organized by the association of newspaper publishers: "Journalists are happy to meet other people, even from other companies. They feel less alone" (M6).

Conclusions

The results presented above reveal a situation full of contrast. News organizations have different approaches to data journalism, in terms of definition, worthiness, or training. Unsurprisingly, we find such polyphony at all levels: journalists, editors, and human resources coordinators did not speak with one voice.

The definitions of data journalism themselves prove to be slippery. There is a sharp tension between each part of the doublet, *data* and *journalism*. The emphasis on *data* underlines specific challenges and needs, whereas the emphasis on *journalism* sees the idea as yet another trendy tool for doing good journalism that does not necessarily require particular attention, specific training, or strong organizational policy.

The (short) history of data journalism in Belgium indicates a trend that seems to plateau at the stage of the early adopters who engage in the production of "ordinary" data journalism, with no indication that it would evolve towards a wider adoption, let alone a mainstream practice. For those who have engaged in the concrete practice of data journalism, there seems to be an overall feeling of resignation. There might have been a brief euphoric phase after the first encounter with the concept of data journalism, but journalists who return from trainings full of ideas and ambitious projects are quickly caught again in the constraints of routinized news production. Such disenchantment is further accentuated by the lack of institutional or structural support; if news organizations do not explicitly disregard data journalism, they clearly consider it as a low priority. As a result, we see the emergence of a loose commitment and the original ambitions are revised downwards by sometimes radically widening the scope of what counts as data journalism: the production of slightly enhanced charts and visualizations (including those printed in the newspapers or displayed in televised news bulletins) counts as artefacts of data journalism, the collection of numbers (even on a small scale) or *any* piece of information qualifies as *data*.

The discourses on data journalism reveal a number of obstacles. Among those, the difficulty to access data appears as the sole obstacle that is really specific to data journalism—though it could be compared to the overall issue of access to sources that fundamentally shapes newsmaking. The other impediments relate to broader difficulties currently encountered by news organizations: a lack of financial resources that result in a constant pressure, a generalized lack of time to be spent on activities that do not directly result in quick, effective output, and a need for trained manpower to keep up with the pace of innovation. These generic traits of contemporary media organizations are further accentuated by the particular context: French-speaking Belgium is a small media market, where modestly sized news organizations that have to cover the full spectrum of news are consequently short of resources.

There is no doubt that data journalism exists in French-speaking Belgium. It is a notion discursively populated by many people, tools, and organizations—all enrolled in the way data journalism *matters* and hence constituting its material reality. Some of these actors are even shared, showing that there is a (modest) consensus on what data journalism is made of. Data journalism undoubtedly constitutes a "matter of concern" (Latour 2005), which exists in spite of the relative lack of actual undertaking. The absence of data journalism artefacts, convenient "matters of fact" that we could gather and display as evidence, does not mean that data journalism does not exist: if "highly uncertain" and "loudly disputed," matters of concern are "real, objective, atypical and above all, *interesting* agencies" (Latour 2005, 114, original emphasis). Data journalism, as a socio-discursive practice, is being constructed by the interactions of a small group of very diverse actors that interpret, imagine, and try out ways to explain what can be done with data in journalism. The definitions they propose are as varied as their positions, and the interrelations among their discourses, and how they end up appropriated in their practices, are the concrete mechanisms that shape data journalism.

Our assumption that any number of these observations may be specific to small media markets should be further explored, if only by conducting similar research in neighbouring countries with different market sizes (France, the Netherlands, Germany, or the United Kingdom) that would include larger newsrooms with *a priori* more resources to devote to data journalism. The arrival of data journalism should also be seen in the larger context of other instances of new or evolving professional practices (e.g., multimedia, engagement with the audience) associated with the adoption of networked digital technologies in the newsrooms.

The journalists we approached for this study were remarkably cooperative and interested, which could indicate that the current disarray and confusion in the news industry might constitute a real opportunity to develop and secure the fragile links between academic research and the various stakeholders of journalism.

NOTE

1. When referencing the interviews conducted for this study, respondents are identified by a unique number and by a (set of) letter(s) that reflect(s) their role(s): J = journalist, T = trainer, M = manager, X = other. The codes are sometimes combined, as some respondents had more than one role.

REFERENCES

Anderson, Christopher W. 2013. "Towards a Sociology of Computational and Algorithmic Journalism." *New Media & Society* 15 (7): 1005–1021. doi:10.1177/1461444812465137.

Cooren, François, Gail Fairhurst, and Romain Huët. 2012. "Why Matter Always Matters in (Organizational) Communication." In *Materiality and Organizing*, edited by Paul M. Leonardi, Bonnie A. Nardi and Jannis Kallinikos, 296–314. Oxford University Press.

Davenport, Lucinda D., Fred Fico, and Margaret H. DeFleur. 2002. "Computer-Assisted Reporting in Classrooms: A Decade of Diffusion and a Comparison to Newsrooms." *Journalism & Mass Communication Educator* 57 (1): 6–22. doi:10.1177/107769580205700103.

Domingo, David, Pere Masip, and Irene Costera Meijer. 2014. "Tracing Digital News Networks. Towards an Integrated Framework of the Dynamics of News Production." *Digital Journalism*. doi:10.1080/21670811.2014.927996.

Fink, Katherine, and C. W. Anderson. 2014. "Data Journalism in the United States." *Journalism Studies*. doi:10.1080/1461670X.2014.939852.

Karlsen, Joakim, and Eirik Stavelin. 2014. "Computational Journalism in Norwegian Newsrooms." *Journalism Practice* 8 (1): 34–48. doi:10.1080/17512786.2013.813190.

Latour, Bruno. 2005. *Reassembling the Social: An Introduction to Actor-Network-Theory*. New ed. Oxford University Press.

Latour, Bruno. 2013. *An Inquiry into Modes of Existence: An Anthropology of the Moderns*. Cambridge, Massachusetts: Harvard University Press.

Le Cam, Florence. 2009. *Le Journalisme Imaginé: Histoire D'un Projet Professionnel Au Québec* [Imagined Journalism: A History of a Professional Project in Quebec]. Montréal: Leméac.

Lewis, Seth C., and Nikki Usher. 2013. "Open Source and Journalism: Toward New Frameworks for Imagining News Innovation." *Media, Culture & Society* 35 (5) (July 1): 602–619. doi:10.1177/0163443713485494.

Lewis, Seth C., and Nikki Usher. 2014. "Code, Collaboration, and the Future of Journalism: A Case Study of the Hacks/Hackers Global Network." *Digital Journalism* 2 (3): 383–393. doi:10.1080/21670811.2014.895504.

Nygren, Gunnar, and Esther Appelgren. 2013. "Data Journalism in Sweden: Introducing New Methods and Genres of Journalism into 'Old' Organizations." Paper presented at the Future of Journalism Conference, Cardiff, September 12–13.

Parasie, Sylvain, and Eric Dagiral. 2013. "Data-Driven Journalism and the Public Good: 'Computer-Assisted-Reporters' and 'Programmer-Journalists' in Chicago." *New Media & Society* 15 (6): 853–871. doi:10.1177/1461444812463345.

Parasie, Sylvain. 2014. "Data-driven Revelation? Epistemological Tensions in Investigative Journalism in the Age of 'Big Data'." *Digital Journalism*. doi:10.1080/21670811.2014.976408.

Powers, Matthew. 2012. "In Forms That Are Familiar and Yet-to-Be Invented." *Journal of Communication Inquiry* 36 (1): 24–43. doi:10.1177/0196859911426009.

Rebillard, Franck. 2007. *Le Web 2.0 En Perspective: Une Analyse Socio-économique De L'internet.* [Web 2.0. in Perspective: A Socio-Economic Analysis of the Internet]. Paris: L'Harmattan.

Ringoot, Roselyne, and Jean-Michel Utard. 2005. *Le Journalisme En Invention: Nouvelles Pratiques, Nouveaux Acteurs [Journalism in Invention: New Practices, New Actors].* Rennes: Presses universitaires de Rennes.

Ruellan, Denis. 2014. *Le Journalisme Défendu* [Defended Journalism]. Rennes: P U De Rennes.

Royal, Cindy. 2010. "The Journalist as Programmer: A Case Study of the New York times Interactive News Technology Department." Paper presented at the International Symposium on Online Journalism, Austin, April 23–24. http://online.journalism.utexas.edu/papers.php?year=2010.

Smit, Gerard, Yael De Haan, and Laura Buijs. 2013. "Visualizing News: Make It Work." Paper presented at the Future of Journalism Conference, Cardiff, September 12–13.

Trédan, Olivier. 2014. "Quand Le Journalisme Se Saisit Du Web: L'exemple Du Datajournalism." [When journalism takes hold of the web: the example of data journalism] In *Changements Et Permanence Du Journalisme* [Change and Permanence of Journalism], edited by Florence Le Cam and Denis Ruellan, 199–214. Paris: L'Harmattan.

Zelizer, Barbie. 1993. "Journalists as Interpretive Communities." *Critical Studies in Mass Communication* 10 (3): 219–237. doi:10.1080/15295039309366865.

BIG DATA AND JOURNALISM
Epistemology, expertise, economics, and ethics

Seth C. Lewis and **Oscar Westlund**

Big data is a social, cultural, and technological phenomenon—a complex amalgamation of digital data abundance, emerging analytic techniques, mythology about data-driven insights, and growing critique about the overall consequences of big-data practices for democracy and society. While media and communication scholars have begun to examine and theorize about big data in the context of media and public life broadly, what are the particular implications for journalism? This article introduces and applies four conceptual lenses—epistemology, expertise, economics, and ethics—to explore both contemporary and potential applications of big data for the professional logic and industrial production of journalism. These distinct yet inter-related conceptual approaches reveal how journalists and news media organizations are seeking to make sense of, act upon, and derive value from big data during a time of exploration in algorithms, computation, and quantification. In all, the developments of big data potentially have great meaning for journalism's ways of knowing (epistemology) and doing (expertise), as well as its negotiation of value (economics) and values (ethics). Ultimately, this article outlines future directions for journalism studies research in the context of big data.

Introduction

Big data, the buzzword *du jour*, carries with it all manner of hype and hope—and hesitation about its social consequences (Crawford, Miltner, and Gray 2014). By one account, "Big data is poised to reshape the way we live, work, and think" (Mayer-Schönberger and Cukier 2013, 190), and by another, "The data explosion [will change] how we do business. Every interaction, every communication, every touchpoint creates a digital breadcrumb—a piece of data that can be analyzed and manipulated" (cited in Dwoskin 2014). While it is impossible to know the prescience of such predictions, there is a growing body of evidence that *something* important is changing in the nature of data —in the volume and variety of its digital representation, in its collection and analysis on a massive scale, and in its ultimate potential for yielding social, cultural, and monetary value, even as these developments simultaneously raise troubling questions about privacy, accuracy, and ethics (boyd and Crawford 2012). Big data is made available by the growing ubiquity of mobile devices, sensors, "smart" machines, digital trace data, digital repositories and archives, and other fragments of social and natural activity represented by clicks, tweets, likes, GPS coordinates, timestamps, and so on (for a related discussion of the "internet of things," see Howard forthcoming). The sheer volume of digital data and its boundless growth is staggering (Mayer-Schönberger and Cukier 2013), and just as significant is the increasing ease with which standard computer software can manage and manipulate data sets that once required supercomputers, thereby magnifying this episode of digital data exploration (Manovich 2012).

This "big data moment" is not merely a technological transition toward data deluge. Rather, it is a sociotechnical phenomenon with cultural, economic, and political origins and implications; it is, indeed, a mythology as much as a science or business (boyd and Crawford 2012; Crawford et al. 2014, 1664). As such, the very term "big data" deserves scrutiny of the kind applied to the likes of "Web 2.0" (Coleman 2013). While we take up such concerns later in this article, for now it suffices to suggest, as Boellstorff (2013) does, that even while "there is no unitary phenomenon 'big data' ... the impact of big data is real and worthy of sustained attention." Moreover, questions of data privacy and surveillance raised by the Edward Snowden revelations, among other incidents, make big data a matter of public as well as professional concern.

In this article, we focus on four concepts that highlight the (potential) implications of big data for journalism: *epistemology*, *expertise*, *economics*, and *ethics*. These "Four E's," chosen from our review of the literature and observations of changes in different news, media, and information technology industries, appear to touch on salient dynamics of big data and its meaning for journalism, both for academic theory and professional practice. While the big-data phenomenon raises many relevant questions for news media, some of the most essential have to do with the legitimation of new claims about knowledge and truth (epistemology); the negotiation of occupational status, authority, and skill sets as new specializations are developed and deployed (expertise); the potential for and challenges of new efficiencies, resources, innovations, value creations, and revenue opportunities (economics); and the concerns raised by these developments for the norms and values that guide human decision-making and technological systems design (ethics). These four concepts serve as a dynamic set of lenses through which to view contemporary developments and envision future research opportunities.

Defining Big Data

Big data is a rather plastic concept, assuming different meanings in different contexts for different purposes—from policing to city planning to predicting preferences for breakfast cereal (Crawford et al. 2014). In strict computing terms, big data refers to data sets that are too large for standard computer memory and software to process. Or, put another way, "when the *volume*, *variety* and *velocity* of the data are increased, the current techniques and technologies may not be able to handle storage and processing of the data" (Suthaharan 2014, 70, emphasis added). Beyond technical specifications, however, big data can refer as much to *processes* surrounding data—and the resulting *products* of information about a great many people, places, and things—as to the scope of data itself. As Mayer-Schönberger and Cukier (2013, 6) describe it: "Big Data refers to our newfound ability to crunch a vast quantity of information, analyze it instantly, and draw sometimes astonishing conclusions from it."

From yet another perspective, and one perhaps more relevant for social researchers trying to understand the wider implications involved, big data can be defined as a social, cultural, and technological phenomenon that sits at the interplay of three dynamics:

(1) *Technology*: maximizing computation power and algorithmic accuracy to gather, analyze, link, and compare large data sets.

(2) *Analysis*: drawing on large data sets to identify patterns in order to make economic, social, technical, and legal claims.

(3) *Mythology*: the widespread belief that large data sets offer a higher form of intelligence and knowledge that can generate insights that were previously impossible, with the aura of truth, objectivity, and accuracy (boyd and Crawford 2012, 663).

The third of those—mythology—calls up a critical stance that is essential but often lost amid the clamor in business, policy, and even some scholarly corners for "big data solutions" (Crawford et al. 2014). Such a critique means worrying less about the "bigness" of data and attending more to how data comes to be seen as "big" in social relevance and normative valence. Moreover, this means recognizing the discursive work being performed by the term itself: "big data" may be as much a marketing term and a techno-utopian vision as it is a material phenomenon. Like terms such as "platform" (Gillespie 2010) and "digital divide" (Epstein et al. 2011), a term like "big data" does not emerge out of thin air but rather is "drawn from the available cultural vocabulary by stakeholders with specific aims, and carefully massaged so as to have particular resonance for particular audiences inside particular discourses" (Gillespie 2010, 359). Importantly, to follow Gillespie's reasoning on the politics of "platforms" and terms like it, "These are efforts not only to sell, convince, persuade, protect, triumph or condemn, but to make claims about what these technologies are and are not, and *what should and should not be expected of them*" (359, emphasis added).

Big data invokes a wide range of normative claims and practical implications for journalism as a professional practice and an organizational production—from knowledge work and economic rationale to practical skills and philosophical ethics. Because of its contested nature, "big data" as a term is a messy business (Crawford et al. 2014), and yet it remains the most succinct way of referring to a larger and complicated set of factors at play in technology and society as well as in technology and journalism. In this sense, we draw upon boyd and Crawford's definition of big data as a social, cultural, and technological phenomenon—one representing various philosophies, practices, and promises. For journalism, big data embodies emerging ideas about, activities for, and norms connected with data sets, algorithms, computational methods, and related processes and perspectives tied to quantification as a key paradigm of information work. We assume that big data is neither good nor bad for journalism but nevertheless freighted with potential and pitfall, depending on how it is imagined and implemented—and, crucially, toward what purposes and in whose interests.

Big Data in the Journalism Profession and Media Industry

The literature points to the need for a conceptual starting point for the study of big data in the salient case of journalism. Like the scientific, corporate, and government sectors broadly, the media industry must confront the question of what to *do* with all this data. This comes as many legacy news organizations struggle to find their way amid disruptions to the professional authority, business models, and traditional logics of news production and distribution (Anderson, Bell, and Shirky 2012; Lewis 2012; Ryfe 2012; Usher 2014). Journalism has long been familiar with data and databases as an object of news work and journalistic evidence, as evident in decades of computer-assisted reporting (CAR) and even older forms of information visualization (for history and discussion, see Cox 2000; Fink and Anderson 2014; Howard 2014; Powers 2012). But the database—which Manovich (1999) boldly suggests is to the digital era what narrative, in novels and cinema, was to the modern era—has assumed a particularly conspicuous role in contemporary journalism (Schudson 2010). Indeed, the larger turn toward digitization of information in recent times has been connected with a greater role in journalism for the *techniques* of computer and data sciences—from programming and algorithms to machine learning and probability models (Diakopoulos 2014; Stavelin 2014)—as well as the *ethos* of open-source software development and its emphasis on making data sets transparent and interactive (Lewis and Usher 2013; Parasie and Dagiral 2013). This take-up can be seen in the recent formation of data-specialist teams at leading news organizations, the development of data-focused journalism education courses and degrees, and the data-centric practices of "explainer" news startups like FiveThirtyEight and Vox (see Anderson 2013; Gynnild 2014; Howard 2014; Pitt 2014). Thus, *data*—whether "big" in the sense of being too complex for traditional database management software, or simply "big" in its potentially transformative import—has taken on particular relevance for news. "The open question in 2014," one report noted, "is not whether data, computers, and algorithms can be used by journalists in the public interest, but rather how, when, where, why, and by whom" (Howard 2014, 4).

Beyond the data-driven journalism on the editorial side of news media organizations, data manipulation has equal if not greater interest for business-side strategies and applications, particularly as market considerations have come to the fore amid declining revenues and fragmenting audiences (for a discussion of contemporary advertising and marketing dynamics, see Turow 2011; Couldry and Turow 2014). Moreover, as big data gains significance, technologists are needed to identify and appropriate suitable technological systems and solutions from external providers, or develop and reconfigure such systems and solutions themselves. These technologists, in turn, may form an important bridging function in negotiating technological systems and solutions across the editorial and business domains of the organization (Lewis and Westlund 2014; Westlund 2011)—potentially complicating sharp divisions that have long existed (or been assumed to exist) between news and business/marketing departments (Coddington, forthcoming; Klinenberg 2005). Big data as a social, cultural, and technological phenomenon (boyd and Crawford 2012) thus serves as a conceptual lens through which to understand how journalism—as both professional field and commercial enterprise—is seeking to make sense of, act upon, and derive value from the growing array of digital data in public life.

This article, like this special issue as a whole, does not celebrate or fetishize big data in the context of journalism. Nor do we assume that most news media organizations are "working" with big data in the same way that astronomers, biologists, and corporate data-miners are analyzing vast troves of data. Rather, we argue that the implications of big data for journalism, while in many cases still hypothetical, require conceptual heuristics that can guide future research. Just as journalism is trying to make sense of big data, so too must journalism studies develop toolkits for understanding what it means to the practice and perception of news. The various agents in news media organizations may make sense of the big-data phenomenon in diverse ways, and consequently also approach it in different ways: by resisting, adapting to, intervening against, or shaping it. Moreover, they may act proactively or reactively, focusing on none, one, or several of the strategic objectives that reside at the intersection of editorial, business, and technological interests and practices (Lewis and Westlund 2014). What is needed, therefore, is a conceptual starting point.

Conceptual Lenses

The full spectrum of research at the interplay of data, computation, and journalism has been reviewed and covered well by Coddington's (2014) contribution to this special issue. Instead, this article will introduce concepts and future research questions for exploring this sociotechnical phenomenon in journalism. There are, of course, a great number of entry points for such an undertaking. In the journalism studies literature thus far, related conceptual development and research agendas have mostly focused on "computational journalism" (Anderson 2013; Flew et al. 2012; Stavelin 2014) or "computational exploration in journalism" (Gynnild 2014). But missing in these analyses of "computation" is a more focused treatment of "big data," as a concept and a phenomenon (with some exceptions, such as Fairfield and Shtein 2014). By contrast, in the media and communication literature more broadly, scholars have critically examined such things as big-data target marketing and media production (Couldry and Turow 2014), the role of smartphone users as appropriators of big data (Nafus and Sherman 2014), big data's metaphorical framing (Puschmann and Burgess 2014), and the implications of big data for communication research methods (González-Bailón 2013). Our review of these analyses reveals a recurring focus on at least four themes that have particular relevance for the case of journalism, as introduced above: *epistemology*, *expertise*, *economics*, and *ethics*. These concepts open up lines of inquiry for understanding journalism in the context of big data.

In the sub-sections that follow, we (1) introduce the concepts generally; (2) discuss their meaning for big data and journalism; (3) provide examples or possible applications, often in the context of news production and distribution; and (4) raise questions for future research. In doing this, we build on our previous work in the context of news media organizations by keeping an eye on inter-relationships among types of social *actors* (e.g., journalists, businesspeople, and technologists), technological *actants* (e.g., algorithms and content management systems), and *audiences* (e.g., whether passive or active)—all interpolated through the *activities* of media production and distribution (Lewis and Westlund 2014; Westlund and Lewis 2014).

Epistemology

Epistemology, as a theory of knowledge, differs from ontology. In the philosophy of science, ontology refers to fundamental inquiries into the nature of existence. That is, ontology refers to what is said to "be" in the world, or the "science of what is" (Smith 2001, 79). While the world undoubtedly exists in the form of nature, people, or events, any attempt to represent the world will, in fact, turn into some sort of re-presentation, with inherent limitations. Epistemology thus points to the nature and boundaries of human knowledge about the world and the determination of truth in that process of re-presentation. The term derives from the Greek *episteme*, which means knowledge, and *epistanai*, which means to understand. A fundamental issue in epistemology concerns the work of legitimizing certain types of information as knowledge relative to others. The academy, like other knowledge-producing fields of practice, long has developed epistemologies that shape what counts in this regard (Schon 1995).

Among the most influential knowledge-producing institutions of the modern era, journalism has a distinct epistemology. It outlines the *"rules, routines* and *institutionalized procedures* that operate within a social setting and decide the form of the knowledge produced and the knowledge claims expressed (or implied)" (Ekström 2002, 260, original emphasis), as well as shapes the justifications that journalists make—to themselves and others—in defense of their truth claims (Ettema and Glasser 1998). Put simply, this epistemology is about how journalists know what they know—and why that matters for the knowledge practices and products in which they are engaged. Research into news production has shown how journalists develop methods for adjudicating knowledge claims in a routinized fashion (Tuchman 1978), for instance by adhering to ideals such as objectivity and practices such as multiple sourcing (Wiik 2010). However, the introduction of various technologies into news work has raised questions about the relative knowledge value associated with "technologically specific forms of work," from photojournalism of the past to programmer-journalism of the present (Powers 2012). The introduction of computers into news work, in the form of early computer-assisted reporting (CAR) nearly a half-century ago, pointed to hope for "precision journalism"— the potential for achieving greater accuracy through the use of databases, surveys, and an overall combination of computer and social science (Meyer 1973). While computers and their capacity for data analysis have improved significantly since that time, journalists have found it challenging to move beyond their established epistemology. This is true of the CAR tradition, one built on the belief that "data have no journalistic value on their own" and therefore journalists must work to find the story "hidden" in the data (Parasie and Dagiral 2013, 859); and it is true of the normative paradigm that positions journalists as essential knowledge-producers for society, bound up in their professional control of news information (Lewis 2012). Amid this tension are questions about the role that technology might play in developing the capacities for and practices of knowledge production in journalism—for example, in the form of augmented reality for digital storytelling (Pavlik and Bridges 2013) or technological systems for customizing diverse types of news for diverse types of audiences (Westlund 2013; Gynnild 2014).

By extension, big data offers similar opportunities for rethinking the epistemologies of journalism. For example, the extraction, combination, and analysis of big data may reveal new possibilities for investigative journalism (Parasie 2014), and with it a potentially stronger link between the production of social facts in journalism and matters of "science" and "precision." Beyond the realm of investigative journalism, where data has long held a special role in the CAR tradition, such beliefs about the power of data are spreading to other types of news amid the "quantitative turn" in journalism broadly (Coddington 2014). While ideas about "data" and corresponding "computation" enabling greater and more rigorous forms of knowledge are commonplace among some academics, practitioners, and pundits (see discussion in Anderson 2013), these ideas should be scrutinized for their underlying assumptions. Data should not to be taken as a proxy for the "science of what is," in the ontological sense, but rather as one form of epistemological knowledge in which numbers carry great significance. Big data, like any data, does not represent an objective truth. As Gitelman (2013) and others have stressed, "raw data is an oxymoron." The figures yielded by big data—even if enormous, robust, and highly correlated—still require interpretation.

Big data, as a set of technological processes as well as a key source of power, thus opens new paths for imagining how journalistic investigations develop epistemologically relevant revelations. More broadly, big data has implications for rethinking the epistemologies of news production and news distribution.

First, news production may be understood as a process of access/observation, selection/filtering, and processing/editing (Domingo et al. 2008)—each component connected with journalistic epistemology. Consider four brief examples: first, access/observation may involve computerized gatekeeping, or "watchdogging in code," through which journalists use actants to continuously and automatically monitor what politicians are doing, as Stavelin (2014) explored in the Norwegian context. A second example, involving all three steps of news production, regards programmer-journalists at *The Los Angeles Times*: they developed an algorithm to record earthquake notifications, process such alerts into epistemological facts, and facilitate easy editing and rapid publication upon human approval. A third example relates to how organizations may offer customers and readers forms of technology-led customization of news (Westlund 2013), as in Narrative Science's automated publishing of news stories based on financial reports released by public companies (Carlson 2014). A fourth example involves the Truth Teller prototype at *The Washington Post*, which combines speech-to-text algorithms with databases of "facts" to fact-check political speech in real-time. In each case, big data and related approaches present new facets for understanding the epistemology of transforming raw *information* into journalistic *truth*.

Turning to news distribution, big data is connected with emerging representations of digital journalism such as infographics, interactive data visualizations, and customizable probability models, among others (Howard 2014; Smit et al. 2014). These news products, in turn, carry certain epistemological assumptions about how audiences might acquire knowledge, as users are encouraged to "play" with the data to comprehend a particular and personalized version of the news narrative. For instance, some news organizations have sought to make data sets more accessible, transparent, and exploratory for users, in line with the ethos of open-source software and open-government advocacy (Lewis and Usher 2013; Parasie and Dagiral 2013). Others have invited audiences to participate on a massive collaborative project, as in the case of the public radio station WNYC asking listeners to build small DIY computer sensors to contribute local temperature readings to help predict the arrival of cicadas (Pitt 2014). Processes of news delivery and audience engagement in this big-data context thus present new questions not only about participation in journalism but also, and perhaps especially, about the legitimation of knowledge in and through such data-driven participation.

This brings us to a set of emerging research questions. In his analysis of television news, Ekström (2002) conceptualized journalistic epistemology in three parts: form of knowledge (i.e., medium-specific concerns, in his case those associated with television as a media form), production of knowledge (i.e., professional norms and routines), and public acceptance of knowledge claims (i.e., the conditions for social legitimacy). Each of these perspectives, brought into conversation with our agent-oriented emphasis above, leads to various questions for future research: How might the particular form of big-data journalism be associated with particular types of knowledge claims? What are the institutionalized routines and procedures that social actors adopt to guide the production of data-backed knowledge claims, and how are such routines conditioned to ensure that claims are legitimate and justified? In what ways do audiences learn from certain knowledge claims made via big-data news products, and what types of conditions must be satisfied to ensure that publics accept such claims? Ultimately, to care about how and why publics come to accept certain knowledge claims is to care about the social actors behind such processes: the experts and their expertise.

Expertise

In the broad sense, the term "expertise" comes from the Latin root *experiri*, meaning "to try," and generally refers to "the know-how, the capacity to get a task accomplished better and faster because one is more experienced"—hence *expertus*, or "tried" (Eyal 2013, 869). Because *expert* (the social actor) is connected with *expertise* (the specialized know-how), the study of expertise has long been associated with the sociology of professions, or the study of how some actors become seen as experts relative to others. This line of research has examined how occupations (and the experts who constitute them) work to forge and maintain "jurisdictional control" over the boundaries around a body of abstract knowledge and the application of that knowledge through work practices—thus allowing professionals to claim autonomy, authority, and other social and material benefits associated with being granted special recognition in society (Abbott 1988, 60). Whether in an occupational context or beyond, expertise thus functions as a key boundary marker setting apart those possessing specialized knowledge and experience. If epistemology directs attention to the *process* through which information becomes recognized as legitimate knowledge, expertise points to the *people* behind the processes. Even more broadly, as Eyal (2013, 863) has shown, expertise may be less of a professional attribution or a "real" thing possessed by individuals and more of "a network linking together agents, devices, concepts, and institutional and spatial arrangements."

Are journalists truly experts then? Just as journalism holds contested status as a profession, lacking many of the protective trappings enjoyed by professions such as law and medicine, journalistic expertise also has something of an in-between nature: while journalists are known for certain skills, such as storytelling, that distinction tells us little about whether journalists are actually experts *in something* (Schudson and Anderson 2008). Moreover, journalism's claim to social expertise through its "professional logic" (Lewis 2012), a bargain to control the production and distribution of news on society's behalf, is beset by challenges to authority (Carlson, forthcoming). Against that backdrop, Reich (2012) has offered a new picture of journalistic expertise. Drawing on Collins and Evans' (2007) influential typology of expertise—one that presumes expertise is a "real" feature of socialization and experience, and therefore may be classified across social domains—Reich argues that journalists can be understood as "interactional" experts:

their expertise lies in their ability to work with and among other types of experts, ultimately synthesizing and translating others' specialized knowledge for non-experts. Furthermore, Reich suggests that journalists develop a *bipolar* form of interactional expertise because they also must manage interactions with lay audiences, thus negotiating a dual process of engagement that constitutes its own kind of expertise. Finally, within the sociology of knowledge, there is a greater recognition for a competence-based approach: "Expertise is now seen more and more as something practical—something based on what you can do rather than what you can calculate or learn" (Collins and Evans 2007, 23; Reich 2012). Skills, technical or otherwise, are thus recognized as key benchmarks of expert distinction, in journalism as in other social domains.

These frameworks, whether constructivist or normative in nature, offer useful entry points for conceptualizing what may become of journalistic expertise amid big data. These might be described as (1) social interactions, (2) networked interactions, and (3) skill sets.

Social Interactions

As Reich (2012) notes in elaborating on journalism as bipolar interactional expertise, some newsworkers may have primarily source-interactional expertise (e.g., long-time beat reporters), others may have primarily audience-interactional expertise (e.g., editors who hear from readers), and others may have some combination (e.g., columnists and commentators). How might the social, cultural, and technological nature of big data affect the character of these interactions with sources and audiences? For example, consider what journalists, long oblivious to their readers and viewers (Lowrey 2009), now know about their audiences via digital metrics, and how that affects decisions about what and how to present as news (Tandoc 2014). Moreover, what of the interactions around expertise that may be happening internally? Large news companies increasingly are hiring data scientists and other technical experts to make sense of data—both data as source material for journalistic storytelling as well as data on audiences for business purposes. How might expertise be developed and made manifest in and through these emerging types of interactions with data? For instance, at what point does a journalist become conversant in the "language of data" such that she can claim expertise in "interviewing" data as an expert source?

Networked Interactions

Next, consider the more socio-technical interactions of expertise that might occur between journalists (as actors) and machines (as actants). From Eyal's (2013) approach, the growing deployment of algorithms and automation in journalism might entail new arrangements of "networked expertise," altering how we imagine what it is that journalists know and how they represent that knowledge to the world. In this vein, Anderson (2013) has shown how the dividing lines of expertise between "original" reporting and "parasitic" news aggregation are hardly clear-cut. In fact, networks of social actors and technological actants, when viewed holistically, yield complicated renderings of journalistic expertise under different conditions of digitization. Thus, big-data forms of journalism, such as data journalism (Howard 2014) or computational journalism (Stavelin 2014), raise questions about how human expertise is embedded in and through technical capacities, some of which may be programmed to perform relatively autonomously.

Skill Sets

Finally, as Collins and Evans (2007) remind us, expertise is manifest in actual, practical skills. Big data as a phenomenon and approach prioritizes certain skills, such as data analysis, computer programming, and visualization, drawn from disciplinary origins such as computer science, mathematics, and statistics (Mayer-Schönberger and Cukier 2013). What might these mean for journalism? Journalists have long worked with "data" of various kinds, building many Pulitzer Prize-winning investigations around data-driven analyses of public institutions. What is different now is that news organizations increasingly need computer programming, sophisticated back-end databases, and data science techniques—in essence, "code"—to comprehend increasingly ubiquitous data, and to publish it in ways that allow users to explore the data for themselves (Parasie and Dagiral 2013). *Data* and *code* thus constitute skills-based forms of expertise that news organizations are working to cultivate. Yet bridging the skills gap between journalists and technologists, or helping journalists develop such data-and-code skills, is neither easy nor broadly institutionalized as yet (Howard 2014; Lewis and Usher 2014). Nevertheless, consider how journalistic expertise might change if more journalists learned to write basic software, as Stavelin (2014) proposes, or if external "algorithmists"—expert reviewers of big-data analysis and predictions (Mayer-Schönberger and Cukier 2013)—were invited to critique computational journalism, much as ombudsmen function for news organizations today. To incorporate such skills into the news production and distribution process not only might lead to technological innovations but also alter the notion of what truly *counts* as expertise in journalism, perhaps complicating notions of status and authority both within and beyond the newsroom and the field at large (Ananny 2013a). Ultimately, perhaps these shifts have less to do with adapting interactional expertise through revised relationships between journalists and non-journalist experts, and more to do with the development or public display of a kind of "original" contributory expertise (Collins and Evans 2007), in which computationally minded journalists *are* the experts as they follow the methods of computer science.

Economics

Economics, with its etymology in the "management of household," is a discipline that studies the behaviors of agents in households and organizations, focusing on how resources are managed to achieve certain ends. Typically these agents are assumed to act rationally, making choices about how to use limited resources toward desired outcomes and strategic goals. Applied to the context of communication, *media economics* is defined as "the study of how media industries use scarce resources to produce content that is distributed among consumers in a society to satisfy various wants and needs" (Albarran 2002, 5). In all, such a focus takes up questions of media management, media business studies, and media innovations—covering the range of managerial strategies and tactics associated with media organizations and industries.

Many legacy news media companies around the world—especially local newspapers—have benefited financially from their standing as oligopolies or monopolies in a distinct geographical market, leading to impressive profit margins relative to other industries in recent decades (Picard 2010). Contemporary research, of course, has shown how such firms face a shrinking advertising base, fragmenting audiences, and rising competition from mobile, social, and digital media (Anderson et al. 2012). Amid a general call for media companies to innovate (Storsul and Krumsvik 2013; Westlund and Lewis, 2014), big data represents an opportunity for value creation through revised business processes as well as new products and services. Big data has obvious relevance for business-side revenue opportunities, allowing media companies to better understand and serve particular audiences and advertisers. Nevertheless, these developments come with corresponding concerns about the ultimate social and political outcomes of a world dominated by personalized digital media, where targeted advertising based on data mining leads to pressures on media companies (including news organizations) to personalize content in response (Couldry and Turow 2014). The march toward big-data personalization, in this view, threatens the very ecology of common knowledge upon which representative democracy depends (Sunstein 2009).

But seen another way, how might big data afford new value creation without undermining the church–state divide between business and editorial concerns that, for many journalists, is central to professional autonomy? Big data, in a basic sense, promises economic efficiency by enabling "more observation at less cost" (Crawford et al. 2014, 1666), as in the case of labor-saving "robot journalism" (Carlson, 2014) and technologically automated forms of journalism more generally (Westlund 2013). In another sense, big data may be associated with augmenting, rather than displacing, human labor by catalyzing new types of technologically enabled forms of news work (Powers 2012) or by allowing journalists to function more like "knowledge managers" who better gather, organize, and analyze disparate information flows in a community (Lewis and Usher 2013). Altogether, big data raises questions about the relative status and precarity of journalistic labor (Deuze 2008) amid the pursuit of new value propositions.

We consider, in brief, two ways of envisioning the value-creation opportunities for a journalism leveraging big data.

The first involves social actors, especially journalists but also technologists, manually drawing upon large data sets to report and present news in ways that differentiate their work from the traditional storytelling paradigm, thereby creating value for audiences interested in new types of news as well as creating distinction relative to commodity news in the marketplace. This shift has been called "method journalism" (Madrigal 2014), moving from an *area of coverage* (a topic, beat, or location of interest) to focus instead on the *method of coverage*. Several news startups are emblematic of this change, built around method-oriented objectives. FiveThirtyEight is "a data journalism organization," per founder Nate Silver's manifesto; Circa focuses on structuring news "data" (i.e., quotes, facts, and other atomic units of information) for mobile devices; and The New York Times' The Upshot emphasizes "plain-spoken, analytical journalism" based on data-driven analysis (quoted in Madrigal 2014). While those are US examples, there is growing evidence of similar data journalism efforts emerging in Europe and elsewhere (Lewis and Usher 2014). In these and other ways, data-focused initiatives may emerge as key forms of differentiation, traditionally held as essential for companies to succeed (Porter 1980; Dimmick 2003). News media organizations, for the most part, have yet to realize the potential strategic value of data as a business model, both for attracting audiences and for providing database resources that can be monetized via subscription and consulting services (Howard 2014; see also Aitamurto and Lewis 2013; Ananny 2013a).

The second approach involves using technological actants such as algorithms and applications to automatically gather, link, compare, and act upon big data of interest to audiences (Lewis and Westlund 2014). These algorithms can be tailored to fit with the personalized preferences and behaviors of individuals, promoting specific types of news to specific individuals (Thurman 2011). Importantly, journalists and technologists need to actively assess what actants they are to use for such purposes (if acquired from external providers), or how they are to be configured (if developed internally). A diverse set of social actors within the organization—from journalists to data analysts to marketers—may need to collaborate in inscribing the technological actants with logics and values for their operation, raising questions about how journalistic values are built into algorithmic news products. Settling such matters across the editorial–business divide, and in conjunction with technology design teams, is no small feat, as Westlund (2012) found in his study of a Swedish newspaper's development of a mobile news app. Nevertheless, as Anderson et al. (2012) have argued, automation offers an important yet underexplored avenue for news media to cut expenses (e.g., by no longer wasting resources on stories that a robot could write just as well) and simultaneously create value (e.g., by redeploying humans toward projects where they uniquely can contribute).

Ultimately, economics directs us to questions about how news media organizations might strategically manage their human and technological resources in relation to big data. The economics of big data is a challenge for media innovation that potentially involves the full range of social actors: journalists to derive editorial value from growing bodies of data, technologists to configure actants for automation and audiences in new ways, and businesspeople to negotiate marketers' demands for increasingly precise audience data and personalized media experiences. All of these developments raise overlapping questions relevant to research and theory. For journalism studies, to what extent do big-data processes contribute to a weakening wall between editorial and business concerns, with what kind of outcomes for news values and judgment as well as revenues and profits? How does an emphasis on value creation influence the distinct practices and products of news work, and how do such things compare across countries or cultures? For media economics and management, how do the development and deployment of big-data approaches correspond with certain theories of strategic management, innovation, and organizational behavior? What is uniquely relevant about the intersecting contexts of economic logics, news media, and big-data tools, technologies, and techniques?

Ethics

The term "ethics" derives from the Greek *ethos*, meaning "character" or "personal disposition" on the part of the individual, and relates to the Latin *mores* (or "morals") and its emphasis on the customs of a group. In this way, Ward (2010) notes, ethics is both internally concerned with the personal decision-making of the individual and externally situated in relation to the rules of society. While the study of ethics encompasses a vast terrain of moral philosophy and theory (e.g., Williams 1973), it suffices for our purposes to conclude that ethics is concerned with appropriate practice within a framework of moral principles.

Ethical behavior and moral reasoning have long been a concern in communication, media, and journalism (Christians et al. 1983). As the foundation for norms and values, ethical standards serve an essential function in orienting journalists, especially, to work in ways that promote honesty, accuracy, transparency, and public service, among other ideals (Singer 2007; Ward 2010). For journalists, ethical codes and conduct serve not only to guide their choices but also to define who they are as professionals. In this latter sense, ethics are associated with professionalism and its power as a form of boundary work, delineating insiders from outsiders and encouraging journalists to distance themselves from people and practices considered inferior or unfamiliar (Carlson and Lewis, forthcoming). The challenge, however, is that journalists are facing all manner of unfamiliarity in the media landscape, not least with regard to technological processes and practices. To reflexively resist or reject such change, framing the unfamiliar as a threat to normative principles, is "to cross the line from using ethics as a legitimate cause for concern to using ethics as a crutch" (Singer 2014, 67), forgoing opportunities to think productively, from the beginning, about how to adapt to and along with innovations as they arise.

Big data, of course, augurs potentially big changes for journalism: from shifting articulations of knowledge (epistemology) to highly technical skill sets and analytical understandings (expertise) to vexing questions of value creation, monetization, and media innovation (economics)—all of which are related to larger transitions in technology and society of which journalism is but one part (Couldry 2012). Such change is neither positively inevitable nor inevitably positive, and yet the specter of it raises questions about how the agents in news media organizations might respond to it all: pragmatically in transforming activities of media production, and philosophically in transforming norms and values that guide behavior. Moreover, the big data phenomenon is freighted with its own set of ethical quandaries—about user privacy, information security, and data manipulation, among others (Crawford et al. 2014)—that deserve scrutiny and reflection as journalists determine how to negotiate innovations associated with it.

Below, we briefly discuss three examples that illustrate the intersecting norms of journalism and big data.

First, consider the process of publishing data or making large data sets publicly available online. An ethos of openness is shared among many data journalists (Howard 2014), though journalists broadly have struggled to embrace such openness as a professional norm (Lewis 2012). In the spirit of open source, data journalists often seek to make complete data sets and programming code open to public examination —creating, in some cases, an invitation for users to contribute and collaborate. Such a movement may help journalism reinvent itself for the digital era, Lewis and Usher (2013) suggest, by integrating norms such as iteration, tinkering, transparency, and participation that are connected with the social, cultural, and technological framework of digital technologies. Yet often there are underlying problems with such public data, whether provided to news organizations by governments or political institutions

(Schudson 2010), or perhaps assembled by news organizations through crowdsourcing, data-scraping, or other means. Such problems may go unnoticed either because of the size of the data involved or because of the attractiveness of making it freely available. For example, big data—such as millions of tweets collected around a particular event—are often assumed to represent the social world, yet they have deeply structural "signal problems," with little or no representation coming from less-connected communities (Crawford 2013). Meanwhile, journalists must weigh the benefits of open data against the risks of personal harm that may come with publication, particularly at a time when private information can be so easily shared and searched (Howard 2014). Altogether, even well-intentioned efforts to revise journalistic norms through big data run up against ethical questions embedded in the organization, analysis, and dissemination of such data.

Second, consider social science research ethics. Drawing on social science methods is not new for journalists, but the process has accelerated and expanded in this data-rich environment (Howard 2014). Meanwhile, at the same time that journalists are embracing such techniques, "social scientists are undergoing a fundamental shift in the ethical structure that has defined the moral use of these techniques," rethinking what it means to protect individuals from harm and allow for informed consent in a world of big-data research methods involving millions of human subjects (Fairfield and Shtein 2014, 38). Journalists, of course, are not subject to institutional review boards, yet they should be cautious: just because certain content is publicly accessible does not mean that it was intended to be made public to everyone (boyd and Crawford 2012).

Third, consider the ethics of technological systems design, or how computer systems come to embody certain values (Nissenbaum 2001). To the extent that big data implies a large-scale, technology-led turn in journalism (Westlund 2013), what happens as humans embed technological actants like algorithms with some assumptions, norms, and values, and not others? In effect, as machines take on a greater role in news judgment, encouraging certain kinds of news selection and consumption over others, how are they "taught" to act ethically? Is there an ethics of algorithms (Kraemer et al. 2011)? Such an ethics will need to unpack various factors of selection, interpretation, and anticipation, revealing "how algorithms structure how we can *see* a concern, why we think it *probably matters*, and *when* we might act on it" (Ananny 2013b, 6, original emphasis), all issues of deep relevance for journalistic decision-making. Altogether, this attention to code and structure behind technology encourages a study of the "black boxes" of big data, working to uncover "the power structures, biases, and influences that computational artifacts exercise in society" (Diakopoulos 2014).

Ultimately, many issues remain to be addressed in future scholarship on ethics at the intersection of big data and journalism. At its core, ethics is concerned with appropriate practice; researchers thus may examine how social actors in diverse news media firms make sense of, domesticate, and innovate in relation to big-data practices. Importantly, scholars should seek to understand the moral reasoning and ethical decision-making among the full range of media-work agents (Lewis and Westlund 2014), each representing relatively distinct positions with regards to epistemology, expertise, and economics. How are data-centric ethics constructed and rationalized (and also written into technological actants) comparatively across national, sociocultural, and technological contexts? Assuming ethical constructs change over time as the big-data phenomenon unfolds, what characterizes this change, and what implications does it have for journalism at large?

Conclusion

This article has defined and discussed big data as a social, cultural, and techno-logical phenomenon, in the particular context of journalism. Introducing and applying four conceptual lenses—*epistemology, expertise, economics*, and *ethics*—the article has systematically explored both contemporary and potential applications of big data for the professional logic and industrial production of journalism. The discussion of these distinct yet inter-related conceptual lenses has shown how journalists and news organi-zations are seeking to make sense of, act upon, and derive value from big data during a time of exploration in algorithms, computation, and quantification. In all, the develop-ments of big data potentially have great meaning for journalism's ways of *knowing* (epistemology) and *doing* (expertise), as well as its negotiation of *value* (economics) and *values* (ethics). Observers such as Howard (2014) argue that data and associated activities will only matter more in the years ahead, with results that may be utopian, dystopian, or otherwise. To assess such significance and outcomes going forward, scholars may benefit from considering the distinct contributions of epistemology, expertise, economics, and ethics as conceptual footholds, while acknowledging and applying the holistic interplay among them. These approaches, we have argued, are but starting points for undertaking future research on big data and the opportunities and challenges that it poses for journalism, media, and society.

ACKNOWLEDGEMENTS

The first author was supported in this work by an Emerging Scholars grant from the Association for Education in Journalism and Mass Communication, as well as funding available through the Hubbard and Charnley faculty fellowships in the School of Journalism and Mass Communication at the University of Minnesota. This article also benefited from a number of comments, including those of the first author's reading-group associates (Josh Braun, Andrea Hickerson, Aynne Kokas, Matt Powers, and Jen Schradie) as well as other readers (Mark Coddington, Anna Popkova, Jane Singer, and Rodrigo Zamith).

REFERENCES

Abbott, Andrew D. 1988. *The System of Professions: An Essay on the Division of Expert Labor.* Chicago, IL: University of Chicago Press.

Aitamurto, Tanja, and Seth C. Lewis. 2013. "Open Innovation in Digital Journalism: Examining the Impact of Open APIs at Four News Organizations." *New Media & Society* 15 (2): 314–331. doi:10.1177/1461444812450682.

Albarran, Alan B. 2002. *Media Economics: Understanding Markets, Industries and Concepts.* Ames, IA: Blackwell.

Ananny, Mike. 2013a. "Press-Public Collaboration as Infrastructure: Tracing News Organizations and Programming Publics in Application Programming Interfaces." *American Behavioral Scientist* 57 (5): 623–642. doi:10.1177/000276421246936.

Ananny, Mike. 2013b. "Toward an Ethics of Algorithms: Observation, Probability, and Time." Paper presented at the Governing Algorithms Conference, New York, May 16–17.

Anderson, C. W. 2013. "Towards a Sociology of Computational and Algorithmic Journalism." *New Media & Society* 15 (7): 1005–1021. doi:10.1177/1461444812465137.

Anderson, C. W., Emily Bell, and Clay Shirky. 2012. *Post-industrial Journalism: Adapting to the Present*. New York: Tow Center for Digital Journalism Columbia University.

Boellstorff, Tom. 2013. "Making Big Data, in Theory." *First Monday* 18 (10). http://firstmonday.org/ojs/index.php/fm/article/view/4869/3750.

Boyd, danah, and Kate Crawford. 2012. "Critical Questions for Big Data: Provocations for a Cultural, Technological, and Scholarly Phenomenon." *Information, Communication & Society* 15 (5): 662–679. doi:10.1080/1369118X.2012.678878.

Carlson, Matt. 2014. "The Robotic Reporter: Automated Journalism and the Redefinition of Labor, Compositional Forms, and Journalistic Authority." *Digital Journalism*. doi: 10.1080/21670811.2014.976412.

Carlson, Matt, and Seth C. Lewis, eds. forthcoming. *Boundaries of Journalism: Professionalism, Practices, and Participation*. New York: Routledge.

Carlson Matt. forthcoming. *Journalistic Authority*. New York: Columbia University Press.

Christians, Clifford G., Kim B. Rotzoll, and Mark Fackler, eds. 1983. *Media Ethics: Cases and Moral Reasoning*. New York: Routledge.

Coddington, Mark. 2014. "Clarifying Journalism's Quantitative Turn: A Typology for Evaluating Data Journalism Computational Journalism and Computer-assisted Reporting." *Digital Journalism*. doi: 10.1080/21670811.2014.976400.

Coddington, Mark. forthcoming. "The Wall Becomes a Curtain: Revisiting Journalism's News–business Boundary." In *Boundaries of Journalism: Professionalism, Practices, and Participation*, edited by Matt Carlson and Seth C. Lewis. New York: Routledge.

Coleman, E. Gabriella. 2013. *Coding Freedom: The Ethics and Aesthetics of Hacking*. Princeton, NJ: Princeton University Press.

Collins, Henry, and Robert Evans. 2007. *Rethinking Expertise*. Chicago, IL: University of Chicago Press.

Couldry, Nick. 2012. *Media, Society, World: Social Theory and Digital Media Practice*. Cambridge: Polity.

Couldry, Nick, and Joseph Turow. 2014. "Advertising, Big Data and the Clearance of the Public Realm: Marketers' New Approaches to the Content Subsidy." *International Journal of Communication* 8, 1710–1726. http://ijoc.org/index.php/ijoc/article/view/2166.

Cox, Melissa. 2000. "The Development of Computer-assisted Reporting." Paper presented at AEJMC, Phoenix, August 9-12.

Crawford, Kate. 2013. "The Hidden Biases in Big Data." *Harvard Business Review*, April 1. http://blogs.hbr.org/2013/04/the-hidden-biases-in-big-data/.

Crawford, Kate, Kate Miltner and Mary L. Gray. 2014. "Critiquing Big Data: Politics, Ethics, Epistemology." *International Journal of Communication* 8, 1663–1672. http://ijoc.org/index.php/ijoc/article/view/2167/1164.

Deuze, Mark. 2008. "Understanding Journalism as Newswork: How it Changes, and How it Remains the Same." *Westminster Papers in Communication and Culture* 5 (2): 4–23.

Diakopoulos, Nicholas. 2014. "Algorithmic Accountability: Journalistic Investigation of Computational Power Structures." *Digital Journalism*. doi: 10.1080/21670811.2014.976411.

Dimmick, John W. 2003. *Media Competition and Coexistence: The Theory of the Niche.* Mahwah, NJ: Lawrence Erlbaum.

Domingo, David, Thorsten Quandt, Ari Heinonen, Steve Paulussen, Jane B. Singer, and Marina Vujnovic. 2008. "Participatory Journalism Practices in the Media and Beyond: An International Comparative Study of Initiatives in Online Newspapers." *Journalism Practice* 2 (3): 326–342. doi:10.1080/17512780802281065.

Dwoskin, Elizabeth. 2014. "Beware 'Big Data' Hype, Report Warns." *The Wall Street Journal*, May 27. http://blogs.wsj.com/digits/2014/05/27/beware-big-data-hype-reports-warn/.

Ekström, Mats. 2002. "Epistemologies of TV Journalism: A Theoretical Framework." *Journalism* 3 (3): 259–282. doi:10.1177/146488490200300301.

Epstein, Dmitry, Erik C. Nisbet, and Tarleton Gillespie. 2011. "Who's Responsible for the Digital Divide? Public Perceptions and Policy Implications." *The Information Society* 27 (2): 92–104. doi:10.1080/01972243.2011.548695.

Ettema, James S., and Theodore L. Glasser. 1998. *Custodians of Conscience: Investigative Journalism and Public Virtue.* New York: Columbia University Press.

Eyal, Gil. 2013. "For a Sociology of Expertise: The Social Origins of the Autism Epidemic." *American Journal of Sociology* 118 (4): 863–907. doi:10.1086/66844.

Fairfield, Joshua, and Hannah Shtein. 2014. "Big Data, Big Problems: Emerging Issues in the Ethics of Data Science and Journalism." *Journal of Mass Media Ethics* 29 (1): 38–51. doi:10.1080/08900523.2014.863126.

Fink, Katherine, and C. W. Anderson. 2014. "Data Journalism in the United States: Beyond the 'Usual Suspects'." *Journalism Studies*. doi:10.1080/1461670X.2014.939852.

Flew, Terry, Christina Spurgeon, Anna Daniel, and Adam Swift. 2012. "The Promise of Computational Journalism." *Journalism Practice* 6 (2): 157–171. doi:10.1080/17512786.2011.616655.

Gillespie, Tarleton. 2010. "The Politics of 'Platforms'." *New Media & Society* 12 (3): 347–364. doi:10.1177/1461444809342738.

Gitelman, Lisa, ed. 2013. *"Raw Data" is an Oxymoron.* Cambridge, MA: MIT Press.

González-Bailón, Sandra. 2013. "Social Science in the Era of Big Data." *Policy & Internet* 5 (2): 147–160. doi:10.1002/1944-2866.POI32.

Gynnild, Astrid. 2014. "Journalism Innovation Leads to Innovation Journalism: The Impact of Computational Exploration on Changing Mindsets." *Journalism* 15 (6): 713–730. doi:10.1177/1464884913486393.

Howard, Alexander B. 2014. *The Art and Science of Data-driven Journalism.* New York: Tow Center for Digital Journalism, Columbia University.

Howard, Philip N. forthcoming. *Pax Technica: How the Internet of Things May Set us Free or Lock us Up.* New Haven, CT: Yale University Press.

Klinenberg, Eric. 2005. "Convergence: News Production in a Digital Age." *The ANNALS of the American Academy of Political and Social Science* 597 (1): 48–64. doi:10.1177/0002716204270346.

Kraemer, Felicitas, Kees van Overveld, and Martin Peterson. 2011. "Is There an Ethics of Algorithms?" *Ethics and Information Technology* 13 (3): 251–260. doi:10.1007/s10676-010-9233-7.

Lewis, Seth C. 2012. "The Tension Between Professional Control and Open Participation: Journalism and its Boundaries." *Information, Communication & Society* 15 (6): 836–866. doi:10.1080/1369118X.2012.674150.

Lewis, Seth C., and Nikki Usher. 2013. "Open Source and Journalism: Toward New Frameworks for Imagining News Innovation." Media, Culture and Society 35 (5): 602–619. doi:10.1177/0163443713485494.

Lewis, Seth C., and Nikki Usher. 2014. "Code, Collaboration, and the Future of Journalism: A Case Study of the Hacks/Hackers Global Network." Digital Journalism 2 (3): 383–393. doi:10.1080/21670811.2014.895504.

Lewis, Seth C., and Oscar Westlund. 2014. "Actors, Actants, Audiences, and Activities in Cross-Media News Work: A Matrix and a Research Agenda." Digital Journalism. doi:10.1080/21670811.2014.927986.

Lowrey, Wilson. 2009. "Institutional Roadblocks: Assessing Journalism's Response to Changing Audiences." In Journalism and Citizenship: New Agendas, edited by Zizi Papacharissi, 44–67. Mahwah, NJ: Lawrence Erlbaum Associates.

Madrigal, Alexis C. 2014. "Method Journalism." The Atlantic, June 10. http://www.theatlantic.com/technology/archive/2014/06/method-journalism/372526/.

Manovich, Lev. 1999. "Database as Symbolic Form." Convergence: The International Journal of Research Into New Media Technologies 5 (2): 80–99. doi:10.1177/135485659900500206.

Manovich, Lev. 2012. "Trending: The Promises and the Challenges of Big Social Data." In Debates in the Digital Humanities, edited by M. K. Gold, 460–475. Minneapolis, MN: The University of Minnesota Press.

Mayer-Schönberger, Viktor, and Kenneth Cukier. 2013. Big Data: A Revolution that Will Transform How We Live, Work, and Think. Boston, MA: Houghton Mifflin Harcourt.

Meyer, Philip. 1973. Precision Journalism: A Reporter's Introduction to Social Science Methods. Bloomington: Indiana University Press.

Nafus, Dawn, and Jamie Sherman. 2014. "This One Does Not Go Up To 11: The Quantified Self Movement as an Alternative Big Data Practice." International Journal of Communication 8, 11. http://ijoc.org/index.php/ijoc/article/view/2170.

Nissenbaum, Helen. 2001. "How Computer Systems Embody Values." Computer 34 (3): 120–119.

Parasie, Sylvain. 2014. "Data-Driven Revelation: Epistemological Tensions in Investigative Journalism in the Age of 'Big Data'." Digital Journalism. doi: 10.1080/21670811.2014.976408.

Parasie, Sylvain, and Eric Dagiral. 2013. "Data-Driven Journalism and The Public Good: 'Computer-assisted-reporters' and 'Programmer-journalists' in Chicago." New Media & Society 15 (6): 853–871. doi:10.1177/1461444812463345.

Pavlik, John V., and Frank Bridges. 2013. "The Emergence of Augmented Reality (AR) as a Storytelling Medium in Journalism." Journalism & Communication Monographs 15 (1): 4–59. doi:10.1177/1522637912470819.

Picard, Robert G. 2010. "A Business Perspective on Challenges Facing Journalism." In The Changing Business of Journalism and its Implications for Democracy, edited by A. L. David Levy and Rasmus Kleis Nielsen, 17–24. Oxford: Reuters Institute for the Study of Journalism, University of Oxford.

Pitt, Fergus. 2014. Sensors and Journalism. New York: Tow Center for Digital Journalism, Columbia University.

Porter, Michael E. 1980. Competitive Strategy. New York: Free Press.

Powers, Matthew. 2012. "In Forms that are Familiar and Yet-to-be Invented': American Journalism and the Discourse of Technologically Specific Work." Journal of Communication Inquiry 36 (1): 24–43. doi:10.1177/0196859911426009.

Puschmann, Cornelius, and Jean Burgess. 2014. "Metaphors of Big Data." International Journal of Communication 8, 20. http://ijoc.org/index.php/ijoc/article/view/2169.

Reich, Zvi. 2012. "Journalism as Bipolar Interactional Expertise." *Communication Theory* 22 (4): 339–358. doi:10.1111/j.1468-2885.2012.01411.

Ryfe, David M. 2012. *Can Journalism Survive? An Inside Look at American Newsrooms.* Cambridge; Malden, MA: Polity Press.

Schon, Donald A. 1995. "The New Scholarship Requires a New Epistemology." *Change* 27 (6): 27–34.

Schudson, Michael. 2010. "Political Observatories, Databases & News in the Emerging Ecology of Public Information." *Daedalus* 139 (2): 100–109. doi:10.1162/daed.2010.139.2.100.

Schudson, Michael, and Chris Anderson. 2008. "Objectivity, Professionalism, and Truth Seeking in Journalism." In *Handbook of Journalism Studies*, edited by Karin Wahl-Jorgensen and Thomas Hanitzsch, 88–101. New York: Routledge.

Singer, Jane B. 2007. "Contested Autonomy: Professional and Popular Claims on Journalistic Norms." *Journalism Studies* 8 (1): 79–95. doi:10.1080/14616700601056866.

Singer, Jane B. 2014. "Getting Past the Future: Journalism Ethics, Innovation, and a Call for 'Flexible First'." *Comunicação e Sociedade* 25: 67–82.

Smit, Gerard, Yael de Haan, and Laura Buijs. 2014. "Visualizing News: Make it Work." *Digital Journalism* 2 (3): 344–354. doi:10.1080/21670811.2014.897847.

Smith, Barry. 2001. "Objects and their Environments: From Aristotle to Ecological Ontology." In *The Life and Motion of Socio-Economic Units*, edited by Andrew Frank, Jonathan Raper and Jean-Paul Cheylan, 79–97. London: Taylor and Francis.

Stavelin, Erik. 2014. *Computational Journalism: When Journalism Meets Programming.* Unpublished dissertation. Bergen: University of Bergen.

Storsul, Tanja, and Arne H. Krumsvik. eds. 2013. *Media Innovations.* Gothenburg: Nordicom.

Sunstein, Cass R. 2009. *Republic.com 2.0.* Princeton: Princeton University Press.

Suthaharan, Shan. 2014. "Big Data Classification: Problems and Challenges in Network Intrusion Prediction with Machine Learning." *SIGMETRICS Perform. Eval. Rev.* 41 (4): 70–73. doi:10.1145/2627534.2627557.

Tandoc, Edson C. 2014. "Journalism is Twerking? How Web Analytics is Changing the Process of Gatekeeping." *New Media & Society.* doi:10.1177/1461444814530541.

Thurman, Neil. 2011. "Making 'The Daily Me': Technology, Economics and Habit in the Mainstream Assimilation of Personalized News." *Journalism* 12 (4): 395–415. doi:10.1177/1464884910388228.

Tuchman, Gaye. 1978. *Making News: A Study in the Construction of Reality.* New York: Free Press.

Turow, Joseph. 2011. *The Daily You: How the New Advertising Industry is Defining your Identity and Your Worth.* New Haven, CT: Yale University Press.

Usher, Nikki. 2014. *Making News at the New York Times.* Ann Arbor: University of Michigan Press.

Ward, Stephen J. A. 2010. *Global Journalism Ethics.* Montreal: McGill-Queen's University Press.

Westlund, Oscar. 2011. *Cross-media News Work: Sensemaking of the Mobile Media (r)evolution.* Gothenburg: University of Gothenburg. https://gupea.ub.gu.se/bitstream/2077/28118/1/gupea_2077_28118_1.pdf.

Westlund, Oscar. 2012. "Producer-centric Versus Participation-centric: on the Shaping of Mobile Media." *Northern Lights: Film and Media Studies Yearbook* 10 (1): 107–121. doi:10.1386/nl.10.1.107_1.

Westlund, Oscar. 2013. "Mobile News: A Review and Model of Journalism in an Age of Mobile Media." *Digital Journalism* 1 (1): 6–26. doi:10.1080/21670811.2012.740273.

Westlund, Oscar, and Seth C. Lewis. 2014. "Agents of Media Innovations: Actors, Actants, and Audiences." *The Journal of Media Innovations* 1 (2): 10–35. doi:10.5617/jmi.v1i2.856.

Wiik, Jenny. 2010. *Journalism in Transition: The Professional Identity of Swedish Journalists.* JMG Book Series no. 64. Gothenburg: University of Gothenburg.

Williams, Bernard. 1973. *Ethics and the Limits of Philosophy.* Hoboken: Taylor & Francis.

Index

Page numbers in italics refer to figures. Page numbers in bold refer to tables.

For Product Safety Concerns and Information please contact our EU
representative GPSR@taylorandfrancis.com
Taylor & Francis Verlag GmbH, Kaufingerstraße 24, 80331 München, Germany